MW01272922

THE BOTTOM LINE

Robert Meyer

Order this book online at www.trafford.com/06-0726
or email orders@trafford.com

Most Trafford titles are also available at major online book retailers.

Note for Librarians: A cataloguing record for this book is available from Library
and Archives Canada at www.collectionscanada.ca/amicus/index-e.html

Printed in Victoria, BC, Canada.

ISBN: 978-1-4120-8970-8

*We at Trafford believe that it is the responsibility of us all, as both individuals
and corporations, to make choices that are environmentally and socially sound.
You, in turn, are supporting this responsible conduct each time you purchase a
Trafford book, or make use of our publishing services. To find out how you are
helping, please visit www.trafford.com/responsiblepublishing.html*

*Our mission is to efficiently provide the world's finest, most comprehensive
book publishing service, enabling every author to experience success.
To find out how to publish your book, your way, and have it available
worldwide, visit us online at www.trafford.com/10510*

 www.trafford.com

North America & international
toll-free: 1 888 232 4444 (USA & Canada)
phone: 250 383 6864 ♦ fax: 250 383 6804 ♦ email: info@trafford.com

The United Kingdom & Europe
phone: +44 (0)1865 722 113 ♦ local rate: 0845 230 9601
facsimile: +44 (0)1865 722 868 ♦ email: info.uk@trafford.com

10 9 8 7 6 5

WHAT THEY WROTE

Benjamin Britten:
"Robert Meyer proved himself a considerable musician and a fine player. I can recommend him most warmly."

Buckingham Palace:
"By command of Her Majesty the Queen the accompanying Medal is forwarded to Robert J. Meyer Esquire to be worn in commemoration of Her Majesty's Coronation."

Gary Karr:
"A British icon - one of the all-time great masters of the double bass."

Greater Victoria Youth Orchestra:
"Many thanks for your wonderful coaching of the contrabass section this season."

Yehudi Menuhin:
"I was delighted to hear of your management and to hear that you are particularly interested in young musicians."

Mistislav Rostopovitch:
        "... with warm gratitude."

Sadlers Wells Opera:
        "We have very much appreciated the work you have done for us and you have certainly been a tower of strength of which everyone concerned is most grateful."

Vancouver Province:
        "Meyer is a virtuoso player with a musicianly approach to the purely virtuoso writing in the pieces he plays. Sparkle aside, however, it was the accuracy of his intonation and the way he made the heavy strings sing with dignity and splendid warmth of tone that impressed most."

Vancouver Symphony Orchestra:
"Your efforts and enthusiasm have certainly contributed to the growth of the Orchestra."

ACKNOWLEDGEMENTS

I am deeply indebted to: Deryk Barker for his encyclopædic knowledge of music and recordings, plus all his useful suggestions, Anne Cassady, Professor Emeritus James V. Chambers, Van and Jim Gimlett, and Isabel Young for her tireless enthusiam in transcribing the book from audio-tapes. Last but by no means least my thanks go to Catherine Foster for her painstaking research and helpful suggestions in preparing the text, and to Carol Sill of AlphaGlyph Publications for assistance in the final preparation of the book and CD.

To my son, Nicholas Meyer, with gratitude.

Every effort has been made to identify the sources of all materials, photographic and other, utilized in this book. Any omissions will be gratefully acknowledged.

Robert Meyer

About Robert Meyer

Robert Meyer, born in 1920, lived through the Great Depression and was at the battlefront in WW II. He graduated from the Royal College of Music, London as a double bass soloist and has spent a lifetime playing with famous orchestras, conductors and soloists throughout the world. He has a wealth of anecdotes to recount and gives sketches of many of the great orchestras, conductors and soloists of his day, some droll, some sad. He was there!

Among the highlights of his career: he was commanded by Queen Elizabeth II to play at her Coronation, was Benjamin Britten's solo bassist and librarian, played with the Moscow Chamber Orchestra, the London Philharmonic, London Symphony, BBC Symphony, Sadlers Wells Opera, San Carlo Opera, the English Chamber Orchestra, the Vancouver Symphony and many more. He played at Carnegie Hall and the United Nations, and was invited to tour the White House, the Gulistan Palace, Iran, by the Shah of Persia, and The Vatican. He gives a vivid and insightful look into a musician's everyday life that readers may well find astonishing. For musicians, musical historians and anyone interested in music and life generally this is a must read.

Robert Meyer still performs and gives lectures. Any free time he has is devoted to painting Chinese watercolours, playing the harpsichord and gourmet cooking. He now lives in Vancouver, British Columbia, Canada.

'It could be said of me that in this book I have only made up a bunch of other men's flowers, providing of my own only the string that ties them together'

Michel de Montaigne 1533-1592

THE BOTTOM LINE

Dedicated to Betty, for without her I would never have enjoyed the success that came my way.

CONTENTS

PART ONE

THE BOTTOM LINE

PART ONE

The Bottom Line

INTRODUCTION

There is an old Spanish proverb that says every man should have a son, plant a tree and write a book. I accomplished the first two many years ago; I have one son, and the trees that I first planted for posterity in many different places have long since matured. It only remained for me to write the book.

I first decided to write a series of pastiches, recounting some occurrences behind the scenes not previously recorded of famous orchestras, conductors and soloists, but as time went on it became obvious to me that the book would have to take the form of an autobiography. Not that the life of a mere bass player would be found to be all that interesting, but because, chronologically speaking, events and people are inevitably bound up with it. So I shall start from the very beginning, my birth, and give you, dear reader, an account of the tangled web that constitutes a professional musician's life. If by any chance any of my readers are contemplating taking up music as a career, don't be put off by some of the sordid happenings that I sometimes mention, and which you, too, could well experience, because to compensate for the down side there are many plusses.

It would have been impossible for me to include every one of the many great musicians and other people I have encountered in my long lifetime and after all, there is a threshold, beyond which the endless recounting of anecdotes can become boring. Like Topsy, the book "just growed" but as I was not contemplating writing a book of gargantuan proportions some judicial pruning became necessary, thereby omitting many famous characters, which I regret.

Perhaps some of my comments on the great personalities of music in my day may seem to be opinionated and even impertinent. Remember that all judgements are subjective, and whatever my feelings may have been regarding artists from my perspective on my side of the footlights, they may be totally different from those of a member of the audience on the other side, or even another member of the orchestra for that matter. Nothing is engraved in stone and if my comments are deemed to be sacrilegious so be it.

As I sit on my sundeck looking over the beautiful harbour surrounded by trees and mountains I am constantly thankful for the privilege that has allowed me to settle in this lovely spot in British Columbia, Canada.

Sometimes I ponder on the people and events that contrived for me to end up here. True, the waters are not always placid, there are storms and rough weather as indeed there are in the musical profession, but there is always eventually a rift in the clouds and a patch of blue sky overhead.

In England, where I worked for many years, there were over eight hundred bassists on the Musicians' Union's books besides a lot more that were not in the Union, but I always took heart from my teacher and mentor, Eugene Cruft, who told me that to succeed in music one has to try to be better than anyone else, also to constantly practice and have money in the bank, besides always having a solo ready in case you were suddenly called upon to audition. These are maxims that I found to be of great help to me in my career and they still hold true today.

Robert Meyer

Chapter 1

Early Days. I pick up the bass.

I was born in London in 1920. My father went to England in 1912 from a small town near Dresden, Germany, to learn the language and study the hospitality industry. He had met and married my mother in 1913. She was an Englishwoman born in London. When the Great War broke out in 1914 he was stranded in England and interned as an enemy alien for five years. After his release from the internment camp following Germany's defeat, my father considered returning home but in the chaos that ensued there were not many jobs available back in Germany, so he was advised by his family to stay where he was, in England. My mother, of course, was a British subject and didn't want to leave England to go to Germany. After desperately hunting for work my father at last found a job in Scotland just as they were about to book tickets to Germany, so the family was destined to stay in England. Not long afterwards my father found a better job in London.

During WW1 two of my German uncles, Horst, and Robert, after whom I was named, were killed. Naturally my father was very upset at losing two of his brothers and often used to refer to them.

Growing up in England so soon after WW1, I was troubled, as a child, to see so many men begging on the streets, some blind, some amputees, all wearing their war medals and selling boxes of matches with a tin box in front of them for passers-by to drop in coins. Practically everyone in uniform, the bus and tram conductors and drivers, the police, the railwaymen and the commissionaires all wore their medals in public as a reminder that they had "done their bit" in the War.

We were dirt poor as a result of the War, but we were united as a family. One thing that held us together was music. One paternal cousin was a staff pianist on the Dresden Radio named Helga Meyer. I never met her. My father also played the violin and piano and he could sing quite well. There were concerts and operas performed in the enemy alien camps where he was held and I remember he told me he took the part of Frosch the jailer in the operetta *Die Fledermaus*. My mother played the piano and my maternal grandfather played the violin and piano. Gramps was a very clever man. He designed and made vases and bas-reliefs of biblical scenes and he also fired terra cotta pieces of sculpture for prominent sculptors.

My maternal grandmother's father was a stained glass window artist and his work can still be seen in some of the churches in the Gloucester area. I suppose I must have inherited my love of art from my mother's side and music from both sides of the family.

We often had musical evenings; Uncle Fred with one hand over his heart would sing such Victorian ballads as *Friend o' Mine*, his daughter, my maternal cousin Gladys, became a professional pianist, my grandfather would sing *Hearts of Oak*, and my father and I on violins with my sister on piano would play Strauss waltzes after which we would be asked, nay commanded, to play pieces by composers such as Charles Dancla, Corelli, and various selections from Verdi's *La Traviata* and *Il Trovatore*.

Entertainment in those days was mainly in the home. True, there was the silent cinema, vaudeville shows, amateur concerts, a few classical concerts and opera at Sadlers Wells sung in English and aimed at the proletariat. There were limited opera seasons at Covent Garden but they were mainly élitist; many of the women in the audience went there because it was 'the thing to do' and to show off their clothes. They would arrive late, make their entrée very noisily in order to attract attention to themselves and Sir Thomas Beecham at last became very exasperated, stopped the opera, turned round and told them to "shut up." It was in all the newspapers but it put an end to the well-heeled latecomers.

Radio or 'the wireless' as it was then called, was in many homes in the late twenties, it had a piece of crystal and beside that there was a thin wire 'cat's whisker' and according to where the cat's whisker probed on the crystal so you received your station. This apparatus required a big aerial with a long wire stretching the whole length of the garden but reception was poor, still, people were thrilled with it at the time and pointed to the marvels of modern science.

Most homes possessed a gramophone (phonograph) that had to be wound up by hand and the discs, or records as we called them were made of a flimsy kind of Bakelite. A fresh metal needle had to be inserted into the sound box before it was placed on the record and the sound was not very good.

Living was quite different to today. We had gaslight for illumination and coal fires for heat. Itinerant vendors came round the houses with a horse and cart; there was the greengrocer, and the oilman who delivered paraffin (kerosene), candles, washing soda, kindling, matches and a host of other household items then considered necessities. In the summer he would bring round long bean-poles for the garden. The milkman came with a cart upon which was a huge polished brass urn full of milk, and he would ladle the milk into lidded metal cans yodelling "be-you-lay-ee" at the top of his voice.

Then too there was the rag and bone man calling out "any old iron, rags and bones"; he sat on a rickety cart drawn by an even more rickety nag that seemed to be ready for and even wanting to be sent to the knacker's yard.

The baker had a very smart brown horse-van, and to cap all this off was the muffin man who came round every Sunday afternoon carrying on his head a tray of muffins covered by a cloth, ringing a bell and crying out, "Muffins!"

Following him was the ice cream vendor crying out, "Hokey Pokey!" He later went up in the world by coming round on a tricycle with an icebox on front. Then there was the inevitable French onion seller who walked round with braided onions hung round his neck. At dusk the lamplighter came on his bicycle to light the street gaslights with a long wand and then again at dawn to extinguish them.

I went to the local school at the age of five and my parents gave me the choice of either taking up the violin or the piano. I chose the violin. There was a peripatetic violin teacher who went round the schools teaching the violin and I was enrolled as a pupil. I made reasonable progress, and was later given private lessons. Eventually I was able to struggle through the Mendelssohn violin concerto, which to me at that time was a landmark.

Saturday mornings became the bane of my young life. In those days the fashion was to have a brass fender with brass tongs and a shovel in the fireplace, we also had a brass plant pot in the shape of a lion's head that contained an aspidistra. It was my job to polish these items with 'Brasso', a chore for which I was given my weekly pocket money – all of a penny!

When the chores were done my father would stand over me and my sister (who was a good pianist) listening to our limited repertoire and exclaiming, "Wrong note! Wrong note!" or, "Zis rhythmus is wrong, it should be ta-di-ta- di –ta." After two hours of this purgatory we were allowed to go our separate ways. I would often go to a matinée at the local cinema or to the Congregational Church to a silent film show which we nicknamed the "tuppeny rush" (admission was two pence)[1] to see such epics as the Keystone Cops or Charlie Chaplin.

Talking of Church, ostensibly we were of the Anglican faith but I became an apostate and joined the Baptists because they gave better treats. There was a weekly meeting of the "Band of Hope," an organization to promote abstinence from alcohol and other activities considered as sinful and we were told stories of the Demon Drink and how it affected family life. There were lantern slides; some of Hogarth's *Rakes Progress* and later on we were given copies of Émile Zola's *Dram Shop* to read. We finished off the evening by singing a tune called *Ne'er a Drop Shall Pass my Lips*. Unfortunately, in later life I have been known to imbibe the occasional glass of wine despite all the admonitions of burning in Hellfire if I did so.

There is no free lunch, or free Sunday school treats come to think of it, so I was inveigled into joining the Boy's Brigade which had a band, consisting of three side drummers, a bass drummer and five buglers, and we went on parade once a month on a Sunday morning followed by a route march of a few blocks. It is a wonder that the hard working populace who were looking forward to a quiet lie-in bed put up with the frightful cacophony and disturbance of the peace. There was one boy aged eighteen, Norman, who besides being the chief bugler was nominally in charge of us "nippers" as he called us. He must have had the makings of a future sergeant-major as when we arrived on parade with shining morning face and a belt polished with Brasso the night before, he would hiss into our ears, "I'll make you little sods smarten up!" It was fortunate that Mr. Stevens the Sunday school superintendent never heard him, otherwise I'm sure Norman would have been consigned to the fiery furnace in the nether regions which was always being talked about both in Sunday school and at the Band of Hope. Indeed, I sometimes had nightmares of Mr. Stevens wearing a tail and horns and stoking up an immense fire aided by the parson who always made Hellfire the favourite topic of his sermons.

Every year the Boy's Brigade held a summer camp run in a quasi-military manner situated on the Sussex coast; I hated it. At night there would be a campfire that we would gather around listening to poems and songs recited by the officers, all good church-going men. I remember Alfred, Lord Tennyson's *Charge of the Light Brigade* was a favourite, also *The Heathen Chinee*[2], *The Green Eye of the Little Yellow God* and the song, *The Road to Mandalay*. After this came inevitably the Victorian ballad *Excelsior* and when the song's burden 'Excelsior' arrived, we sang it in chorus with great gusto repeating it twice. Even the hymns had a martial air such as *Fight the Good Fight* and *Onward Christian Soldiers Marching as to War*. All this prepared us for the real thing that was to come not long afterwards.

Often we went on a family holiday to Brighton on the South Coast where there was always an orchestra playing in a band shell. Jan Hurst and his orchestra played pieces such as selections from *No, No Nanette*, *The Desert Song*, Strauss waltzes, the *Lustspiel* overture by Kéla Béla and *Symphonic Rhapsody* by Fetras. You never hear much of that stuff played nowadays but there is a movement afoot to revive it.

One evening we were taken to the Palace Pier in Brighton where an orchestra was performing. My father said to me (I was nine at the time) '"You are going to see a very famous man tonight, and never ever forget it." He turned out to be Albert Ketélbey who delighted us by conducting a performance of his *In a Monastery Garden*, followed by *In a Persian Market*. I can see him now, a bent old man, nearly blind; the packed audience was spellbound. When it came to the part in the *Persian Market* where the orchestra had to sing, "Bakshees, bakshees Alla-a-a," I could see some of them smiling, particularly the bass player and I remarked to my Dad that he seemed to have an easy job. Little did I know then that to play the bass properly is a very difficult job.

The school celebrated Empire Day on May 24th every year, and we had to purchase a Union Jack flag for the price of one penny and bring it to school where there was a huge Union Jack on a staff in the playground. We were all ordered to gather round and the ceremony began, consisting of all the jingoistic "old faithfuls". First we all sang *Rule Britannia*, repeating the line which goes, "Britons Never, Never, Never Shall be Slaves." This set the tone for the rest of the ceremony. The teacher unfolded a huge map of the World showing the British Empire liberally sprawled across it marked in red and we were reminded that this was the Empire upon which the sun never set and how fortunate we were to be British and of all the good works being done by the British in the colonies.

Then we sang *God Bless the Prince of Wales* with great fervour, but from what I had heard my parents remark about him I really wondered whether, instead of being blessed by God, Mr. Stevens might recommend that he be given a glimpse of Hellfire. Then came the song, *Hail the Flag, the Jolly, Jolly Flag of the Red, White and Blue,* during which we were encouraged to wave our penny flags. Sometimes *Jerusalem* was thrown in but always *Land of Hope and Glory* followed by *God Save the King*.

All that being accomplished we were ordered by the teacher to wave our caps and shout "Hooray!" after he had given a preliminary "Hip, Hip!" This was repeated three times and we were then allowed to go home, the day was declared a half-holiday which for us was the best part of the whole proceedings.

Life for the masses was turbulent in those days. I can just remember the General Strike of 1926 brought about by poverty and unemployment. My father wanted to hang on to his job, so he caught a lift to work every day in trucks that were organized to break the strike. I suppose he would have been called a "scab" nowadays, but at least we ate.

Later on I saw large columns of hunger marchers who journeyed on foot all the way down from Jarrow, a shipbuilding town in the North of England, to London to protest to the Government the hardships they were undergoing. Some of the Marchers who chained themselves to the railings outside the classy Ritz Hotel in London were given food, but the March did not achieve much. It was only after Chamberlain's visit to Hitler, when re-armament started in earnest and employment rose that things began to look up.

There was hardly any welfare in those days and the Government brought in the dreaded Means Test which decreed that if there was even one item of furniture in a household such as an easy chair that they deemed to be superfluous, it had to be sold before the family received even a penny.

The Great Depression really made a difference to the majority of people. My family always seemed to have enough food for my mother was a very good homemaker, but even at my tender age I couldn't see myself achieving much in life with the shortage of money that precluded a good education.

Material expectations were different then. There was a spirit abroad that we were all in this together. If there was a passing funeral procession whilst my father and I were walking together he would ask me to remove my cap and stand at the kerb facing the hearse, head bowed. Also whenever a train carrying cattle passed, it was his custom to remove his hat and stand silently contemplating the fate of the animals that were to be slaughtered for our food.

Such were the times that I grew up in, and many of the events are engraved forever in my mind but, ironically, I myself am of the opinion that because some of the customs that were then in vogue are not now observed, spiritually, we, as human beings are now much the poorer for it. Many old people boast of things being different in their young days and how much the world has declined, but it may be a symptom of their own decline so I will change the subject and get on with the narrative.

When I was thirteen my father obtained a better job in Leamington Spa, a pleasant country town about ninety miles North West of London. Gouty colonels retired from India used to frequent the spa to take the mineral waters for a cure. My father at this time frequently asked me what I wanted to do for a living. I told him that perhaps I would like to do something in the Arts, preferably music. My father would have none of this, and used the word "precarious" that always came up when the musical profession was discussed, and insisted that I become an "apprunktis" as he pronounced it.

In his day in Germany it was then the practice to indenture boys as apprentices for seven years after which they were able to enter a trade or profession. There was a scheme at a local engineering factory whereby boys were enrolled at the tender age of fourteen and I, too, was enrolled.

There was practical hands-on teaching in the morning, afternoons were spent examining the mysteries of the calculus, algebra, trigonometry and machine and freehand drawing. Evenings were optional; you could study business English, business French and literature. Thirteen-hour days were unbearable for all of us; it seemed as though we were regarded as receptacles for cramming as much knowledge into as at all possible.

There was one man named Harold Price who had been a violinist at the time of the silent cinema and who was to become my ally and mentor. When talkies arrived, he, with thousands of other musicians, was thrown out of work and had been unemployed for years. I used to play violin in a small orchestra that met at a church on Sunday afternoons that they called "Pleasant Sunday Afternoons". Harold was a good player; he had studied with John Dunn, and always played a solo at the concert.

When I was sixteen I saved up enough money to take the train to London (they were steam in those days and I remember they were pulled by magnificent Great Western Railway Castle class locomotives) to go to a Promenade concert at the Queen's Hall, London. The BBC Symphony Orchestra was playing and the great Eugene Cruft was the principal double bassist. I was fascinated to watch him play, and then and there I made the most momentous decision of my life – that I would take up the double bass and eventually study with Eugene Cruft if at all possible.

My father shrugged his shoulders at this news and re-iterated that he still thought the musical profession to be precarious. My mother, though, was fairly receptive when I told her of my decision and she agreed to help me buy a bass. There was a weekly advertising magazine called the *Exchange and Mart* and in it there were adverts for basses. I selected one that cost seven pounds ten shillings and came with bow and cover. A fine bass would cost over one hundred pounds but there was not that kind of money available, so that was the instrument I had to settle for. I caught the train to London and bought the bass. I didn't fully realize what a momentous step I had taken at that time, but I had a bass, great eagerness to study it, and thought the world was now my oyster.

There ensued many discussions with Harold Price as to what my next move should be. Studying music full time was beyond my means so I eventually plucked up the courage to write to Arthur Cockerill, who was principal bass with the BBC Midland Orchestra and also principal bass with the City of Birmingham Orchestra. He replied saying that he taught the double bass at the Birmingham and Midland Institute School of Music of which Sir Granville Bantock had been the Principal, and that he would be happy to teach me. I was thrilled.

Arthur Cockerill was a fine orchestral player and during the years I spent with him he gave me a thorough grounding. I used to catch the train to Birmingham every Friday and before the lesson went to Joe Lyons, a chain cafeteria to have tea and baked beans on toast. It was the highlight of the week. Every night I would practice assiduously for hours on end and as we lived in a big house I was fortunate that I didn't disturb the family with my practice. After a while Mr. Cockerill recommended that I join a string orchestra class directed by Johann Hock and I went a couple of times and enjoyed it. I was the only bassist and after I had fumbled my way sight reading through a particularly difficult bass part in a Haydn symphony Mr. Hock came up to me afterwards and said in his broken English, "Mr. Cockerill tells me zat you vill be a great bass player, and I agree vith him." Naturally my head swelled upon hearing this but I couldn't afford the fee for the class so I had to leave. However his words gave me the encouragement I needed and I resolved to practice even harder.

Nothing daunted, I had been asked by a local dance band if I would play with them and I eagerly accepted. The going rate then was five shillings an hour. As an apprentice I was only receiving the paltry token sum of seven shillings and sixpence per week, some of which I gave towards my keep so the extra money was to be of great help. Actually it was a good band, the bandleader, Eddie Pratt had been first alto sax with the then famous Joe Loss band, and the tenor sax was Johnny Gray who later became very famous. I looked upon it as musical navvying[3], getting back home at 1.30 a.m. covered with sweat, hands sore with plucking the strings, then having to get up early to go to work next day. As time went on I was busier with the dance band, but as my technique improved I was asked to play with various amateur musical societies. There was one in Leamington and one in Banbury where they had a yearly music festival and where I was fortunate to meet and play under Thomas F. Dunhill, a pedagogue and composer.

I wanted to save up for a car so I accepted every offer that came in. One was to play regularly for a dance band run by a Reg Laight who provided the band for a certain "Professor" Daniels who owned a ballroom dancing academy in Coventry. The "Professor" was a small, chubby man, about fifty years of age, bald and wearing glasses. Nobody thought the fair sex might be at all interested in him, although he thought otherwise. At every dance he gave a demonstration of a tango, paso doble or some other Latin dance. We invariably played *La Cumparsita*; why the name sticks in my memory I don't know but the "Professor", clad in a tail suit with the tails sweeping the floor would steer his partner around with great aplomb.

This caused all the young girls in the class to swoon and at the interval you could count on the Professor to come up to the bandstand and say, "All you young stags have nothing on me; after they've been in bed with me for an hour and a half…" the rest is unprintable. At least though, the five shillings an hour came in handy for the car fund plus all the many expenses I incurred in lessons and upkeep of the bass, so I used to catch the train for Coventry, bass on my back, and catch the late train home to Leamington Spa round about midnight. I eventually bought my first car in 1938 at the age of 18, it was a 1932 Morris Family Eight horsepower and cost all of thirty pounds but it wasn't very reliable and I spent much time underneath fixing it.

Strings were a large expense in those days. The upper strings, G and D, were made of gut and sometimes they would break in a week or maybe they would last three months. After a while, with the sweat of the hand, whiskers would appear on the string and you knew it was time to change it. I was advised by Arthur Cockerill to use almond oil to rub on the strings before playing, this alleviated the problem slightly, but after a time the bow wore a flat on the string making it unuseable. The two bottom strings were made of gut wound with silver plated copper wire and there was a frequent problem with the wire wrapping becoming loose. Then there was the problem of intonation; according to the weather the strings would go out of tune and have to be adjusted frequently during a concert or rehearsal.

When Basil Cameron conducted a rehearsal with the BBC Northern Orchestra there was a difficult passage for the basses and he asked for the basses to play it alone without the rest of the orchestra; one very good bassist had just put on a new string, which of course being gut was stretching with the result that some notes were flat. Cameron complained to the management and the man was fired. When wire strings became in vogue they were a great step forward.

Soon I was getting calls from Leicester, Birmingham and all over the Midlands. In the Spa Pump Room at Leamington there was a ladies trio in residence to play for the "quality" who attended the spa. Suddenly, one day they were no longer there.

It appeared that the violinist of the trio and the spa manager were more than friendly and in those days this sort of thing was frowned upon, so they were fired and a new trio was brought in. The leader of this new trio succeeded in arranging for an octet to play on Sunday afternoons and I was asked to play with them. The fee was ten shillings, a princely amount in those days and on top of that we were regaled with scrumptious pastries and tea in the interval. We played the Tavan arrangements of *Madama Butterfly*, *La Traviata* and selections from such musicals as *No, No, Nanette*, *Chu Chin Chow* and *The Desert Song* interspersed with Strauss and Gung'l waltzes and sometimes I was asked to play a bass solo, either *Lucy Long* or *Grandma's Birthday*. I doubt if they are in circulation now, but they always received humorous applause.

The following year due to monetary constraints it was cut down to a quintet but I was still hired. The Pump Room trio was changed and a new man, van der Venn took over and I was asked to play in a little group that performed on Sunday afternoons. We all had to wear a colourful blouse and a sash as it was supposed to be a gypsy band. Van der Venn went round the tables playing to the old ladies as we played a czardas[4] and some of the players used to call out to each other in mock Hungarian. I remember one dear old soul saying, "Fancy, they must be real foreigners!"

I was asked to deputize at the Coventry Hippodrome. It was my first experience of playing at a variety show. The drummer was the star of the orchestra and he managed to get in a cymbal crash or a drum roll whenever the dancer or comedian onstage was kicking his/her leg in the air. The drummer was always paid extra as really good ones were very hard to find. It was fascinating to see and hear him play, timing his percussive volleys to a split second; he really made the show. Another thing I noticed was a tube connected to a barrel of beer outside the pit and the drummer and his cohorts used the tube frequently to slake their thirst.

The Warwickshire Symphony Orchestra, a part amateur group that was conducted by Adrian Beecham, son of the famous conductor, Sir Thomas Beecham, Bart. asked me to play with them. We used to meet once a week at the home of a Mrs. Lamb, a wealthy lady who lived in a huge manor house called Compton Verney near Stratford-on-Avon. Lady Beecham was always there but she and Sir Thomas were estranged at the time, Sir Thomas being partnered with Lady Cunard (of the shipping company) who helped Sir Thomas financially in his musical ventures. I don't think he and his son were very close, in fact we never saw Sir Thomas present at any of his son's concerts. The rehearsals for me at age seventeen were wonderful, especially in the interval when a flunkey, gorgeously attired in a wig, a zebra striped jacket and knee-breeches would serve the most marvellous titbits of food plus iced lemonade in the magnificent garden. Mrs. Lamb sang the aria *Leise, leise* from Weber's opera *Der Freischütz* at the concert which was given at the Stratford Memorial Theatre: at the time I really thought I had died and gone to Heaven!

Then, when I was eighteen, in the early part of 1939 I received a telegram, (there were not many phones in those days so communication was mainly by telegram or letter), and it read: "Can you play a concert with the Coventry Symphony Orchestra, directed by W.B. Major?" You wouldn't think that a perfectly innocuous thing like that would change my whole life, but it did.

I caught the train to Coventry, about ten miles away, carrying the bass on my back to the railway station, then upon arrival in Coventry carried it to the concert hall and played the concert. I can remember the programme now: Tchaikowsky's Pathétique Symphony and Mozart's violin and viola *Sinfonia Concertante* played by Major on violin, and a violist whom I have mercifully forgotten. Major was no conductor but he had that air of confidence and a lot of B.S. that enabled him to get through. He was also a prominent teacher of the violin in Coventry.

After the concert Major had a chat with me and informed me that he was also the Bandmaster of the 7th Royal Warwickshire Regiment which was a part-time battalion of the Territorial Army. There was a camp every year and also a bounty of five pounds sterling. He also told me that it really wasn't like the Regular Army at all and that all the part-time soldiers had a wonderful time, there was marvellous camaraderie and enjoyment, indeed, the way he described it, it sounded like the next best thing to achieving Nirvana. Well, it certainly wasn't, as it turned out, but I made my way to the local H.Q. of the 7th Royal Warwicks in Leamington, accepted the King's shilling (an ancient custom going back to medieval times when a shilling was worth a lot of money), made my oath of allegiance on the Bible to King and Country and that was it. I was a soldier in the King's Army, but I thought to myself that if my family had made the move back to Germany I would have been a German soldier. Such are the vagaries of life.

Chapter 1 Notes:
1. Pre-decimal currency was 12 pence to the shilling, 20 shillings to the pound
2. "Heathen Chinee", slang for a Chinese person, not politically correct nowadays
3. A "navvy" was the name for a labourer employed in the early 1800s to dig canals.
4. A Hungarian dance of Magyar origin.

CHAPTER 2

All the King's Men. Some bloody fighting. I escape from Dunkirk.

In my later years I cannot help equating Major with that famous picture of Millais entitled *The Boyhood of Raleigh*. It shows the boy Raleigh and a friend sitting on a Devonshire beach by the sea whilst an old salt is pointing with outstretched hand over the horizon to a mythical El Dorado; one gets the impression that he is implying that they too can reap the glorious plunder to be obtained just by following his suggestions. So it was with Major, but once I had signed up his attitude changed noticeably; so much for my youthful naïveté.

We went to camp in the July of 1939 at Arundel, Sussex, the country seat of the Duke of Norfolk. There was the occasional drill and the band was expected to play for the officers' mess. The programmes consisted of marches, waltzes and such pieces as *Nola* and Luigini's *Ballet Égyptien*.

Back from camp we were sent one Saturday afternoon to "fire our course" at Budbrooke Barracks, the home of the 8th Warwicks, a regular battalion. This consisted of firing five shots at a target. It was the only target practice we would ever receive due to the shortage of ammunition. The rifles were 1912 Lee Enfields. Later on when we were to encounter the German Army we found that they were equipped with the latest automatic firearms with plenty of ammunition, so much so that they would fire bursts seemingly for the fun of it.

Meanwhile the news was becoming graver day by day and war seemed inevitable. Neville Chamberlain came back from Munich after signing the Munich Agreement with Hitler on September 29th 1938 and upon alighting from the airplane he waved what was to be called his "Piece of Paper" to the crowds and declared that there was to be peace in our time. He has been much maligned but I think one of his objectives must have been to gain time to re-arm, which then commenced with a vengeance. Maybe in retrospect he will be re-evaluated by historians because at the time of Munich we were in no way ready to wage a war, neither were we in 1939.

A week before September 3rd, 1939 we were called up. I had to report to the H.Q. Drill hall situated in the Butts, Coventry. This is the site where King Henry VIII forced every able man to practice with a bow and arrow at a bull's eye target called a butt; hence the name "Butts". We were medically examined and issued with our kit, which consisted of a greatcoat, hat, uniform and boots, underwear, iron rations, a water bottle, gas mask, gas cape, pack, blanket, a 1912 Lee Enfield Rifle plus a bayonet and five rounds of ammunition.

I well remember Sunday, September 3rd, 1939 when we were paraded and marched in our serried ranks bearing our Colours which were to be laid up in Coventry Cathedral. I can still see in my mind's eye its beautiful Warwickshire red sandstone exterior and the magnificent interior. Little did we realise then that it would be soon made into a pile of rubble. Hitler gave a name to it when he later bombed other cities - they were said to have been "Coventrated".

That day, September 3rd 1939, the sirens went off and everyone scrambled to a shelter. It turned out to be a false alarm but it brought it home to us that now we really were at war.

Shortly afterwards we were sent to Swindon in Wiltshire to do our training which consisted of marching up and down, various manoeuvres with a rifle and several 60-mile route marches; "Toughen the men up, don't ye know," so said our Colonel, the Honourable Cyril Siddeley who was a member of the wealthy Armstrong, Hawker, Siddeley family. The Hon. Cyril must have thought he was tough enough already because he drove up and down in a staff car to 'supervise'. Foot blisters were numerous but we were advised by the Medical Officer to prick them with a pin and swab them with iodine.

Christmas came and we were given leave and told to say our farewells to our families because we would be shortly on the move, where to we were not told. Arriving back from leave we were marched down to the railway station and then sent to a port to embark for France. When we arrived at the port we were mustered and waited for hours because H. M. King George 6th was coming to inspect us. I caught a glimpse of the King who was heavily made up with a kind of pancake make-up. We were ordered, "On the command cheer, you must cheer, raise your cap and go on cheering until you are told to stop." That done, we embarked for France.

It was bitterly cold on the ship. Other ranks were herded on deck whilst the Hon. Cyril and his officer cohorts were down below. There was

The Bottom Line

very little food but we were ordered not to touch our iron rations, with threats of dire consequences if we did.

Eventually we docked at Le Havre, France, and were then marched to a waiting train with cattle trucks marked *24 hommes et 12 chevaux*. The journey seemed to be interminable, but at last we arrived at the village of Râches near Douai in the Pas de Calais not far from the Maginot Line. The temperature was about 40 below and the roads were covered with slippery ice that caused some of us to fall over as we marched to our destination, an enamel factory situated by a canal. This didn't prevent 'Queenie', our Sergeant-major, from barking out commands to impress the locals that we were indeed a fighting force.

My first impression of Râches was that of a desperately poor community resigned to its poverty. Another thing that struck me was the number of men who had been crippled in the First World War hobbling about on crutches or without an arm or with a facial disfigurement.

The population was friendly and some of the local ladies would do our laundry for a few centimes. Our bathing facilities were at a coalmine pithead shower near Douai where we were taken once a week. There was about half an inch of coal dust on the floor so you had to be careful you didn't drop your towel or clean underclothes because they were immediately transformed from white to coal black thereby necessitating another visit to the *blanchissage* lady to get them re-laundered.

The mines were the Mines d'Aniches. Later on in life when I read Émile Zola's novel *Germinal* it occurred to me that this was the area in the Pas-de-Calais where *Germinal* was set. The bleakness and sense of meek acceptance of their lot amongst the population was still there when I saw it in 1940.

In England too, there had been that air of despondency in the Great Depression but the rush for re-armament and the prosperity it brought to the workers, together with a lot of pro-war propaganda, seemed to have transformed Britain with a will to fight. In the London parks they were digging trenches which proved to be useless. A total black-out at night was rigorously enforced with many road casualties as a result, and various propaganda placards appeared. I remember one in which a man is declaring "Be like Dad, keep Mum"[5], which nowadays would certainly not be politically correct.

But reverting to France, the millions of casualties they had suffered in WW1 was uppermost in the minds of those French people with whom I spoke and there was fear of another war taking place on their soil. In Belgium, just over the border, it seemed even worse. There was a man digging an air raid shelter for his family. As we had an hour or two off I offered to help him, but I was met with a curt refusal.

Our sleeping quarters were in a huge room with broken north light windows in an unused part of the factory. Work was still going on in another part of the factory where they were enamelling coffee pots and jugs a bright orange colour. We were issued with straw to put on the concrete floor to sleep on and at night covered ourselves with a blanket and then a gas cape.

By morning there were icicles on the gas cape from our breath and our water bottles were frozen solid. Reveille was at 6 a.m. and we were expected to be on parade at 6.30, washed, dressed and shaved for inspection, after which we ate breakfast. But the problem was that there were no washing facilities. There was no running cold water and the only water we could obtain for our ablutions came from siphoning off the coolant water from a diesel engine that was running for the factory. Inevitably some of the 100 men of our HQ company were late on parade, 'Put on the Peg' as it was called, and then sentenced to do so many days 'Jankers' which meant running round each day at the double for an hour or so wearing F.S.M.O.[6] which consisted of your pack and all its contents, your rifle, bayonet, water bottle, blanket, gas mask, gas cape etc. totalling about 60 pounds.

Needless to say the Hon. Cyril was nicely billeted at some chateau, but I'm quite sure he was pleased to see that the men were being toughened up. Food or lack of it was another matter. The cooks consisted of one, Monty, who suffered from bad acne and whose hands and nails were absolutely filthy, but he was a pleasant soul, although somewhat lacking in intellect. Supervising Monty was a Sergeant-Cook. There were field kitchens, huge pots into which went anything that Monty could lay his hands on and then topped it all up with copious amounts of water, this was called 'Pontoon' and was served with bread that had green mould on it. The next day, Monty added curry powder to it and it went under the name of 'Curry'.

As I could speak French tolerably well I was asked to go into Douai with W.B.Major to buy bread, as even the officers had noticed the mould. At every mealtime an officer went round asking if there were any complaints about the food. No-one ever did complain, as it was not politic to do so. If you did, there was always the possibility of a charge of 'frivolous complaint' being laid against you. Later it was discovered that the Sergeant-Cook had been selling our rations so he was court-martialled and reduced to the ranks.

Looking back, I am reminded of Edward Gibbon's history, *The Decline and Fall of the Roman Empire* wherein he comments on the Emperor Commenus, "In every deed of mischief he had a head to contrive, a heart to resolve and a hand to execute." This describes the Honourable Cyril wonderfully well. For instance, when war broke out we were paid the princely sum of seven shillings per week that was shortly increased to fourteen, but Siddeley decreed that he didn't agree with us having all that money to spend in a foreign country. "Got to keep the Pound strong, don't ye know." So although it was strictly against Army Regulations we were only allowed to keep seven shillings per week and the rest was sent home to be put in an account for us. This caused us hardship but even with a paltry seven shillings per week we were much better off than our French comrades the *Poilus*[7] who received a miniscule amount.

Another little trick the Hon C. got up to was to order bromide to be put in our tea. I actually saw Monty doing this so I know it to be true. His reason; "Calm the men down, they mustn't get too obstreperous, don't ye know," perhaps he foresaw a mutiny.

Instructions were given to the Medical Officer that too many men were malingering, so all who attended sick parade were to be given M&D.[8] this had a bad outcome for one poor fellow, a corporal, who, although in great pain wouldn't go on sick parade. Eventually someone told the duty officer about it, the corporal was found to have appendicitis and then rushed to hospital but he died en route from a burst appendix.

I was ordered to be the Medical Officer's orderly, or "Pox Doctor's Clerk" in Army parlance. At that time brothels were legal in France and there was one in Douai, the nearest town that we were allowed to frequent. Soon there were cases of venereal disease that I, as the orderly came to be acquainted with. This put me off partaking of the brothel's delights but I did visit it once just to see what the interior was like. It reminded me of a Toulouse Lautrec drawing. There were several bored looking girls and the Madame who was encouraging us to buy drinks and then consort with them, and in retrospect I am glad I didn't. Condoms were provided for the troops who named them variously "French letters" or "Dreadnoughts". They were so thick that the men never used them, hence the numerous V.D. cases.

The band instruments were brought over, so we still played on Sundays for Church Parade and had to act as stretcher-bearers on manoeuvres which were were usually chaotic. We were being trained to man the Maginot Line and surrounding areas, this meant operations with the French with lots of *Entente Cordiale* and all that. One day we were out there doing our thing and there was an officer appointed to be an umpire who would go around randomly throwing firecrackers in imitation of enemy fire. He threw one at me and the other stretcher-bearer and adjudged me to be dead, whereupon the other stretcher half said, "He can't be dead, and I can't carry the stretcher by myself." The reply was, "You're dead too, just for arguing!" In the heat of this charade the Hon. Cyril was brandishing his revolver and ordering men around left right and centre until a high ranking brass hat[9] came round and bellowed for all to hear, "Siddeley, you bloody fool, do you know what you've done, you've led your men behind the enemy lines!"

We had to go on sentry duty to guard the small railway marshalling yard in Râches. It was bitterly cold at night, no open fires were allowed so most of us wore gloves or mittens plus Balaclava helmets that the Friends of the 7th Warwicks had knitted for us and sent over in a huge hamper. This got to the notice of the Hon. C., and an order was posted which declared that wearing non-issue articles of clothing such as gloves or balaclavas was against King's Regulations and any man caught wearing them could expect condign punishment. By this time most of us had the idea that in volunteering to fight in a war we had committed a heinous offence and that we were to be treated as common criminals.

Soon after that some of the officers (I don't know if the Hon. C. was amongst them) "borrowed" an army truck to have a night out on the town, (Lille), but were apprehended by the Military Police and subsequently court-martialled. All were demoted in rank and later the Hon. C. was sent off as Town Major of Dieppe. He was replaced by Lt. Col. Mole, a professional soldier seconded to us from an Irish battalion. He was firm but just, and did a great deal to improve morale but unfortunately he was killed very soon afterwards.

One day the duty officer told me that as I could drive I would be transferred to a trench mortar squad. As well as being the driver I was number three, which meant I activated the fuse as the bombs were passed along to the mortar. I also had to guard the truck which was full of bombs, and even now it makes me break out into a sweat when I think that I used to spread my blanket on the bombs and sleep on them at night!

We were issued seven more bullets making a total of twelve and I used to keep one "up the spout" in case of sudden surprise. This practice was observed by several of the men and there were one or two accidental shootings – "Friendly fire" they call it nowadays. To send a thousand boys with only twelve bullets each to fight the German Army which was so well equipped, was criminal, I think, considering our lack of weaponry.

However, it was war and anything can be done to anybody in a war under the guise of necessity, I suppose.

One happy event took place. My friend, George Ford, who played the French horn, noticed there was a concert taking place one Sunday in Lille. We were given permission to attend it and we thoroughly enjoyed it. I forget most of the programme but one of the items was the *Trumpet Septet* by Saint Saëns that includes a double bass. I had a chat with the bass player who was a French Army sergeant and we shared some finer points of technique.

May arrived and there were whisperings that the Germans might march, and they did. We were all mustered and headed in the direction of Belgium but before we left the band instruments were unceremoniously dumped in the canal; "Scorched Earth," they said. We were not able to move very quickly because of the numbers of refugees, fleeing to where I do not know. I spotted M. & Mme.Descatoire who kept the local estaminet[10] in Râches where we used to supplement our rations pushing a wheelbarrow holding their meagre belongings. I waved, but never saw them again.

The French had huge guns of 1914 vintage that were pulled by teams of twelve horses. The German Stuka dive-bombers swept down with their engines making a terrifying scream and gunned down the horses; after that the roads became impassable. At last we reached the Albert Canal where bitter fighting took place, some hand to hand, that lasted for many days. We were deployed with the mortar which proved to be a formidable weapon, but the German mortars were lighter and more manoeuvrable, requiring fewer men to operate them.

The German strategy seemed to be, at least as I experienced it, to send waves of Czech conscripts over first, followed by the dreaded S.S. Storm Troopers, the German Army's élite troops, wearing their zig-zag flashes and skull and crossbones insignia.

We were out of gasoline and ammunition so I parked the truck in order to reconnoitre. All contact had been lost with HQ but by chance I came across William B. Major and a sergeant named Cliff Edwards. We were holding a council of war as to what we should do when an effete looking captain approached us twirling a revolver. He informed us that we were surrounded and the order had been given to try to make for Dunkirk, "and if any man panics I'll shoot him dead, so there!" This was more suited to a Victorian melodrama than an order given in battle, so not wishing to be shot dead by one of our own we went on our way.

We learned later that being taken prisoner would not be a viable option because an S.S. officer, SS-Hauptsturmführer Wilhelm Mohnke, had allegedly committed a most heinous crime. It was said that he ordered about 80 Warwicks into a barn, set fire to it and had them shot as they fled out. It later became known as the "Massacre of the Warwicks". He was never prosecuted although the United Nations War Crimes Commission declared him a war criminal in 1947. At the end of the war he attained the rank of SS-Brigadeführer and was second to Hitler in command of the German forces defending Berlin, but somehow managed to get out of Hitler's bunker alive. The last I heard of him was in a 1988 newspaper article reporting him alive and well and living in the village of Stemwarde, just outside of Hamburg, Germany. Recently I read they were making a film in Germany, glorifying him.

Dunkirk was far off and I was so glad I could speak French to get further directions. On the journey the farms were deserted and as we were very hungry we purloined the occasional chicken and cooked it over a fire, which was a dangerous thing to do because we would have been in trouble if the Germans had noticed the smoke. One evening at dusk a German truck full of Waffen S.S. soldiers came roaring by us. It was obvious that in their rush and in the failing light they hadn't noticed us, but it put us on our guard.

Shortly afterwards two French soldiers came along supporting a French captain who had recently been wounded. One soldier was saying, "Courage, Mon Capitaine." The captain appeared to be in a bad state, his arm was hanging loose and blood seemed to be coming out of his chest area. The poilu murmured to me "mitrailleuse," which confirmed there was a machine gun emplacement nearby and it sounded ominous to us. Fortunately there was a field dressing station close by and we directed them there but I often wondered what happened to that captain.

It seemed that now the battle had developed into skirmishes. During the Battle of the Albert Canal both sides were in front of their artillery in lines facing each other, and as we became more experienced we could tell by the whine of the shell from which side it came, but now it was risky to walk anywhere because you never knew where the enemy was situated. We had heard the rattle of machine gun fire several times but did not realise it was so close to us.

As dusk was changing to night we came upon a deserted village. Our Guardian Angel appeared to us in the shape of a Frenchman who had stayed behind alone and he beckoned us into his house. He had been chauffeur to Marshal Foch in WW1 and he recounted some of his experiences to us. He hadn't much food in the house but brought out a baguette, some cheese and some onions plus a bottle of vin ordinaire, which we consumed with gusto. He warned us that the whole area was overrun with Germans and that we should move at night but only on by-ways or trails as all the main roads were being constantly bombed and strafed by the German Stuka dive-bombers. Had it not been for this French patriot and the advice and sketch map he gave me I am sure that I would not be alive today.

Because we had expended all our twelve bullets he suggested that we cache our rifles, as he had heard on the radio that there could be reinforcements and ammunition coming, in which case we could double back and pick up our rifles.

The next evening after kissing us on both cheeks and with cries of "Bonne chance","Vive La Grande-Bretagne", "Vive La France" and "À bas Les Boches"[11] he sent us on our way. After a long and arduous journey we eventually reached Dunkirk where there was a boat tied up at a damaged dock. It was carrying a cargo of biscuits and tins of gasoline and although it was already overloaded the crew agreed to take us aboard. Hoping and praying that the Luftwaffe wouldn't strafe us we eventually reached England and home, but our battalion was decimated by the numbers of those killed, wounded and taken prisoner-of-war.

After being sent to a regrouping area in Devonshire, I was called into HQ and told I was going to be discharged from the Army and put on war work. I was given a small sum of money so that I could buy civilian clothes and a railway pass and I found myself back in Leamington Spa. This was 1940 and the war still had a long time to go.

Not long afterwards I received an International Red Cross post card from my friend George Ford. He was a P.O.W and had been marched all the way from Belgium to Thorn, in Poland. A short time later I received another card from the Red Cross to say that he had died. I went to Coventry to visit his heartbroken parents; George had been their only child, and they had had him late in life. When I left they gave me George's collection of miniature musical scores that I still treasure.

I came across W.B. Major years later when I was freelancing in London. He had obtained the job of "fixer" for a brief time with the London Mozart Players and asked me if I would play a concert with them, but I never saw him after that.

Chapter 2 Notes
5. English slang, meaning to keep silent and not give your opponent any information, eg. war secrets.
6. Field Service Marching Order
7. "Poilus", slang for French soldiers
8. M&D, Medicine and Duty
9. A general
10. Cafe
11. À bas Les Boches: Down with the Germans

CHAPTER 3

Back in "Civvy Street". Eugene Cruft. The Carl Rosa Opera Company. I am made an A.R.C.M. Asked to play principal bass in the City of Birmingham Orchestra. The London Philharmonic invite me to play with them.

It didn't take me long to accustom myself to civilian life, which seemed like Heaven after all I'd been through.

I went back to the engineering factory in Leamington Spa where I had been apprenticed before the outbreak of war and was placed in the Drawing Office as I had already some experience in machine drawing, and was set to work designing jigs and tools for the war effort; everyone had to be usefully employed if they were not in the Forces. Because I had been in the Army I was treated very well and allowed to take a little time off for music provided I made it up, this flexibility helped me a lot as time went on.

By this time Harold Price had been taken on for war work and worked in the next office to me. Again, after much discussion I thought the time to study with Eugene Cruft was now or never.

The BBC Symphony Orchestra had been evacuated to Bristol by some clown in its management department. It couldn't have been a worse choice of location because Bristol was a significant port and also there were several factories in the area, some making aircraft engines and 'planes. When Hitler's Blitzkrieg started in earnest the Luftwaffe bombarded Bristol and Coventry. I well remember the Coventry air raid where everything was blown to smithereens; my sister drove an ambulance that night and we could see the sky lit up with fire, searchlights and anti-aircraft guns. We were only ten miles away from Coventry and a stick of bombs was dropped on Leamington, one of which fell near Queen Victoria's statue outside the Town Hall, dislodging it about six inches off its pedestal. Looking down from her Great Niche in the Sky, poor Queen Victoria, I am certain, was not amused.

One of the casualties in the Bristol air raid was Arthur Cockerill's brother, Bert, who was also a bass player in the BBC Symphony Orchestra. After this débâcle it was decided to re-locate the BBC Symphony Orchestra to Bedford, a quiet county town about sixty miles away from Leamington as the crow flies. This made it possible for me to get there and back in a day, so I wrote to the great man, Eugene Cruft, begging him to teach me. He replied, saying he would be glad to accept me as a pupil and his fee would be one guinea[12]. In those days all professional men, doctors, lawyers etc. charged their fees in guineas, for me it was a huge amount.

I was determined to get to Bedford by hook or by crook, but there was one problem that I had to surmount. I could catch a train to Coventry, where I changed for Northampton, but no train ran to Bedford from Northampton. Many trains had been cut due to the coal shortage. What to do? It was 23½ miles to Bedford from Northampton and I was now feeling fit so I decided to take my bicycle on the train, cycle the 23½ miles from Northampton to Bedford, have my lesson, then cycle the 23½ miles back to Northampton, catch the train and get back home to Leamington. Fortunately I didn't have to take a bass.

The great day came. I stopped at a pub halfway, ate my sandwiches and arrived at the splendid house where Mr. Cruft was billeted. I timidly knocked on the door, it opened, and there was Eugene Cruft! He was attired in a Home Guard uniform wearing the rank of Captain; he had a revolver on a lanyard at his side and said rather imperiously, "Ah, Meyer! Good to meet you, come in." After introducing me to Mrs. Cruft the lesson began. He was meticulous in showing me his method of playing which was based on the Simandl method that was, and possibly still is, the definitive one. He had adapted Simandl so that the thumb was employed even in the lower positions and he frequently used extensions, i.e. stretching the fingers to obtain more than one full tone, and also used "fork fingering" as he called it, in the upper range of the bass by swivelling the first two fingers together in one position so that they were vertically in line with the fingerboard. I found this to be most useful later on.

The lesson took at least two hours after which Mrs. Cruft regaled me with tea and seed cake that she had made from her meagre rations, plus sardines. I always remember her saying to me at every lesson. "Do have another sardine, Mr. Meyer." I was overwhelmed with all this, and after arranging another lesson in a fortnight's time I bowed out backwards like one does before royalty. After I had exited the front door I realized that I had not given Mr. Cruft his guinea, so, embarrassed, I knocked on the front door again, apologized, tendered the guinea, got on my bike and rode back to Northampton where I caught the train and eventually arrived back in Leamington.

Practice then began in earnest, and every night I would practice anywhere from two to four hours so that when I went for my lesson I would be note perfect. It was an exhausting life but I felt that at last I was working towards my goal, to be a bass player par excellence. Sometimes before I had my lesson, Mr. Cruft would obtain a ticket for me to a concert given by the BBC Symphony at the Bedford Corn Exchange, a large, drab hall. Usually Sir Adrian Boult would conduct, but sometimes there were guest conductors. I remember Sir Henry Wood conducting William Walton's oratorio, *Belshazzar's Feast* with Dennis Noble, the baritone, who had also sung in the first performance at Leeds in 1931. Sir Henry was getting on in years and sported a grey beard. He was much revered by the Orchestra and was affectionately known to them as "Old Timber" and although not regarded by them as being a virtuoso conductor he was, nevertheless, very competent.

After the concert we would repair to the Cruft residence where the two-hour lesson would begin. After a time Mr. Cruft suggested that I should now tackle a bass concerto. He decided on an arrangement by Francis Baines of the Capuzzi Concerto adapted from the original violone version. I made rapid progress with it and one day he told me I should consider applying at a later date to become an Associate of the Royal College of Music as a Double Bass Soloist. I needed to work on all the Richard Strauss, Wagner, Beethoven, and Mozart etc. excerpts, as well as double bass concertos that I had to learn to play from memory. Music was mostly unobtainable in the war; there were no Xerox machines in those days so I remember having to laboriously copy them by hand from the parts Mr. Cruft loaned me.

I had to make a decision regarding tuition in music theory, harmony, composition and keyboard. Fortunately Dr. Alan K. Blackall, who had succeeded Sir Granville Bantock at the Birmingham Midland Institute School of Music, was also organist at St. Mary's Church, Warwick, about three miles away from Leamington. I found him unforgiving as a teacher, although looking back, he taught me well. I remember cycling to his house one day when the bike chain broke, so I had to walk the rest of the way and arrived fifteen minutes late. Despite the fact that there was no pupil following me he just gave me the remaining fifteen minutes of what would have been my lesson. Dr. Blackall later held a high position in the English School of Church Music.

With Eugene Cruft there was an entirely different attitude. On one occasion I arrived at his house absolutely soaked and he gave me a hot bath and some clean clothes. One day when the roads were very icy and I'd had a couple of falls from my bike he made allowance for my tardiness.

As time went on Mr. Cruft would tell me tales of his past. The Cruft family was musical; his father had been a violist in the Carl Rosa Opera Company and consequently as they were always touring he was sent to whatever school was at hand in the nearest town and when the Company moved on he was sent to another school.

He was always keen on physical fitness and had performed in music halls as a trick cyclist when he was young and had also toured with a boys' band. He took an ice cold bath every day and also maintained that playing the bass was good for the cardio-vascular system. He told me once that when he used to play the Proms at the old Queen's Hall in the years before WW2, the concerts went on for six weeks, the programmes were very long and arduous and near the end of the season the orchestra was feeling very tense, having been allotted only one three hour rehearsal for what were difficult concerts. He used to go home after the morning rehearsal on the day of the concert, have lunch, remove all his clothes, put on his pyjamas and go to bed for two hours; this kept him going. In one season when I played both the LSO and LPO Prom concerts, I followed his advice and it worked admirably.

Samuel Sterling was Cruft's first teacher, and he told me that Sam knew a lot about the bass, as I was to find out for myself later when I played next to him. He made an arrangement of the Bach 'cello suites for bass and they are in print still --a standard work for the double bass. When I knew him, Sam was Professor of the double bass at the Royal Academy of Music and was friendly with Edouard Nanny the famous French bassist whom he had often visited in Paris.

Sam was nicknamed the "Domino King"[13] for he had a reputation for making false entries. One notable occasion was when he was playing the opera *Rigoletto* by Verdi, who is famous for introducing the *cesura*, which is a sudden halt in the music, sometimes when least expected, and it occurs at the end of every verse in the aria *La Donna è Mobile*, after which the 'celli and basses come in with a decisive down beat to start things off again, but not Sam, who would come in on the silent bar much to the mirth of the bass players and the chagrin of the conductor, but although 'Tell Sam" was written in all the bass parts to remind him he still persisted.

He also ate a lot of garlic and there is a legend that on one occasion he cleared the front row of the stalls at Covent Garden with his garlic breath.

Sam was an innovator and experimenter. Having seen the great Octobass in a Paris museum he decided that he would try to extend the lower compass of the bass from E to G.

The Octobass, made by J.B. Vuillaume in 1849 is a giant of an instrument with three strings operated by levers and pedals and was intended to give the double bass a 32-foot register to the orchestra. A similar experiment with a 15- foot high bass was made in the U.S.A in 1889, but both this and the Octobass were not a success. Sam decided to put a low string on a five-string bass tuning it G D G D G but his experiment failed also. In those days, as I mentioned before, the lower strings were made of gut wound with wire, and Sam's bottom 'G' string was too flabby to make a good sound. He was before his time, because I'm sure that nowadays with all the modern technology in metal string-making, Sam's idea could have been made to work.

Hector Berlioz in his *Memoirs* mentions a remarkable double bass virtuoso named August Müller whom he met in 1843 in the Darmstadt Orchestra. He describes him as a giant of a man who played a four stringed bass with marvellous facility, from this we must infer that the three string bass was gradually being supplanted by the four stringed instrument and that attempts were being made even in those days to extend the double bass compass downwards, employing a fourth string on the double bass, as we know it today; a fifth string was to come later.

Eugene's next teacher was Claude Hobday[14], who was later to play second to him when the BBC Symphony was inaugurated in 1930. I never had the good fortune to meet Hobday but all the bass players spoke of him with great respect. I heard tales about him cycling with Fritz Kreisler in what were then the country lanes of Surrey. Hobday was a very sensitive player and much in demand for playing chamber music and was Professor of the Double Bass at the Royal College of Music at the time I first met Eugene Cruft. It was a bone of contention, particularly with Mrs. Cruft, that Claude Hobday, well into his seventies, should still be teaching at the Royal College of Music, and this was hinted to the Powers that Be, possibly by Eugene, and a rule was introduced that all the professors should be retired at age seventy. Eugene was awarded the position but he was eventually hoisted by his own petard because when he attained the magic age, even though he was sprightly and playing well, he had to step down, much to his chagrin.

In 1942, I was asked to play with the Carl Rosa Opera Company. Their repertoire consisted of *Rigoletto, Tales of Hoffman, Faust, Lohengrin, Cavalleria Rusticana, Il Pagliacci, Madama Butterfly* and *La Bohème*. The conductor was Walter Susskind, whom I adjudged to be a very good conductor, although I had had little or no experience in opera at that time. His beat was very clear and there was cohesion between the stage and the pit. There were none of the catastrophes that sometimes happen in Opera and he also kept things moving so that the performance was alive. All in all he was one of the best opera conductors I ever came across and was also an excellent pianist. He could be rather acerbic and once accused Zisolfo, the first bassoon, of making lavatory noises. Zisolfo and the first trumpet, Bruno, both Italians, were veterans of the pre-war company. Zisolfo himself came from Sicily where at a very early age he learned to play on a miniature bassoon, he was deformed, a hunchback, and I thought he was very unkindly nicknamed "Rigoletto". Years later when I formed Robert Meyer Artist Management Ltd. I wrote to Susskind and reminded him of the Carl Rosa and I received a very cordial reply.

A Maltese, Joseph Satariano, sang the part of Rigoletto, and for me, even today, he is the definitive Rigoletto. Although there are others with better voices that I have heard and worked with, including Tito Gobbi, the way Satariano clung to the courtiers, giving a Rubini sob as he asked for his daughter to be given back to him was truly moving. Another singer was the soprano, Joan Hammond, a rather large lady who was embarrassed when the bed collapsed in *La Bohème*. Now, after performing over 140 operas I still like the Verdi operas, although some of the highbrows contemptuously refer to them as being all sex and gunpowder.

A Mr. And Mrs. H.B. Phillips ran the Carl Rosa, and every Friday night the word got round that the "Ghost was walking", which in theatrical terms meant we were being paid. The whole company, singers and musicians alike would line up and were handed their pay in cash in a small brown envelope and everybody was given a grateful "Thank you" by Mrs. H.B. as she was called by the Company. She took a great interest in the welfare of the "Young ladies of the Chorus" as she used to call them and was determined that Sex would never raise its ugly head. Once, she spoke in a motherly tone to one of the young ladies; "Miss X, it has come to my notice that you were taking tea in a certain tea shop with Mr. Z the tenor; you know, we cannot really tolerate these goings on." It was a far cry from today's sexual freedom but there was a genuine camaraderie that permeated the whole Company, we all felt we were barnstorming the Provinces as itinerant players, or mummers as of old.

This was my first introduction to touring with a musical company. There were theatrical "digs", (B&B's) and all the old hands kept note of the better ones and would compare them and pass on the good word to other touring companies. There was always a good breakfast served late, a light lunch- cum- tea and then a big dinner after the show and a comfortable bed. The cost was remarkably cheap.

One day I received a letter from Sir Ivor Atkins, the Organist and Music Director of Worcester Cathedral asking me to play for him at Worcester Cathedral. I played for him often, taking part in works such as Parry's *Blest Pair of Sirens, the Messiah, the Creation* and *Israel in Egypt*.

Another orchestra in which I was asked to play principal bass was the semi-professional Leicester Symphony Orchestra conducted by Alfred de Reyghere. The concerts took place in the de Montfort Hall, Leicester, which in my opinion has one of the best acoustics of any hall I have ever played in. There are many fine halls around the world with good acoustics, but there are also many new halls built of hardwood, concrete and glass designed by so-called acoustic experts that are not good, their sound is hard and brittle. A good hall gives you a sense of good feeling, for you can sense the vibrations as you play in a manner that is hard to describe.

When I was engaged for the first concert with the Leicester Symphony I was asked what would be my fee, I replied "Two pounds." When I told my father, he was shocked and he said, "How can you ask for that money, you are not yet a meister spieler on the kontrabass." I pointed out that I had to pay for my rail fare plus a taxi and a hotel but he told me that I had to pay for my experience and even if and when I became a master bass player I should give back any of the talents I had by sometimes playing for charities. I didn't think so at the time but in hindsight it was good advice and I have attempted to follow it in my career – I have found that what you give, without any thought of remuneration, it sometimes comes back to you in many other ways

I was advised by Arthur Cockerill to write to the City of Birmingham Orchestra (CBO) to audition, which I did in front of George Weldon the conductor and Norris Stanley the concertmaster. To my surprise I was immediately offered the job of principal bass but was unable to accept the offer because of my war work. I was offered the weekly Sunday afternoon concerts with them which I enjoyed, and was able to learn some of the orchestral repertoire.

The Cockerill's were a musical family. Arthur's brother Bert, as I have already mentioned, was also a bass player, his cousin, Winnie, played the harp in the London Philharmonic, and another cousin, John, was principal harpist in the London Symphony Orchestra. I never met Bert but I knew Winnie well. She concerned herself with the welfare of the men in the orchestra; for example, when we went on a two-week tour of Scotland, Winnie drew me to one side and pointed to the small backpack that Richard Adeney, the first flute, was carrying. "You know Bob," she said, "I wonder how he can possibly be carrying enough underwear to last the fortnight." John Cockerill was a fine harpist who dressed immaculately and was of a gentle mien. I was very amused one day when we were playing a programme of ballet music, John was singing naughty little ditties to some of the tunes and I was surprised that someone whom I had regarded as being a perfect gentleman and a pillar of the profession would be having such fun on stage. Some of those icons that were household names when I first entered the profession I discovered to be human like everybody else.

The City of Birmingham Orchestra was going to be made a full time orchestra. Up until then its nucleus was made up of members of the BBC Midland Orchestra, a Mozart sized orchestra with eight first violins, six second violins, four violas, three cellos and two basses, two each of woodwinds plus two horns, two trumpets and timpani. During WW2 the BBC Midland Orchestra was disbanded and Arthur Cockerill was sent to the BBC Scottish Orchestra in Glasgow. After the war it was re-formed as the BBC Midland Light Orchestra, but with smaller personnel.

The BBC Midland Orchestra's conductor was Leslie Heward[16], a fine musician and an excellent conductor who gave some wonderful, insightful performances. The orchestra thought very highly of him, but unfortunately he suffered from the demon drink like so many other musicians. There is a legendary tale of one of his radio performances. The programme had been pre-empted at the last minute although it had been very well rehearsed but Heward said to the orchestra, "Ladies and gentlemen, I know our broadcast has been cancelled but instead of going home let us play it anyway for the music's sake." It was given a superb performance. This story has made an indelible impression on my mind.

The CBO as it was called then had renowned soloists including Albert Sammons[17] and Ida Haendel, violinists; Moura Lympany, Myra Hess, Moiseivitch and Pouishnoff, pianists. I remember a particularly fine performance of the Beethoven violin concerto given by Albert Sammons, who played the cadenza beautifully. Even now, years later, and having heard so many solo violinists I still think he ranks with the best.

Ida Haendel lived opposite me in Radford Road, Leamington Spa, after being evacuated from the London Blitz. We smiled at each other sometimes when we passed, each carrying our instruments, but I never had the nerve in those days to speak to a woman walking alone because the social mores of the time forbade it. Her father, who also was her manager, was always fussing around her at rehearsals, so much so that years later when I was playing with the BBC Symphony, Sir Adrian Boult had to tell him to go away and not interrupt the rehearsal.

George Weldon, the conductor of the City of Birmingham Orchestra, was born with a silver spoon in his mouth. I believe the family money came from Weldon's Fashions, which were very popular as patterns for women's dresses. Again to quote Gibbon who writes of the Emperor Theodoric, "He loved the virtues he possessed and the talents of which he was destitute." He would tackle anything in the orchestral repertoire, sometimes not making a good job of it, his tempi and beat being rather erratic, but he conducted a lot of Delius and Elgar. I remember him conducting a performance of Elgar's *Falstaff*, and I was struck by its beauty. I only played it once again in my whole career, under Sir Adrian Boult. It is a pity that it is not performed much nowadays, indeed, there is a wealth of music out there that is never performed and should be; the listening public doesn't know what it is missing.

The time came in 1944 when Eugene Cruft decided that I was ready to take the auditions and examinations necessary to be made an Associate of the Royal College of Music even though I was an outsider, having been unable to attend the College because of the war. After practicing intensely I went in for the exam and, having satisfied the examiners after performing a concerto or two from memory and doing the necessary theory examination I was made an A.R.C.M.

Not long afterwards I received a telegram from the London Philharmonic Orchestra asking if I could play with them in their Sunday afternoon concerts at the Albert Hall, and of course, I was delighted. He never mentioned it to me, but I suspect Eugene Cruft had recommended me to them. Owing to the scarcity of trains, in order to be on time for a 10 a.m. rehearsal I had to catch a train that left Leamington at 3.30 a.m. and arrived in London at 6.00 a.m. I would go to bed at 8.30 p.m. on Saturday night, and I am forever grateful to my father who always awakened me at 2.30 a.m. to ensure I caught the train. I would leave home at 3.00 a.m. with the bass on my back and walk the mile to the station. On arrival in London I would have breakfast in Paddington Station buffet then catch a taxi to the Albert Hall.

The LPO, despite the war, still had some very fine players, and the sound was much better than the CBO, but their life was a hard one as they were constantly on tour and had suffered their share of the Blitz. Sometimes they were without accommodation and often had to spend the night on a railway station but somehow they survived. Many of the old diehards were replaced by younger players after the war, which was rather a pity after all they had done to keep the orchestra alive.

At my first concert with the LPO, after audition, I was asked to sit with the principal bass, Victor Watson during a rehearsal beforehand so that they could have some idea of how I played in the orchestra. There were catcalls from the sub-principal bass, Gerald Brooks, who just for this occasion was sitting on the last desk, of "dumbo pizzicato" and "Brylcreem on his bow" but notwithstanding all this I was given the O.K. by Mr. Watson, as I then called him.

I had listened to Victor Watson play bass solos at Stratford-on-Avon Memorial Theatre earlier on in the war and never thought that I might meet such an illustrious player in the flesh. He was nicknamed "The Master". His right hand forefinger was missing, but he made a big sound and a glorious tone. One of his interests was backing horses and consuming a pint of beer after the concert and later on, when I got to know him better I used to listen to some of his many stories over a pint of beer.

Because he had no trigger finger Mr.Watson was exempt from military service in World War 1 and had to serve as a special policeman. One day he was called to a tram to eject a drunk who would not pay his fare. The drunk was a brawny Irishman and the tale goes that Victor volunteered to pay his fare rather than have a confrontation. Discretion is sometimes the better part of valour. Soon after I joined the LPO, as an excuse to leave and go to the Phiharmonia Orchestra Brooks gave an ultimatum to the LPO directors that either I be fired or he would leave. Mr. Watson told the Board that they could go ahead and fire me if they so wished but he refused to say I was a bad player, so I stayed and Brooks left.

I'm sure Brooks had psychological problems. To annoy his wife he would practice the tuba sitting on the stairs of their home late at night. She had caught him in *flagrante delicto* and since then would have nothing to do with him, but whether his tuba practicing had anything to do with this I never knew. He could keep all the orchestra amused because he had a very good voice and during rehearsals would sing very naughty ditties to the pieces we were playing. Sometimes if there was a fanfare he would kneel and Mr. Watson would dub him knight on each shoulder with his bow.

Messrs. Brooks and Watson, in the *March to the Scaffold* from Berlioz' *Fantastic Symphony* would make a great flourish and present their bows in imitation of swords when the brass sounded a fanfare just before the end of the movement when the unfortunate victim is supposed to mount the scaffold. Then they would make a great display of the final bass pizzicato which indicates the victim's head falling into the basket. During the march in *Lohengrin* when the knights and their ladies parade around the stage, Brooks and Watson would bow to each other and imitate the stage action. All this may sound a trifle childish but there is often great tension at lengthy rehearsals and they certainly relieved it.

It was rather anomalous that later on in my career when I joined the Philharmonia Orchestra, that I was designated to sit with Brooks. In fact I was known as the "Barmpot's Keeper" because I had to look after him on tour. His nickname, "Barmpot"[18], I believe, was a term of friendly abuse common in Lancashire. He owned some farmland in Oxfordshire. Mine was the "Baron" probably because I owned a large house. I remember having to get him drunk in order to get him on a 'plane when we flew to the United States. When we went up the Empire State Building he had an urge to throw himself off and this also happened at the Eiffel Tower. He once got into fisticuffs with another bassist at rehearsal and I had to separate them, so you can see I had my hands full.

When the pre-war LPO played in Berlin with Beecham the orchestra stayed at the posh Adlon hotel and Brooks and some colleagues were waiting for an elevator. When the doors opened a German officer stepped out and shouted "Heil Hitler" giving the Nazi salute. At this, Brooks who had been in the British Army and either was very brave or very foolish, (the latter, I think) punched the German on the chin knocking him back into the elevator and then pressed the down button. Remember that Germany and Britain were not yet at war and this could have caused an international incident, but nothing further came of it.

Incidentally it is worth recording that whenever the Berlin Philharmonic went on tour there was a curfew and the hotel corridors were patrolled at night to ensure there were no high jinks and that they would be fresh for the concert the next day.

On one occasion when we were playing at the Lucerne International Festival, that old tyrant Fritz Reiner was conducting *Also Sprach Zarathustra* by Richard Strauss. Brooks had taken the music home to practice but had forgotten to bring it back with him. There is a solo for two five-stringed basses in *Zarathustra*, which we both played from memory at the rehearsal and fortunately it went without a hitch.

If I were to be asked who was the most obnoxious conductor I have ever encountered, the answer would have to be Fritz Reiner; mind you, there were many who ran a close second, but I must give Reiner that doubtful honour. Reiner was in his 'fifties when I first ran in to him. Of middle height, stocky build with thin, graying hair, he had a permanent frown on his face and when he came into rehearsal never said "Good morning," or gave any other greeting but would gruffly state the piece he wished to rehearse and then commence. At rehearsal, he certainly knew his job; he would not waste time on trivia but always went through the programme thoroughly, giving great attention to detail. In Wagner, Richard Strauss, Mahler, Liszt and all the "biggies" he was superb and certainly in the front rank of conductors; but in say, Mozart, Haydn, Rossini where that extra sparkle is needed he never could deliver. This, I think, was due to his miserable temperament. Freud, no doubt, would have had a wonderful time trying to sort him out.

The reason, I believe, for his nasty attitude was that he never really succeeded in establishing himself as one of the truly "greats", and also because of his unfortnate manner he had lost some good jobs over the years. He was infamous for calling on-the-spot auditions, which certainly never enamoured him with the orchestra.

Although he knew exactly what he wanted, sometimes he couldn't (or wouldn't) convey it to the orchestra because of the microscopic, miniscule beat he used - the tip of his baton never seemed to move more than an inch; some of the musicians thought it was deliberate and put it down to his cussedness. There is a tale that was often told in bass playing circles: At one concert a bass player (who was about to retire) drew from his pocket a small telescope and directed it at Reiner's baton, thereby conveying to him the general concensus of opinion of his beat, which up till then no-one had dared to do.

We were recording *Petrouchka* with Ernest Ansermet. In one of the scenes called *Peasant and Bear* Brooks walked around his bass imitating the bear much to the amusement of all, Ansermet included. This recording of Petrouchka using Decca Recording Company's new FFRR system was a best seller at the time and I am told it is now regarded as archival. It was one of the last 78 rpm's that I made before the vinyl 33 1/3 rpm long-playing records were introduced. One of the drawbacks of the 78's was that no splices could be made. This meant that a "take", which lasted about 10 – 13 minutes, had to be perfect and this caused great tension among the musicians.

Ernest Ansermet was rather more of a mathematician than a gutsy, artistic type. He had been a professor of mathematics and could multiply or divide large numbers in his head in a matter of seconds. He conducted many modern works including Schoenberg, Stravinsky, Martinu and Bartok etc., but that being said he never possessed the innate rhythm of, say, a Colin Davis, Malcolm Sargent or Wolfgang Sawallisch, although he tried to convey it sometimes by saying "Gentlemen, I beg you, ze rhythm should be like zis," and then proceeded to sing in a reverbrating bass voice "bing-bong, bing-bong, bugga-bugga-bugga-bugga." Having been a conductor of Diaghilev's Ballet Russe, he often included ballet music in his programmes whenever possible. His Mozart and Beethoven, I thought, were uninteresting. I understood that he married the heiress to a chocolate manufacturer who probably gave him financial support in his conducting career.

There was a tuba player named Micky White in the LPO and Ansermet was conducting the Moussorgsky-Ravel arrangement of *Pictures at an Exhibition*. Micky was getting on in years; in fact he used to boast that he had played at Queen Victoria's funeral. He often used to hark back to pre-1914 days, regaling us with tales of the times when he could catch a tramcar to a music hall, buy a packet of cigarettes and after the show quaff a pint of beer and catch the tram home for less than a shilling. "Those were the days; you wouldn't call the King your uncle!" But back to *Pictures*, one of the pieces in it is called *Bydlo*; it represents oxen plodding along and is one of the big tuba solos in the repertoire, but when it came to playing it Micky made a hash of it. He used to play a very big instrument that we all dubbed the "upright grand" which was not really suitable for playing *Bydlo*. After the concert Micky lamented that he should have brought along a smaller instrument or even a euphonium, but by then it was too late, you are only as good as your last concert. Ansermet complained, quite rightly, and Micky was let go but he continued to revile Ansermet for getting him the sack. If he is up there serenading Queen Victoria with his tuba I'll bet that *Bydlo* won't be one of the pieces!

Chapter 3 Notes
12. One pound one shilling, 1.05 in decimal currency.
13. Domino, coming in at the wrong place
14. Two weeks
15. Claude Hobday can be heard on the November 1935 recording of Schubert's *"Trout" Quintet* with Artur Schnabel, piano and members of the Pro Arte string quartet
16. Heward's 1942 recording of E.J. Moeran's *Symphony* has now been issued on CD
17. Sammons was the dedicatee and gave the premiere of Delius' *Violin Concerto*; he also made the first complete recording of the Elgar *Violin Concerto* in 1929.
18. A term derived from the slang "barmy" meaning mad in a humourous way.

CHAPTER 4

The LPO Tour to France and Belgium. I am offered a contract with the LPO. Some conductors and "characters".

In November 1945 the war in Europe was over and the British Council arranged and paid for the London Philharmonic to visit Paris and Brussels, they were the first orchestra to travel to the Continent after WW2 and I was thrilled when they asked me to go with them. Although the war in Europe was over there was still Japan to be reckoned with. All the British factories wanted to keep their personnel because it was realized that trade would have to be developed again for the country to recover from the war. The local bureaucracy couldn't give me permission to leave, so I took matters into my own hands. Sir Anthony Eden was my Member of Parliament and was in Leamington meeting his constituents and I made an appointment to see him. He was very sympathetic towards me but also appeared to be very sad and was on the verge of tears as he told me of his son who was killed in an airplane accident. He had been working with Churchill, Roosevelt, Stalin and others mapping out the post war world and my problem must have sounded very trivial to him, but nevertheless because of my war record he did act. After that, I arranged an appointment with Mr. Edward Boughton, who was the director in chief of the firm I was with and he too was very simpatico. Mr. Boughton happened to be the brother of Rutland Boughton, the composer, whose opera *The Immortal Hour* I was to have the pleasure of playing at Sadlers Wells years later.

Joy Boughton, Rutland's oboist daughter, with whom I was to play with later in Benjamin Britten's English Opera Group, used to talk of him with reverence as "Uncle Ted the money bags." Sadly, Joy died of cancer at an early age.

The bureaucratic hurdles having been crossed, I was now ready to go on the tour. To say that I was elated would be putting it mildly. "Gay Paree" (although these days "gay" has a different connotation) was where, before the war, Uncle Bert slipped off to for week-ends, returning with a half smile on his face and a faraway look in his eyes. Paris, the home of the

Tuileries, Notre-Dame Cathedral, the Moulin Rouge, Toulouse-Lautrec, L'Opéra etc., and I was actually going there, with a first rate orchestra and none other than Sir Thomas Beecham, Bart. conducting it, to boot! After all my hours of practice I had arrived, or naïvely thought I had, so I heaved my bass on my back, carrying also my suitcase and made my way to Leamington Station and caught the London train. Upon arrival in London I called at the LPO office and was introduced to Felix Apprahamian who then had an administrative job with the LPO. Felix, who was nicknamed the "Bey of Tunis" on account of his swarthy complexion and black beard, was later to become a noted musicologist and music critic with the *Times of London* newspaper. We took a taxi to the Passport Office where a passport had to be expedited, and then I went to rehearse.

Sir Thomas Beecham had returned from America where he had been resident during the War, and was glad to be back conducting the orchestra that he had founded. The orchestra however, was not too enthusiastic about it. Beecham had gone to the U.S., it was said, without paying for recordings the orchestra had made, and the orchestra complained that he had left them in the lurch. Because they were now desperately in need of funds and had taken music to the masses as part of the war effort, Jack Hylton, who had been a bandleader and was now a very successful impresario, came to the rescue and the orchestra survived, but Beecham still thought he should carry on where he had left off without giving too much attention to what the orchestra thought <u>they</u> wanted. In the interval since Beecham had left, the orchestra re-formed itself with a chairman and board of directors made up of elected musicians. There were also outside advisors including J.B. Priestley, the author.

So, the orchestra was rehearsing the programme that was to be played on the tour with Beecham conducting. The British Council dictated the music to some extent and it included Vaughan Williams' *Variations on a Theme of Thomas Tallis*. Beecham sniffed at this, and complained to us that it was a pity all Vaughan Williams' other themes hadn't been composed by Tallis. We were also to play the *Four Sea Interludes* from Benjamin Britten's opera *Peter Grimes*, which Beecham referred to as "The Bugger's Opera". Under his baton, our performances of this wonderfully evocative piece were less than sparkling. The main work was to be William Walton's First Symphony to which Beecham, who didn't like it, gave very short shrift.

Beecham often conducted without a musical score in front of him and he made a pantomime of it. He would come on stage affecting a slight limp and on arrival at the podium the concertmaster would always proffer him the score whereupon Beecham with lordly grace would give it back to the concertmaster, thereby subtly informing the audience that he could conduct the piece from memory. This always got him a round of applause from the audience; music is partly showbiz.

We gave a concert at the Albert Hall and were immediately whisked away to Victoria Station to catch the boat train to Paris. The crossing was miserable for there were high seas and a wind blowing. Mine sweepers escorted us. David John, the second oboist and son of the society painter Augustus John (who painted the well known portrait of Madam Suggia, the 'cellist, whom I had the pleasure of playing with later on) looked very seasick, as was also Jean Pougnet, the concertmaster, who came from Martinique. Jean practiced constantly and when travelling in a railway carriage would bring out a mute practice violin but all this practice caused him to have problems with his hands and when I last I saw him he was conducting a light orchestra at the BBC. I don't think he was offered many dates and later on seemed to go into obscurity.

At last we docked at Boulogne, and boarded the train for Paris. Meals on the train were served at an exorbitant cost, not like pre-war France where everything was so cheap with a favourable exchange rate. Eventually we arrived in Paris and were told that we were to be driven to our hotel, which turned out to be not an hotel at all but some wagons-lits (railway sleeping carriages) drawn up in a siding opposite the main platform in the Gare de l'Est. They were comfortable, but the noise of the trains kept us awake at night, and there were no washing facilities except for the hand basin in the railway compartment. Even the British Army latrines were more hygienic than the facilities in the railway station that consisted of a standing only toilet à la Turque which smelled abominably and was never cleaned.

There was a station restaurant which served up a sort of paté, plus a few vegetables and, of course, the usual French baguette and sometimes some vin ordinaire or Bock beer. Meanwhile Beecham was living it up at the Ritz Hotel and ran up a huge bill which Adolf Borsdorf, the LPO's business manager had to pay.

We were invited to the Quai D'Orsay, the diplomatic quarter of Paris where we were given a lavish reception during which the wine was flowing, and I wondered how they had managed to hide so much wine from the Germans. Then the toasts began; "Vive L'Entente Cordiale", "Vive Les Anglais", "Vive La France", "Vive le London Philharmonic", "Vive L'Orchestre Nationale", "Vive Sir Beecham", "Vive Debussy" and so on, and after all and sundry had been kissed on both cheeks we staggered out to be taken back to the wagons-lits for bed.

Next day we were taken to Versailles and one evening a number of us visited the Pigalle district and went to the Folies Bérgère. We were impressed with the number of American soldiers out on the town. The shops were empty and there was not much fuel. People looked dejected and depressed but this did not stop me seeing all the sights between rehearsals.

One free evening we were all invited to L'Opéra where Claude Debussy's opera, *Pelléas et Mélisande* was being staged. I admired the Grand Staircase and ruminated on all the illustrious happenings that had taken place there.

Afterwards there came the concerts in which we performed, amongst other things, César Franck's *Symphony in D minor*, and it was in this work and also in Mozart, Delius and Rossini that Beecham came into his own. I could see, novice though I was, that he was in the category of top conductors. His conducting technique was very limited; there was no clear beat and sometimes he must have relied on his musicians to pull him through, as indeed, many other conductors do, but when he conducted works that he liked there was a wonderful sparkle. In the César Franck Symphony there is a cor anglais solo. Jock McGillivray, the cor anglais player was puzzled at Beecham's lack of direction and didn't come in, however Beecham, in one of his famous loud stage whispers hissed "Go on'" and the day was saved.

When it came to Walton's Symphony, the Parisian audience seemed to like it less than Beecham, for the Poulailler or top balcony in the Théâtre des Champs-Elysées booed and catcalled. I reflected on the fact that it was at the Théâtre des Champs-Elysées that the first performance of Stravinsky's *Rite of Spring* had been given and that there had been a riot, now famous in musical lore. I was not to know then that at the 50th Anniversary concert of the first performance of the *Rite* I would be playing it with the original conductor, Pierre Monteux.

Monteux was a rubicund little man with thinning, iron-grey hair brushed back; he sported a huge handlebar moustache. He was good both in the German and French classics and particularly good at Stravinsky, having given many performances of his works. I particularly liked his version of the *Fantastic Symphony* where, at the end of the ballroom scene he would make an extraordinary accelerando (speeding-up) that would have swept the dancers off their feet. He had marvellous energy and would call out "C'mon gentlemen!" and immediately life was injected into the music.

It is a pity he parted with his wife of many years, "Ma" Monteux as the LSO used to call her. Unfortunately he died after having to climb the stairs to his New York apartment when the elevator failed, but by then he was a good age, eighty–nine.

Charles Munch conducted the last concert with us at the Théâtre des Champs Elysées. Earlier he had conducted Ravel's *Bolero* and a Tchaikovsky symphony with considerable success. He conducted with great fire which may have been due to the brandy which he consumed both before the concert and in the interval. His conducting technique was excellent and he got on well with the orchestra who always gave him of their best.

Brussels was completely different from Paris. We stayed at the Grand Hotel Metropole, which was like Heaven compared with the wagons -lits at the Gare de l'Est. There were gorgeous delicacies in the patisseries and there was plenty of food - the place seemed to have an air of prosperity so different from London at that time. London had been heavily bombed but Paris and Brussels were unscathed. The Maire of Brussels invited us to a banquet and the food was sumptuous, far better than anything we could obtain in England where there was very severe rationing.

The concerts at La Salle des Beaux Arts went very well and as in Paris we met all their famous musicians and, too, their orchestras were very hospitable. I met a beautiful young lady after one concert and was very smitten with her, but alas, my goal was the double bass and I had no desire to settle down, but I often wondered later, what if?

One morning, I visited the Palais de Justice where a trial of a collaborator with the Germans was in progress. I did not stay until the end of the trial but all and sundry around me had come to the conclusion that the accused was guilty, indeed his demeanour in the dock seemed to go against him, but I suppose that if Germany had won the war he would have been a hero, such is life!

Our next venue was Antwerp where we played in the Opera Flamande which is a very old theatre. I can still see the backstage firemen in their picturesque brass helmets admonishing those in the orchestra who dared to light up. In those days smoking was much more prevalent.

Backstage, after the concert I was very honoured to meet M. Eugène Goossens, a distinguished conductor in his late seventies. He was the doyen of the famous Goossens family, some of whom I knew very well, including Leon the oboist, Marie and Sidonie the harpists and Sir Eugene the conductor whom I later played for. Sir Eugene was something else, for round about the late 'fifties his luggage was searched by Customs in Australia and various sexual paraphernalia were found, including masks. Nowadays nothing would be said but then it was given wide publicity and some of the wags in the Philharmonia orchestra wondered out loud whether he had brought his masks when we were recording William Walton's *Troilus and Cressida* with him soon afterwards. Orchestral musicians can be very cruel.

Apart from the sexual deviation I thought he was a very competent conductor, and always obtained a good, if not memorable performance. He paid great attention to detail and tried to comply faithfully with the composer's intentions, and would sit at the podium, nervously chewing on the temple of his glasses whilst pondering over the score.

It had been a memorable tour for me and I still look back on it to this day, but I soon learned that taking a bass around was a risky business, for on our return as they were unloading the basses overboard from the ship in huge nets; one bass fell out of it. It was Tom Alexander's Maggini and it was very badly damaged, but Tom who was an expert repairer, painstakingly put it together again later.

I should say a word about travelling with a bass. When you "take up" the bass you do so literally and there is also a constant worry that the bass may arrive at the concert hall damaged. Wally Knight, the LPO's orchestral porter often damaged the basses in his hurry to catch a train after the concert. One day the neck of my bass was broken but Wally's only remark to me in his fluent Cockney was, "Well, it's insured ain't it?" I heatedly replied, "Well maybe you're insured too but you wouldn't like your bloody neck broken would you?" I must say that when bass cases began to be made of fibreglass the risk of damage was considerably lessened.

At a concert in Birmingham Town Hall, the timpani started to roll clankety-clonk down the risers, much to Clary O'Neill the timpanist's and the audience's concern, but they were hauled up again, made secure, and everybody treated the matter light-heartedly and the concert resumed. Wally was kept on, however, because he always managed to get the instruments to the hall on time and there were very rarely any complications.

Another time my bass case was opened by Customs in Germany and the bass put back improperly, which caused damage, and the same thing happened once in Holland too. I remember leaving my bass in a safe corner (so I thought) on Euston Railway Station in London and came back to find the neck knocked out. Once I was travelling by train to the English south coast and put it in the guard's (conductor's) van and came back along the train and saw people sitting on it! On another occasion I was leaving Los Angeles airport to fly to Vancouver, Canada, when I happened to see my bass on an Alaska Airlines truck destined for Alaska although it was clearly labelled "Vancouver".

Then there is always the problem of temperature and humidity change. I remember once playing at Carnegie Hall in November. After the concert the basses were taken from the hot hall and put outside in the freezing cold; you could hear popping noises coming from them - it was the patches that had been stuck over old cracks becoming unglued and most of the basses had to be taken for expensive repairs when we arrived back home. The worst casualty at that time was a Strad violin belonging to Micky Freedman which was cracked right down the belly. Micky was in tears.

There seems to be something sinister about a bass too, because the police have often stopped me when I was carrying it. Once, in Iran, I was going into the concert hall to perform before the Shah of Perrsia and his new wife Fara Dibah and had to suffer the bass being searched by an unsavoury looking individual who pointed a machine gun at my head.

I was beginning to find out what a musician's life was really like when, after the tour to Paris, Brussels and Antwerp we arrived back in London and had to rush to play another concert immediately.

Not long afterwards I was offered a contract to join the LPO and had to share a stand with one, Fred Ventris, who was against "All these young chaps with no experience" joining the orchestra. He was not very pleasant to work with and sometimes he would bring down his bow as if to play, hoping I would make a false entry, and another little device he used was to draw a chalk line on the floor to stake out his position, which I did not dare to cross.

A funny thing happened when we were playing in Bournemouth. Fred came on stage wearing dark glasses and it was rumoured that he was trying to avoid one of the fair sex who was pursuing him, but we never ascertained whether it was a wife or some other damsel. In Glasgow at the St. Andrew's Hall, Fred must have fallen afoul of one of the stage attendants because the man took one look at Fred and said, "Oh, that bugger!" and promptly turned off the light that was behind us, making it well nigh impossible for us to see the music. After much pleading from me the light was turned on again and we were able to play the concert.

Like so many other musicians Fred sometimes took to the bottle and on these occasions would go on a binge that lasted for days, then he would remain sober for months afterwards. He could be cantankerous too. I remember a tour of Ireland, where we played first in Belfast and then caught the train for Dublin, in the Irish Republic, a foreign country with its own customs and immigration at entry points. When the train crossed the river that divides the two States it stopped in the middle of the bridge. At this point, the occupants of the train became very excited, shouting that this is where it all had happened, and the name of Cromwell was mentioned. Some threw pennies into the river for good luck. The scene was interrupted when a Customs man came aboard and asked Fred if he had anything to declare at which Fred said,"No." The customs man asked him to open his luggage which riled Fred so much that he pointed to a fat old priest in the seat opposite and said unwisely, "Why don't you look under his cassock?" There followed a lengthy stand-off and the Customs man threatened to have Fred put off the train, but harmony was eventually restored so we played Dublin with our full complement of bass players.

Talking of trains, I was playing with the LPO in Carlisle in the North of England. It had a large railway marshalling yard and unfortunately when I booked a room at a hotel I did not realize that the yard lay behind it. Hotel rooms were scarce so I agreed to share a room with Sam Lovett, a 'cellist, and what with the hiss of steam from the locomotives, the pounding of buffers and the screech of wheels on the rails, neither of us could sleep so we just sat up and talked. Sam was very proud of his son Martin, also a 'cellist, and he told me that Martin had just joined a newly formed string quartet. When I asked him the name of the quartet he replied, "The Amadeus."

The rest is history, not only were they successful but overly so. I occasionally met Martin's wife, the violinist Susan Rosza, when I played with the English Chamber Orchestra, and according to her they were always on the road, sometimes for months at a time. Fame had brought them so much hard work and tension that there was a tale circulating that two of the members of the quartet were engaged in a fight just as the red light went on in a radio studio in Germany. I can well believe this because I, too, had had my share of tension having worked at one period for over three months without a day off, sometimes playing three sessions a day and had also been on tours lasting three months or more.

Peter Schidlof, the violist of the Amadeus String Quartet was a very fine player and when I was playing in the BBC Symphony Orchestra he gave an exceptional performance of the Walton Viola Concerto with us.

Another member of the LPO bass section was Charles Conhoff

who had been a Russian émigré to Paris after the Russian Revolution. Life was not good to him in Paris and he had to take on menial jobs to earn a living. One job was winding bass strings for the firm of Morel for which he was paid ten cents per string. He also helped manufacture Morel's resin, and although he did obtain some playing engagements in Paris, he could never find any regular bass-playing job. After his sojourn in Paris he ever after used the French etiquette of shaking hands with his stand partner after a concert.

Paris not being the Mecca he had hoped for, he crossed the Channel to England, where he fared better. He used to tell the tale of being a member of a Signor Pellegrini's Band that was asked to play at Buckingham Palace. At the intermission a butler came out to the band with twelve glasses and a jug of water - so much for Royal hospitality! In the LPO, Conhoff was known as the "Iron Curtain" because he played so loud.

Charlie made his own resin that contained everything except eye of newt; I persuaded him to give me his recipe that he made me swear never to divulge. He joined the BBC Symphony Orchestra and after he retired (the BBC retiring age was sixty), he went to the LPO. In those days he was the only bassist to use the Horst extension (or fire escape as it was nicknamed) that is tuned down to C. It had metal keys, and when a piece such as the introduction to Stravinsky's *Firebird* is played, the Horst extension sounds like a noisy typewriter. When I came to Canada I introduced it and it is now used extensively, but without the noisy keys.

The LPO contract ran for a year and, providing a player's performance was satisfactory, the contract was renewed every March. Round about the renewal time you would see little knots of musicians saying to each other, "Beware the Ides of March,"or, "I heard so and so isn't getting his contract renewed."

This brings me to the subject of orchestras run by the players themselves versus organizations that employ the musicians direct such as the old Philharmonia Orchestra or the BBC. I would much rather work for them than an orchestras run by its own players, and I'll tell you why.

On a regular basis, self-run orchestras such as the LPO, LSO, the present Philharmonia and RPO, elect a chairman and a board composed of orchestra members, and it did/does happen that one of the board might bear a grudge against an orchestral colleague because of a real or perceived slight that happened perhaps years ago. Such an individual can exercise his power as a board member to give his enemy a very rough time, even to the extent of getting him fired.

Then again auditions. For the most part they are fair, but I do know of cases where it has already been "fixed" in advance. For fairness, particularly in North America, many auditions are held with the player auditioning behind a screen. I disagree with this method, because having been chairman of an audition board myself I believe it is imperative to get some idea of a player's style and approach to the music and this, in my opinion, can only be gained by seeing the person perform. I'll give you an example: A very fine violinist gave an audition before the London Symphony; he played very well, but something puzzled the audition board, somehow he didn't look right. They then realized that it was because he was playing with his bow in his left hand and his violin in his right, the opposite way to everyone else in the orchestra. They wouldn't hire him because he would not fit in. If he had played behind a screen they would have had no means of knowing of this drawback. Eventually he joined a first class string quartet and did very well; perhaps better than if he had been engaged by the LSO.

Sometimes there are so many applicants for one particular job, all playing extremely well, that it might be just as effective to pick out a winner by closing your eyes and sticking a pin in the list of applicants, like picking a winner in a horse race; but one can usually tell in the first few bars whether a player is any good or not. When I was chairman of an audition committee I always tried to imbue the occasion with a little tact and humanity, because bad as some may be, one has to realize they must have been practicing for months for the job, and could also sometimes be a little nervous, so I have to smile at many of the parrot-like job advertisements in the Musicians' Association's magazine which state imperiously that the orchestra has the right to immediately dismiss anyone not coming up to their high standards.

Occasionally a musician would be hired without an audition on the basis of his/her standing and reputation in the profession. Usually this worked out, but there have been occasions when the said musician had become friendly with a director or conductor and later proved to be unsuitable. The saying was that they had talked their way in and played themselves out.

Now that I was a fully fledged member of the LPO I began to realize that a musician's life wasn't all honey. I had thought in my early youth that to belong to a symphony orchestra was tantamount to achieving Nirvana. Mrs. Cruft had told me often and Victor Watson too, that being an orchestral player was a hard, taxing life - I was to find this out very quickly.

To say that life was hectic would be an understatement. There were one or two rehearsals for a prestige concert in London every week either in the Albert Hall, the old Stoll Theatre on Kingsway, or the Coliseum, when a celebrated conductor would be engaged, but otherwise our time was spent playing in the environs of London or going for run-outs (out of town engagements) to Leeds, Birmingham, Cambridge, Brighton, Newcastle, etc. etc. Sometimes we would have a three-hour morning rehearsal and an evening concert and then have to catch an overnight train to, say, Scotland or Ireland.

When travelling by train one could walk up and down the carriage to stretch one's legs and after the concert stay the night in the town and travel back to London or another venue the next day, feeling rested after a night's sleep, but later, for economy's sake, the Board elected to do most of the travelling by bus, which was far more tiring because after the concert we caught the bus back to London, sometimes arriving as late as 1.00 or 2.00 a.m., and as the Underground stopped running at midnight we had to take a taxi home, which was expensive. We were still expected to be on time for a 10.00 a.m. rehearsal next day.

There was a large LPO fan club. I remember two sisters, nice girls whom we dubbed the "Belsen Twins" on account of their being so skinny and undernourished looking. Many of the girl fans travelled the country to listen to us, and I dated a few of them but soon gave up, as most of them wanted to talk about music all the time and I didn't because I had had a surfeit of it.

Many of the soloists I had met in the City of Birmingham Orchestra also played with the London Philharmonic Orchestra. Being strapped for cash the LPO had to bargain fiercely with both conductors and soloists, and Moura Lympany, the pianist, was the only one not to agree to a fee cut, yet she was still engaged for their concerts because she played so well and was in great demand at the time so I suppose she could afford to be adamant over her fee. Mark Hambourg, the pianist, played with us on a few occasions, and although he was no longer young and inclined to thump it out, in his day, I was told, he was a terrific player. I always thought he carried off his performances with gusto, even though there were one or two wrong notes, but the overall impression he left was that of a great musician.

I have played with many viola soloists including William Primrose, Peter Schidloff, Rudolf Barshai and Lionel Tertis, but the finest was undoubtedly Ödon Pártös, a Hungarian born Israeli who played the Walton *Viola Concerto* with us as well as some of his own compositions.

He was a big man and had a marvellous technique, but above all it was the wonderful tone he drew from his instrument that made the whole orchestra as well as the audience applaud him enthusiastically.

Another soloist of note to appear with the LPO about that time, 1945, was Arthur Grumiaux, the Belgian violinist who dazzled us with his technique and gave encore after encore.

The conductors who were engaged for the run-outs were not always of the best quality although there were one or two exceptions. They consisted of men varying from Basil Cameron, Anatole Fistoulari, Karl Rankl, Heinz Unger and Gregor Fitelberg to Malcolm Sargent, Sir Adrian Boult, John Barbirolli and many others. Some of the better conductors always had a list of orchestra personnel in front of them and made a point of addressing the various players by name, which went down very well with the orchestra and placed him in the orchestra's good books.

Basil Cameron received the lion's share of the conducting, mainly I suppose because his fee was very modest. He was adequate, not very inspiring and was neurotic, having the habit of saying, "Please, please!" over and over again. Cameron had been conductor of the Seattle Symphony Orchestra and at one time 2nd violin in the Queen's Hall Orchestra. During one rehearsal intermission our new concertmaster, Jimmie Cooper, a Canadian, somewhat surly in his approach to conductors, accused Cameron of conducting from the 2nd violin part and looking as if he was trying to get out of a sack. Cameron burst out in great fury over this and complained to the whole orchestra. There were accusations and counter accusations, but we, as an orchestra, wanted to finish the rehearsal and go back home to our hobbies, so eventually we packed up our instruments and left after having played our allotted three hours. Years later, though, he conducted the closing scenes from Wagner's *Götterdämmerung* at a Prom concert, and looking back, I think it was one of the best performances of the piece I ever did.

Karl Rankl was not in the front rank as a conductor. He, like Furtwängler, stood with his belly sticking out when on the rostrum, but there was never a great depth to his readings. That being said, he was chosen as chief conductor for Covent Garden Opera and to his credit put on the *Ring*, not that it was a great conception of Wagner's epic but at least he did it. The strain of it all made him somewhat of a martinet and eventually he was let go.

Heinz Unger had the same stance on the dais as Rankl and Furtwängler, not that they should all be classed together. Unger was courteous and gave very good readings of most of the pieces he conducted which were mainly all the German classics, and nothing very venturesome. Indeed, the orchestra could not be very avant garde in its programming in those days, because to quote Sol Hurok, "the audience would have stayed away in droves" and the box office cash was badly needed.

Malcolm Sargent or "Flash Harry" as he was nicknamed was something of an enigma. He was hated by many of the orchestral players, particularly some of the old sweats, the reason being that in the 1930's, when he was comparatively unknown, he contracted testicular tuberculosis and in those days, before antibiotics, the cure consisted of a sojourn in the mountains and a clean healthy diet hoping that Mother Nature would take her course. Many musicians clubbed together to send him to Switzerland for the cure, and he did recover after having one testicle removed, the current talk being that he "only fired on one cylinder." Unfortunately he mentioned to the press (and he may have been misquoted), that orchestral musicians were being paid too much money for what they did. This immediately caused a furore amongst the musicians, who took it as a slap in the face for all they had done for him; he was for ever after regarded as an enemy of musicians in general.

Musicians are notoriously generous when one of their own has a misfortune. In the late 1950's there was a violinist named Donald Sturtivant who contracted polio. Donald was a fine player; he had been concertmaster of the BBC Midland Light Orchestra and was later accepted by the BBC Symphony Orchestra, and it was during a Prom season that he caught polio.

He had bought a house in the suburbs and used to cycle to the Albert Hall, then cycle back home for lunch and work on fixing up his house before cycling back again to the Albert Hall for the Prom Concert. All this proved to be too much for him and he was badly stricken with the disease; he was immediately placed in an iron lung and could move nothing except his teeth, so Sargent kindly donated a device that enabled him to turn the pages of a book by using his teeth on a rubber ball attachment. The BBC Symphony members also contributed to an ongoing fund for him and he was eventually released from hospital.

He came into the studio to see us but could barely drag himself around. His career as a violinist was over and his marriage too, was affected, but the BBC was very good and found him a job in the music library and sent for a taxi every day to take him back and forth.

On another occasion Sargent helped Willem de Mont, in those days principal 'cello of the London Symphony Orchestra. Bill, as we called him, used to run an open Jeep and one day he left his 'cello in the jeep and it was stolen. He asked Sargent if he would help him buy another 'cello; Sargent agreed and I heard him say to de Mont, "You won't let me down, will you?" These are two examples of his generosity and kindness to musicians that are not generally known.

He appeared on stage dressed immaculately. He wore a very high winged shirt collar, always a carnation, his shoes glistened, and he sported an air of sartorial perfection. I once met his valet in a pub near the Albert Hall, (Sargent lived in Albert Hall Mansions), and his valet told me Sargent always had his eye on the "main chance". He was a close friend of Marina, Duchess of Kent, and anyone else who could further his goals.

Walter Legge is on record as saying that the Philharmonia Orchestra sounded like a Salvation Army band when Sargent conducted it.

There are many Beecham/Sargent stories: After Sargent, who had previously been known as <u>Dr</u>. Malcolm Sargent was knighted, somebody informed Beecham, who said 'Oh yes, I knew he had been doctored," obviously referring to his solitary testicle.

It was the custom in those days for the orchestra to stand for a conductor at a concert when he entered only if they thought he was exceptional and worthy of what was considered a mark of considerable respect. The orchestra would get together to decide and the word was given out that we would all stand, giving the conductor a very high accolade that was greatly appreciated by them. Nowadays, at the beginning of a concert, orchestras stand automatically for any Tom, Dick, Jill or Harry who can wag a stick. I think this present practice has taken away recognition from the truly great, for the audience would often remark after the concert upon the honour that the orchestra had bestowed on the conductor.

Sargent, however, tried in vain to get the orchestra to stand for him by saying, "You know, gentlemen, when I enter I would like you to stand and receive the applause with me." The orchestra never fell for that ploy, for when he entered, the orchestra just sat in their seats with poker faces, much to his chagrin.

He was very self-centred. At one Promenade concert in which I played, Sargent spent most of the time discussing with the TV producer in his Victorian English, "At this point I go awf, and then I come on," repeating several times to himself before his entrée, "I'm the greatest conductor in the world." So much for the power of positive thinking.

Despite that, he was very good in what he did, although his performances were not always very inspiring, except perhaps for some Elgar and Sibelius. He always produced a memorable *Nimrod* from Elgar's

Enigma Variations.

His forte was, I think, in his choral conducting. He conducted the Royal Choral Society in such works as Smetana's *The Ferry Man's Bride,* Handel's *Messiah* -always Ebenezer Prout's version with full woodwind; *Israel in Egypt,* Walton's *Belshazzar's Feast* and, of course, Mendelssohn's *Elijah.* He liked to use Elsie Morrison and Isabel Baillie as his sopranos, plus Heddle Nash, the tenor. I recall Isabel Baillie nodding with great vigour when she sang, "I <u>know</u> that my redeemer liveth," from the *Messiah.* He had one of the clearest beats of any conductor I have ever met but, if anything, he over-conducted, that is to say that in any little solo or cadenza that any of the orchestra principals might have, he would insist on conducting them instead of giving them a little leeway.

In Mozart's *Requiem* there is a famous trombone solo in the *Tuba Mirum* that Sargent wanted to change to a French horn solo. This incensed George Maxted, the principal trombone who threatened to sue him, feeling that his ability as a player had been called into question.

Every year when he was conductor of the BBC Symphony, he would take the orchestra for an outing to the London Zoo, of which he was a Member, and delighted to have himself photographed with a boa constrictor round his neck. Some of the bystanding musicians wondered out loud what would happen to Sargent if someone were to deliberately annoy the reptile, but no-one ever did.

On one occasion he was conducting Holst's suite, *The Planets,* and he was visibly discomfited when he turned the page to the *Uranus* section where some orchestral miscreant had written the word "Up"in front of it.

Another conductor who eventually became the LPO's musical director in the 'fifties was William Steinberg, who had conducted the Pittsburgh Orchestra. Steinberg was a large man who devoted his conducting mainly to the German symphonic repertoire and although he had a fairly good stick technique, set reasonable tempi and obtained a good performance, his concerts were just like his build, stolid; I thought at the time that he lacked the verve that may have placed him in the top rank of conductors.

Albert Coates came to the LPO in the late 'forties. He was a big man with a shock of iron grey hair, very courteous to the orchestra, gave a very clear beat and was excellent in his renderings of the Russian classics. He was born in St. Petersburg (his mother was Russian, his father English) and was educated in England but had a very thick accent. We played some of the Tchaikowsky symphonies. I can remember the climax he obtained in

Tchaikowsly's *Fifth Symphony*, last movement, when the march is played for the second time. Coates just folded his arms and let the orchestra play, with wonderful results.

The LPO used to rehearse at a military drill hall just off Kensington High Street, which was very handy to the Albert Hall. One day in 1946 I arrived early for rehearsal not knowing who the conductor was going to be. My readers may raise their eyebrows at this, but some days we had three different conductors, all as fresh as paint and rearing to go. The musicians were only interested in the difficulties presented in the music and did not bother much as to who was going to conduct them, unless it were one of the truly greats, and the phrase "Same poor old horse but with a different jockey" was often repeated. I asked one of the players who had just arrived whether he knew who was conducting that day and he replied, "Oh, some young American chap, a New Yorker, I believe, named Bernstein."

Leonard Bernstein arrived with a retinue of friends. He must have been in his late twenties. Of medium height, thin, with a shock of black hair, he seemed to mesmerize the audience with his vim and pep on the rostrum. At rehearsal he gave off a terrific amount of energy, and to this day I think he was the sharpest conductor I have ever come across. We rehearsed Walton's Portsmouth Point Overture, which is very difficult rhythmically, but with his wonderful stick technique he was able to get through all the traps and difficulties. Years later, when I played his overture to *Candide* I felt as though he had something akin to Walton in his composition.

Despite his quick brain and flawless technique I never thought he had the gravitas or depth of feeling of a Giulini, Walter or Kleiber, but that being said he became a great favourite with the LPO. Victor Watson told me that he was sure Bernstein would go places, which, of course, he did.

Stokowski, whom I played for in the LSO, was a poseur if ever there was one. He started this god-like veneration of the man on the podium who was able to bring out all these heavenly sounds through the film *100 Men and a Girl* made in the 'thirties. Mind you, the image of a man or woman standing as a leader before a group of musicians and directing their every movement appeals to the perception of the masses that a conductor is a god-like figure. The media and publicity people must be blamed for promoting this image. After all, whilst much of it is show biz, to my mind the music is all-important.

Stokowski, in my opinion was a good conductor, in that he obtained some exciting performances and his tempi were always logical.

Nevertheless, he certainly had his faults, mainly compounded by his terrific ego. What old man would go to a mother and tell her he was going to marry her daughter, a young girl heiress, whether she liked it or not? Then there was his phoney accent. It is said he was born "Stokes" in London's East End (nothing against that) but he always spoke with an affected foreign accent. At a recording session it is usual for the musicians to stand around during "takes" waiting for the previous take to be listened to and approved before beginning the next segment. Stokowski came upon two violinists just standing there waiting for the next take and suddenly he said "no vun has privilege" and demanded the violinists be sent home, which to appease him they were, but with pay, I might add.

When I sometimes played as an extra with the London Symphony at Christmas time, he would invite the wives and children to a rehearsal where goodies were dispensed to the kids, but he delighted in lambasting the musicians in front of their wives.

Stuart Knussen, who was principal bass of the LSO at the time became friendly with Stokowski and often had him to his house just outside of London. At dinner, Stuart mentioned that he had broken his mute. The next day at rehearsal, there was a passage written for the basses to be muted. Stokowski immediately demanded to know, to the embarrassment of Stuart, where his mute was.

My friend Simon Streatfeild, who was principal viola in the LSO at one time, told me this tale: Stokowski and a group of musicians were standing around talking in the break, and Stokowski mentioned that he had it on good authority that there was a wrong note in a score. When asked who the good authority was, he said after an embarrassing hesitation, "It vas Finkelstein," obviously a made up name, and the musicians could hardly conceal their mirth.

Although Stokowski's arrangements of Bach for full orchestra are, in my opinion not the real Bach, nevertheless I think they come off with much grandeur.

The first time I met John Barbirolli was at a concert at the Royal Albert Hall, put on by the *Daily Telegraph* newspaper to celebrate the end of the European WW2 and also some anniversary or other. There were three orchestras engaged for the occasion, the LSO, LPO and the BBC Symphony. Barbirolli conducted without a baton, making arcane gestures with his hands, and as a relative novice I couldn't understand what he was trying to convey, but the old sweats in the orchestras did, and the piece, the slow movement from Tchaikovsky's *Serenade for Strings* received thunderous applause.

That was the biggest orchestra I have ever played in. I cannot tell you the numbers of the upper strings but I do know there were twenty-four double basses, led by Eugene Cruft, with Victor Watson sitting beside him. The two were arch rivals, and it was amusing to see them making polite conversation, each knowing full well what he thought of the other. When the BBC Symphony Orchestra was first formed in 1930 Victor was offered the job of principal bass, but was under contract to Beecham at the time and often used to recount how he had sought advice from King's Counsel (in England, a very high priced lawyer) but there was no way he could accept the offer and Eugene got the job instead.

When I was freelancing in London, I occasionally received a call to go up to Manchester to play with the Hallé Orchestra of which Barbirolli was the conductor. The Hallé players worshipped him, as did the members of the Houston Symphony Orchestra.

Once, I was asked to play at some morning and afternoon recording sessions held at the Abbey Road studios of EMI/HMV conducted by Barbirolli. It was said that he drank a bottle of scotch at each session. His wife, Evelyn Rothwell was a very fine oboist, and I remember her exquisite playing at a Promenade Concert. She was totally different from Barbirolli who came over as a rather earthy individual, but she reminded me of a rather prissy schoolmistress.

The Barbirollis were a musical family. John Barbirolli's brother, Peter, was a violist in the Royal Opera House, Covent Garden. Peter was a good player and had inherited the family trait of portliness; he wore a large walrus moustache. But John, although he had a large frame, was not nearly as big as Peter. John Barbirolli was a very fine 'cellist in his day, and a teacher too, for Victor Watson told me that Barbirolli had coached him in his double bass solo playing.

Anatole Fistoulari, a Russian, was at one time the LPO's chief conductor. He was capable, not prone to giving extraordinary performances of anything, but he did a workmanlike job. He would waste time over minor matters and at 1.00 p.m. (rehearsals were almost always 10.00 a.m. until 1.00 p.m.) he would beg for just another ten minutes time, which the orchestra, albeit with rather bad grace, would give him.

Some time after I had left the LPO, Fistoulari asked me if I would play principal bass in an orchestra he was forming to tour Ireland and Scotland.

After the tour I was invited to a party at Fistoulari's apartment. He was married to Gustav Mahler's daughter, Anna, to whom I talked at great length. Naturally, she was a great admirer of her father, the noted composer who was also a talented conductor. She was a fine sculptress and there were many of her pieces displayed in the apartment.

Gustav Mahler, who was before my time, was hated by the Vienna musicians; some of the older ones almost went ballistic at the mention of his name, they told me that he had a penchant for sacking his musicians just before retiring age.

I heard a rather salacious story from the stage manager at the Royal Festival Hall where I had played at a concert that Fistoulari was conducting. The next day I was playing there again but with another orchestra and I got into conversation with the stage manager. He told me how the night before, when he was getting ready to lock up, surmising that Fistoulari had left, he had opened the conductor's room door, it being very late, and there was Fistoulari, in *flagrante delicto* with one of his admirers. Fistoulari just looked round and said,"Geef us anuzzer fife mineet"

Sir Adrian Boult was of quite a different character. He was tall, thinnish with a bald head and fringe, and wore a sizeable handlebar moustache that he was fond of stroking as he contemplated the music. A Quaker of very strict principles, he neither smoked nor drank, both were an abomination to him. He was married to the former wife of Stuart Wilson, a BBC executive. Lady Boult was a charming person as was Sir Adrian, but he had a terrible temper that fortunately he very rarely lost.

On one occasion when the LPO were playing at Hastings on the South Coast of England in a bout of very cold weather, Lady Boult came across the LPO orchestral porters, one of whom did not have an overcoat. She said to him, "My good man, do you not have an overcoat?" Whereupon the porter answered, "No, my Lady." So forthwith Lady Boult gave him a handsome amount of cash and told him to buy an overcoat at Montague Burton's, a men's clothing chain store.

On another occasion when Sir Adrian was chief conductor of the LPO, the orchestra was in financial difficulty and there was no money to pay the orchestra for their summer holiday. The orchestra was so strapped for cash at times that it was forced to make economies such as hiring the flowers that were presented to the soloist onstage but returning them to florist when the concert was over. Boult immediately came to the rescue and provided the necessary money for the holidays on one condition; nobody was to know who the benefactor was. Of course, it came out later, but that was Sir Adrian – he never wanted anyone to know of his many contributions to the well-being of the orchestra. I was told his money came from Duckham's Oil Company.

I have a letter from him that I greatly treasure; in it he wishes me well in my new position as principal bass of the Vancouver Symphony Orchestra. In the letter he mentions Hans Richter, who, to Sir Adrian was one of the "greats", and goes on to say that he is pleased the Vancouver Symphony now has eight basses and recommends that, as Richter suggested, they be placed four on each side of the orchestra thereby giving the bass sound a chance of being evenly distributed.

Boult was always self-effacing, unlike so many of the "virtuoso" conductors who imprint their own egos and personalities over the composer's wishes. He put the composer first and always gave a true rendering of what he adjudged to be the composer's intentions; for this reason alone he was a *rara avis*. He used a long baton, and often gave sweeping accounts of works by Bax, Elgar in particular, Vaughan Williams and many other English composers. He once told us that during his tenure as conductor of the BBC Symphony Orchestra he had to tackle many works that other conductors would have refused. However, for the standard works he would devote as little time as was necessary, and if it were a hot summer afternoon would say to the orchestra, "I'm sure we all know this very well, ladies and gentlemen, let us take advantage of this beautiful weather and leave."

I remember Sir Arnold Bax coming to BBC Maida Vale studio for a rehearsal of one of his pieces. He was a rotund man. I admire his works, particularly the tone poems *The Garden of Fand*, *Tintagel* and his symphonies. Bax, incidentally, was Master of the Queen's Musick and like many other musicians he was a toper. As I mentioned before, Boult hated drink, and, when Bax came up to the conductor's podium to discuss a point in the score, he smelt Bax's breath and said to him, "Go away sir, you stink!"

Bax's music seems to have fallen into disfavour, but lately I have noticed one or two CD's of his works have been issued. Will his works be around a hundred years from now? I hope so. Bax's partner was Harriet Cohen, the pianist. Bill Fussell, the orchestral porter used to say that in the old days at the Queen's Hall she used to pee in the potted palms in the soloists room due to nervousness.

Nervousness does affect many artists in this way; not only musicians, but actors, ballet dancers and speakers, so they usually make a point of visiting the washroom before they go on stage. One violinist in the LPO who had a prostate problem was suspended for two weeks because he peed on stage in the middle of a long symphony. Do not forget that stage folk are only human like everyone else.

I well remember playing in a television show conducted by Eric Robinson with Harriet Cohen as the soloist. She played a concerto for one hand, having unfortunately lost the use of the other. Harriet was placed on a raised dais and the orchestra couldn't help noticing she wasn't wearing any underpants, which caused a lot of hilarity. You could see all the way to Pasadena!

Sir George Dyson's opera *The Canterbury Pilgrims* was performed in the late '40's, early '50's. He was the Principal of the Royal College of Music, and although I'm sure he knew all the rules of contrary motion, not doubling the thirds and consecutive fifths etc., nevertheless, the performances were very pedestrian. In my opinion it is a good work and Sir George would have been well advised to obtain the services of a professional conductor instead of conducting it himself. The work reminds me very much of Vaughan Williams opera *Sir John in Love* - why, I don't know, because Williams and Dyson have dissimilar styles.

Gregor Fitelberg, the conductor of the Polish National Radio Orchestra, came to us in 1946, and immediately rubbed the orchestra up the wrong way. He would shout to the violins "No cross legs when playing!" and "No laugh when I talk." All this didn't go down very well with the orchestra, particularly his rendering of Schubert's Great C Major Symphony in which he made cuts that enucleated the whole meaning of the symphony. He was met with derision by the orchestra for doing so, and consequently was reduced to begging and pleading with them to co-operate. I was fortunate to meet a very fine conductor who was taking the Niagara Youth Orchestra on tour in July 2002, Michael Newnham, who told me when I mentioned Fitelberg that he was a legendary figure in Poland and was delighted to know I had played for him.

Meanwhile Beecham was appearing with the LPO less and less, for behind the scenes matters were becoming acrimonious and slowly coming to a head. Beecham's insistence that he wanted complete control over the LPO became the main stumbling block.

At the Board's direction, Thomas Russell, an ex-violist who was the manager at that time, was engaged in a long dialogue with Beecham to try to resolve the issue, but Beecham remained adamant in his demands. His plea for total direction was not on the orchestra's agenda however, and he then took matters into his own hands, and formed his own orchestra, which he named the Royal Philharmonic Orchestra (RPO). Soon the newspapers were full of reports that Beecham had likened his new orchestra to a Rolls Royce compared with the LPO's Ford. Thomas Russell fired off a letter to one newspaper saying that he would rather have a new Ford than a 1907 Rolls Royce, and so the mud slinging went on.

The Royal Philharmonic was to become the fifth symphony orchestra in the Capital and many wondered if there was indeed room for another orchestra, but the RPO survived because of Beecham's many connections, and also he had engaged some fine players including Arthur Cleghorn on flute, Reginald Kell on clarinet, Dennis Brain on French horn and Steven Staryk as concertmaster. I received a phone call from Staryk one day asking me if I would be interested in joining the Royal Philharmonic Orchestra but had to refuse as I was too busy with other things.

There were repercussions for the LPO, and I don't know what dirty work went on behind the scenes, but it was noticed that the critiques particularly in some of the right wing newspapers were becoming more damning. At one concert for which a particularly bad write-up was given it was proved that the music critic wasn't even there, so all complimentary tickets to that source were immediately stopped.

The Press made much of the fact that some members of the orchestra were communists, which was true. The orchestra had subscribed for a hospital bed and medical supplies to be sent to a Leningrad hospital, there being terrible shortages in Russia, but this didn't help the LPO, for although the war in Europe was now officially over there was a growing concern about Russia's future intentions. Some of the media were saying that Stalin intended to march right to the English Channel.

One day in the fall of 1946 I heard that there was going to be a conductor from Milan coming to us, his name was Victor de Sabata and he was Director and Chief Conductor of La Scala Milan. Berta Geissmar, the author of *The Baton and the Jackboot* who had been Furtwängler's secretary in Berlin and then held a position in the LPO's office was instrumental in bringing over de Sabata and, later on, Furtwängler. The orchestra didn't realize at the time what a tremendous effect he would have on them, and even now I think about him often and still admire him so much that I named my boat the "Victor de Sabata" after him. Out of all the conductors I have worked with, and there are many, I can only think of a mere handful that I became excited about: Victor de Sabata was at the forefront of these.

He was around fifty-three years of age at that time, thin, with aristocratic features which reminded me of a Roman senator, of medium height, bald, with a fringe of white hair, he walked with a limp caused by the poliomyelitis he had contracted years before, and had a magnetic, aesthetic presence.

At his first rehearsal, which I can remember as if it were yesterday, we began with Dvorak's New World Symphony, then followed Elgar's Cockaigne overture and Berlioz's *Carnival Romaine* overture without de Sabata stopping even once to comment. At the end of the rehearsal I asked Victor Watson, who was steeped in experience (I was allowed to call him "Victor" by then) and a good judge of a conductor, what he thought of de Sabata; he replied, "Oh, another typical Italian," and we left it at that.

Next day, however, there was a far different de Sabata on the podium. He said, "Gentlemen, yesterday I was just getting to know the orchestra, now we rehearse," and rehearse we did, with a vengeance. He dissected Dvorak's New World Symphony correcting printed mistakes that had been played for years, and the results were remarkable. The overture Cockaigne, which hitherto had been thought of as a lesser work of Elgar's became alive - a thrilling piece and to crown it all Berlioz' *Carnival Romaine*. The audience went wild after his first concert at the Albert Hall.

One of the crowning pieces in his repertoire was the *Verdi Requiem*. I have never forgotten the *Dies Irae* where he had a throng of trumpets situated in the boxes on either side of the Albert Hall stage. He created such energy and electricity that it made shivers run down one's back.

He was particularly fond of Ravel's works. On one occasion a choir was brought over from Paris to sing in Ravel's one act opera, *L'Enfant et les Sortilèges*. De Sabata had conducted its first performance and he even corrected the choir's pronunciation. In Ravel's *Bolero* his performances were memorable. He would start with the side drum playing pianississimo[19] and then each of the soloists would come in playing gradually louder. His right hand would keep a rigid tempo for the side drum but his left hand would give a rubato[20] indication especially on the repeated notes and all the while the frenzy would build up until a blaring fortissimo[21] evolved towards the end of the piece which would then fizzle out in the last few notes. His Bolero performances always brought the house down.

After the rehearsal I tried to beat separate tempi[22] with each hand in front of a mirror but could not, and I venture to suggest there are also not many conductors out there who can. Ravel's *Rhapsodie Espagnole* was another piece in which he excelled. In the last movement, *Feria*, there is a slow section in which a solo bass plays a glissando[23], this, de Sabata explained, was to represent the sound of a bull in its pen near the bullfighting arena, and whenever I have played this little solo since, my mind has always gone back to de Sabata. I have mentioned it to some well-known conductors who did not know this was the composer's intention, to imitate a bullpen.

He always conducted without a score; his memory was prodigious. For instance, sometimes he would stop and say "Gentlemen, there is a mistake, shall we commence at bar 207?"

One felt that he had an instinctive knowledge of each player's ability; it was as though those huge brown protruding eyes of his could delve into the very mind of a person.

One great thing in his favour though, was that whilst he expected the maximum from everyone he could be sympathetic with any musician or soloist who, although giving of his/her best just couldn't deliver what he wanted of them. One case in point was a once famous tenor who was now "over the hill", and I felt so sorry for him not being able to produce, try as hard as he might, but de Sabata was extremely compassionate towards him and helped him to be at ease, and at the concert the tenor gave a superlative performance.

Not so with von Karajan. We were recording the Strauss operetta *Die Fledermaus* in 1955 when I was in the Philharmonia Orchestra, and he wanted to take the tenor soloist's part abnormally quickly, but the tenor couldn't keep up. There was just one run through and that was it; the tenor was gone by lunchtime and Walter Legge, the Founder and Artistic Director brought in a replacement.

At the end of his series of concerts de Sabata was crowned on stage with a laurel wreath and given a reception by the orchestra backstage. That was the only reception given by an orchestra for a conductor (apart from Toscanini) that I know of.

On one occasion de Sabata was chatting with some of the orchestra members and declared to us "You know, I only conduct at concerts for fun, my real job is the opera." Someone asked him how a conductor started his career in opera and he thought for a minute and then with his infectious laugh said, "Well, for the first seven years, after he has gone through rigorous tests, he sweeps up the stage, then, he may be given part of a rehearsal and if all goes well he is later entrusted with a matinée. This could make or break him but if he is successful, then, maybe they will entrust him with an opera the next or some subsequent season and perhaps he will make his reputation and eventually build up a career."

He was very fond of the fair sex. Once, when he was staying at the Hyde Park Hotel in Knightsbridge, he discovered he had forgotten his pyjamas, so Felix Apprahamian crossed over the road to Harrods, the exclusive department store, bought a pair of silk pyjamas and presented them to de Sabata, who said earnestly "Well, where is the woman?" Felix told me he didn't think he was joking either.

One season an auburn haired actress accompanied him and he was much happier than of yore. At one rehearsal he went over to a soprano soloist and put his hand over her ample bosom, then gave a discourse on the music. This soprano sometimes sang Hector Berlioz's *The Death of Cleopatra*, a vocal epic of Cleopatra's suicide by clutching a poisonous snake to her bosom. One wag in the orchestra deemed it to be all asp and tit.

I was incredulous when Adolf Borsdorf told me that he accompanied de Sabata in a limousine to York Minster where he was to conduct the London Philharmonic in a performance of Verdi's *Requiem*. Half way to York there was a motor bike in front of them and riding pillion was an attractive girl who turned round and smiled at them. Immediately de Sabata ordered the driver to follow the motorcycle and said to Adolf "You never know this could be all right." Adolf replied,"Maestro, you have to conduct the Verdi *Requiem* in York and we may be late." According to Adolf de Sabata reversed his instructions to the driver and they headed for York. I questioned Adolf about this but he asserted vehemently that it was true.

He could be disagreeable at times and at one concert he stopped conducting and muttered a lot of presumably swear words and then spat at a 'cellist whom he thought was not paying attention. For de Sabata the music was everything.

During a period of recording sessions at Walthamstow Town Hall (Walthamstow is a suburb situated on the north-east side of London) we recorded Richard Wagner's *Ride of the Valkyries* and I had never heard anything like it in my life before. The LPO was greatly augmented for this occasion and I still possess the recording on vinyl and it is superb. At one of the sessions we recorded the *Eroica* symphony and de Sabata said, "Contrabassi, you can play that passage all in one position, why do you move?" and to the English horn player he said, before recording Sibelius' *Swan of Tuonela*, "You should employ fork fingering for this passage."

One sad note lingers in my memory. The contrabass trombonist committed suicide the next day after the *Ride of the Valkyries* recording, why, I do not know, but some musicians tend to be suicidal. I can think of one contrabassoonist in the Philharmonia Orchestra who committed suicide and others too. Perhaps there is that constant aim for perfection that obsesses them, or it could be the constant lack of money and the uncertain lifestyle that some musicians experience which causes depression.

There are many instances of de Sabata's amazing knowledge and talent; two of these were recounted on the sleeve of a re-issue CD of de

Sabata's by Felix Apprahamian and I can vouch for the truth of it because I was there and saw and heard it all. The principal 'cellist remarked that a certain passage was unplayable. The maestro thought for a moment and then said, "Give me your 'cello, I will show you." The same happened with a difficult horn part that Charlie Gregory the principal horn said was unplayable. De Sabata said, "Mr. Gregory, give me your instrument and I will show you," which he did. Felix added that all the LPO of those days must be dead by now, but I wrote him and told him I was alive and well and living in Sooke, British Columbia, Canada. I never received a reply and I wondered whether he too had departed for a better life but Deryk Barker, the music critic of the *Victoria Times-Colonist*, contacted the Delius Society of which Felix was a board member and he was told that Felix was in poor health following a stroke, but he was still alive. He passed away in January 2005.

Respighi's *Pines of Rome* calls for a recording of a nightingale to be played during part of the piece, and Felix was entrusted with the nightingale. Nowadays with our advanced equipment it wouldn't present a problem, but somehow or other the nightingale didn't come in on time much to de Sabata and Felix's consternation.

Digressing about advanced equipment, the use of body microphones has certainly helped many stage performances, as has the use of closed circuit television. To my mind there is nothing worse in opera than to have an over zealous prompter who can be heard quite clearly by all and sundry. The TV and microphones have obviated this problem to a large extent.

There was one débacle that occurred when Berlioz' Fantastic Symphony was being played by the LSO. In the last movement, the *Witches' Sabbath*, there is a very important entry by the bells played backstage. The orchestra manager at the time was John Cruft, a former oboist and son of Eugene. He was directing the bell player, but unfortunately the bells came in at the wrong place and caused chaos because the conductor was not visible from where John and the bells were situated. If there had been a closed circuit TV behind stage I'm sure that this domino would not have happened.

Upon de Sabata's departure the LPO players returned to their humdrum existence with Basil Cameron conducting the lion's share. De Sabata was sorely missed. The audiences loved him, the orchestra loved him, but the Press for some reason or other, panned him. One reviewer called him the "Dancing conductor from Milan", and subsequent concerts were all given bad reviews, so much so that he came for a year or two more and then gave up. Walter Legge once told me that he had offered de Sabata any fee he wanted, choice of any programme, venue or time, and that he, Legge, would fly over personally to Milan to bring him over by private plane, but de Sabata was obdurate and would not come.

When I was playing at La Scala Milan with von Karajan and the Philharmonia Orchestra I attended a reception in honour of Toscanini. There I met de Sabata's wife and his daughter, a very good-looking girl. I asked her why her father would not come to England any more and she just shrugged and said "It is the Press."

Apart from music he had a remarkable brain and could add or multiply large numbers in his head. When he retired to Santa Margherita, in Italy, he devoted his time to solving mathematical puzzles.

Some time later Wilhelm Furtwängler came over from Germany to conduct the London Philharmonic. Let me set the scene: The war had not been long over, Britons and Germans were not very friendly disposed to each other due to the terrible havoc wreaked on both sides and the many civilian and military casualties. Many cities had been bombed and as a result there were thousands of homeless, so it could be said that the timing of Furtwängler's visit was inopportune to say the least. Added to that, he had been Hitler's favourite conductor and connected with the Bayreuth Opera House, the seat of Wagner Opera that at the time seemed to be viewed by Hitler's opponents as a hotbed of German expansion and nationalism.

After the war there were de-Nazification courts and Furtwängler was tried as a Nazi but was acquitted. He was never a member of the Nazi party; in fact he had supported Hindemith (whose wife Gertrud was Jewish) against Goebbels and the Nazis, which resulted in his having to give up the conductorship of the Berlin Philharmonic in 1934 but he was later re-instated. It became obvious that the man lived only for his music and it seemed to be only fair for him to be exonerated from war crimes.

During the war the Berlin Philharmonic Orchestra suffered many casualties when an Allied bomb hit a factory where they were performing.

At his first rehearsal with us he came onto the platform very nervously, looking tense as if expecting us to boo him, but to a man and with no pre-arranged signal the orchestra rose and applauded. A big sigh of relief came over him; it was wonderful to see his face, and then he just said, "Meine Herren, bitte, die Neunte Symphonie." (Please gentlemen, the Ninth Symphony). This was one of the most poignant moments in my long musical life.

We started to rehearse Beethoven's *Ninth Symphony* and it was a revelation. Whilst most Italian conductors of note I have played for seemed to get their feet in the right position by looking down and then adjusting their stance very carefully before they commenced (I can think of amongst others, de Sabata, Giulini, Tullio Seraphin, Nino Sansogno and Guido Cantelli), Furtwängler just ambled on looking very inelegant on the podium, gave a little wriggle and then commenced. He was a tallish man, lank and balding, and had an ungainly way of sticking out his belly when he conducted. He spoke very little, and was very quiet and even humble when addressing the orchestra. Despite the fact that he didn't have a great stick technique and never indulged in pyrotechnics the end result was astounding.

The next concert was devoted to Wagner. In the programme were the closing scenes from *Götterdämmerung*; to say the concert was wonderful would be an understatement.

There is an interesting tale to tell about the Wagner tubas: The LPO possessed a set of these but would not lend them to the Philharmonia, because they were a rival orchestra. Legge, however, always had a set flown in from Germany whenever they were required. Looking back, it all seems very petty, but that is what the music profession was like and still is; cut-throat.

I next played for Furtwängler when he was conducting Beethoven's *Ninth Symphony* at the Lucerne International Festival with the Philharmonia some years later and that was the last I was to see of him. Kirsten Flagstad the great Wagnerian soprano came to London soon after Furtwängler to record with us but by that time she was past her prime. I do not remember the recordings ever being issued, although in her day she was a legend.

Another conductor who came to the LPO about that time was Edouard van Beinum who was principal conductor of the Concertgebouw Orchestra and would have been in his early 'fifties at the time. He had been a cook in the Dutch Army and was very down to earth and had none of the mannerisms that some conductors affect. Sometimes, just before going on stage, musicians will joke, "Let's follow the beat just for fun, and see what happens," but the orchestra could always follow van Beinum.

Van Beinum was very popular with the orchestra because apart from being a fine conductor he could understand where the musicians were coming from. He had begun his career by conducting some of the lesser-known Dutch orchestras and once told a joke about an elderly trombonist whose pay was poor but was asked to play a certain passage better. The trombonist replied, "What do you think, black bread in and white bread coming out?"

His health was not good- he had heart trouble, I believe, and he used to slip a tablet in his mouth before starting to conduct, but he never spared himself, and got some truly great performances. He once gave a very good performance of Berlioz's Fantastic Symphony. At rehearsal he would point out little details in the score. For instance the bassoons representing the old crones knitting around the scaffold, the bass pizzicato at the end of the *March to the Scaffold* indicating the victim's head falling into the basket after being guillotined, and the horns playing cuivré[24] in the *Witches Sabbath* imitating the demons.

He was very friendly with Benjamin Britten, the noted composer, and conducted us in the first English performance of Britten's *Spring Symphony*. Once I was called in to play a concert with the LPO with no rehearsal. Britten's *Young Person's Guide to the Orchestra* was on the programme, and when it came to the bass variation van Beinum seemed to turn all his attention towards me. He wagged his stick and looked at me like a hawk but fortunately I knew the piece and at the end of it he smiled at me, so I suppose he must have been satisfied. This underlines the fact that when freelancing one must be prepared to deliver the goods at short notice, there is no quarter given - make a mistake and you are out!

Malcolm Arnold, the great composer, was in those days the LPO's principal trumpet and seemed to be very friendly with van Beinum telling him rather risqué jokes in English, a language in which van Beinum was not very fluent. Malcolm was a jovial, daredevilish character. Someone bet Malcolm and two others that they would not jump into the fountain outside Watford Town Hall, Hertfordshire, in their tuxedos. They did, and won the bet. Sitting next to Malcolm was Dennis Egan, also a fine player. Dennis had a high, squeaky voice and on one occasion when Sargent was coming onto the platform to conduct the LPO he had to pass by the trumpets; Malcolm mimicked Dennis and said "I think Sargent is a #!@*$>" much to Sargent's discomfiture.

On another occasion at a rehearsal with de Sabata conducting, Dennis had to climb to the top balcony to play the off stage trumpet in Beethoven's *Leonora No. 3 Overture*. He didn't make it in time and de Sabata cried angrily, "Where is the trumpet?" at which Dennis, now having arrived, leaned over and said, "Wait for it you bastard you'll get it when it comes." De Sabata asked what Dennis had said, and when he was told, instead of becoming angry he broke out into paroxysms of laughter.

Other conductors of note for whom I have played include

Ferenc Fricsay who conducted once at the Lucerne Festival. Although I don't think he was in good health at the time he gave some outstanding performances, as did Rafael Kubelik, Rudolf Kempe, Karl Böhm and Hans Swarowsky. I met these gentlemen only on rare occasions, and nothing much about them comes to mind at the present time. It is amazing to me how some make an impression and others leave no memories behind, but by and large the really great ones tend to stick in one's mind. Not that I am denigrating any of the former, who were certainly great conductors. When freelancing, one plays a concert and then goes on to the next pitch the following day putting behind what happened on the previous day, particularly if something difficult is on the next programme.

I must mention Aaron Copland. He was a tall, stooped man with a thin, lined face, a rather long nose, darkish, thinning hair and a crackly voice. He conducted the LSO in recordings of his own works. He was an amiable man and obtained good results from the orchestra, and naturally he had his own ideas about his own works that he was easily able to convey to the orchestra. Altogether I enjoyed playing for him.

There were often funny occurrences, and overall the musicians got on well with each other, but it was a punishing schedule. When the next contract came around I was suffering from a bout of the'flu that I may have caught while playing in some of the frigid halls on our circuit. Because of the fuel shortage many halls remained unheated, and we often had to play in our overcoats. I couldn't see my musical life being forever on such a treadmill, but what to do? I thought I might try freelancing for there seemed to be plenty of work about.

From all this, the reader can infer that a professional musician's life is not the sinecure that it is purported to be. An iron constitution and perfect health are needed to withstand the rigours of it. Another thing, if you didn't work in those days there was no pay unless you happened to be in the BBC or LPO. Most of the work was done by successful freelancers who had left the orchestras, partly because of burnout, but also there was also much more money and flexibility to be had freelancing.

There was a big rate of turnover, particularly with the wind and brass principals, many of whom left to freelance or to take up other jobs. The rank and file also suffered from burnout and left to take on jobs outside music. Some of the jobs the disenchanted and discarded ones took were varied, such as gardeners, working in a leather factory, orchestra managers, restaurateurs, administrators, taxi drivers, insurance agents, realtors, chicken farmers and night watchmen etc. etc. Those to whom I talked seemed happier with their lot. My wife often used to say to me that she wished I had a nine –till– five job because she and the kids hardly ever saw me. Needless to say there were many marriages ruined because of the gypsy life we were forced to lead.

There is one violinist living in Victoria, B.C. who was a pupil of Heifetz and concertmaster in one of the BBC Orchestras. Despite having risen to the top of the musical profession he came to the conclusion that it wasn't for him so he studied and became a dermatologist.

One bass player, Paddy Rush, emigrated to Australia. I can remember him auctioning off his tailcoat and selling his bass after his last concert. That was that; no more double bass for him! Nobody ever heard from him since, so how he fared I don't know, but he certainly vowed never to play the bass again.

It is very rare to see wind players over sixty years of age in orchestras, particularly brass players, but double bass players seem to have longevity; I can quote Eugene Cruft still playing at eighty-nine, Dragonetti at eighty-three, and myself at eighty-seven. Some humourists used to say that old bass players never die, they only lose their endpins.

Other candidates for longevity seem to be harpsichordists. Last year I was recommended to a harpsichord technician who lives in Seattle and who came to my house in Sooke to voice my harpsichord. He was asking about all the harpsichordists I had encountered and I mentioned some including Wanda Landowska, George Malcolm and Colin Tilney plus Mr. Gough the harpsichord maker, all of whom lived to a good age. It was almost like the *Thousand and One Nights*, for he stayed two whole days whilst I regaled him with fish and chips and plenty of Merlot; he made an excellent job of my harpsichord, it played like velvet.

In a pub over a pint of beer I talked to Victor Watson about my dilemma; I wanted to try freelancing but needed some security. He said that his son Roy, also a fine bassist, would like to join the LPO but there were no vacancies. This gave me my opportunity - I suggested that I would like to do all the LPO extra work when the basses were made up to eight from six at the important concerts; this would then give me the nucleus of an income and allow me to work under the more famous conductors as well as freelance, and that way Roy could fill my vacancy. We struck a deal and that was another turning point in my life.

Chapter 4 Notes
19. Very, very soft
20. Robbed, taking liberties with the tempo
21. Very, very loud
22. Italian for the speed at which a piece of music is performed
23. Gliding
24. Brassy

CHAPTER 5

Mixed feelings on leaving the LPO. I am offered the job of solo bass in Benjamin Britten's English Opera Group. Behind the scenes of the EOG. I meet my future wife at Glyndebourne.

After leaving the LPO I felt absolutely exhausted; I had caught the 'flu and was feeling tired and run down, so I decided to visit with my parents in Leamington Spa, not knowing what the future would bring. I had nothing in my diary except the promise of extra work with the London Philharmonic, which at least would keep the wolf from the door, so I spent some pleasant days at home, and was beginning to get all my vim and vigour back.

A few days had passed when I received a telegram from my landlady in Chelsea; it read "Please telephone Mr. John Francis in London about an important engagement." I phoned him and he told me he was in charge of the London Harpsichord Ensemble, which was to be the nucleus of a chamber orchestra directed by Benjamin Britten; it would be playing for a new opera company called the English Opera Group. Britten had written a comic opera, *Albert Herring*, which was to be premièred at the Glyndebourne Opera House. We arranged that I would go to Francis' house for an audition in two days' time, which gave me enough time to travel back to London and do a little practice.

On the appointed day and hour I arrived at John Francis' house in St. John's Wood, an affluent suburb just outside of London. He ushered me in, introduced me to his wife, Millicent Silver, who played the harpsichord, and also to George Roth, who played the 'cello in the ensemble. They didn't wish to hear any party pieces or concertos but wanted me to accompany the harpsichordist in playing continuo parts. One or two were selected from various operas and oratorios and they seemed satisfied, so Francis offered me the job immediately. The pay was excellent, and that was it, I was to be Benjamin Britten's solo bassist.

There were to be no less than thirty-two rehearsals for Albert and another Britten opera, *The Rape of Lucretia*, that were to begin soon in London and then be continued at Glyndebourne. Meanwhile I received a phone call from Morris Smith, the orchestral manager of the Royal Opera House, Covent Garden.

He offered me a ballet season at Covent Garden as principal bass, one of the ballets was to be Tchaikowsky's *Swan Lake*. He also offered me sub-principal bass with the Southern Philharmonic Orchestra who were to play Gluck's opera *Orfeo* that was alternating with Britten's *Albert Herring* and *The Rape of Lucretia* at Glyndebourne.

Besides being the "fixer" for Covent Garden, Morris also contracted many other orchestras and musical groups; he was an important man to get to know.

Doris Greenish, the lady who was to be playing principal bass in *Orfeo* was quite a character. She was of uncertain age, but I would think that then she would have been in her mid-fifties and was famous among the bass playing fraternity for wearing long khaki bloomers, or "taxi cheaters" as they were called in those days, that went down to her knees so that when she played, her bloomers were displayed, much to the mirth of the bass section.

She had been very friendly with Charles Winterbottom whom she called her "cuddy". Charlie Winterbottom was a very famous bass player in his day and was active before I went into the musical profession. He was principal bass with the London Symphony Orchestra for years and was known as the "Rock" because he could always be relied upon to come in like a ton of dynamite on any important entry. My very first Simandl bass tutor that I bought seventy years ago for what was then the exorbitant price of twelve shillings and sixpence was edited by Charles Winterbottom.

Doris' friendship with Charlie was the subject of much speculation. Although she was very prim and proper, used no make-up and had straggly bobbed hair, it was widely discussed as to whether Doris and Charlie had been a "couple", and the bass players in the Southern Philharmonic Orchestra would often hotly debate the matter in the train returning from a concert.

The rehearsals and shows I had booked all fitted in nicely and it meant I was going to be one very busy bass player, but I didn't mind that - I was young, fit and eager. At the first rehearsal for the ballet I was bowled over by one of the prima ballerinas, "D", and we struck up a friendship that I thought might develop, it did, and we became very close. After the show was over I used to wait at the stage door until she had removed her make up, showered etc. and we would repair to the local pub, "The Nag's Head", to discuss the night's performance.

I must say that when she was doing the "hearts and flowers" stuff in the pas de deux with the male dancer in *Swan Lake*, I became extremely jealous. Looking up from the pit, did I imagine his hand going too far up her leg in the lift? I would play resounding pizzicati with much vibrato during these episodes, and in my jealous way compared myself to Spartacus whose woman in the adjacent cell was being raped by a Roman soldier. Such are the passions of youth, and I would look forward to the curtain calls when she was making her curtsey for the smile she gave in my direction, like a dog that waits for a pat on the head. She chided me for being so jealous although I'm sure she quietly enjoyed it. After we had finished our drink and discussion we went our different ways home, and, to quote Pepys, "And so to bed" for there was no shacking up in those days!

When I worked later on with another ballet company I was friendly with one of the male principal dancers whom I had known years before. Often some of the orchestra or the ballet people would go to the stage door for a breath of fresh air during the interval and I bumped into my ballet friend and noticed he was cursing and swearing to himself. When I asked him what on earth was the matter, he replied, "Fat old cow, I'm nearly ruptured, she won't jump." The female has to jump in the hoist so that she doesn't become a dead weight for the male, but much depends upon the conductor for this and it might not have been entirely the woman's fault.

Some of the ballet conductors I worked for were John Lanchberry, Robert Irving, Warwick Braithwaite and Constant Lambert. Irving was a quiet, courteous man who was well thought of by the dancers. But the real favourite amongst the ballet dancers in those days was Constant Lambert who was not only a fine conductor, but also a good musician and composer; his *Rio Grande* is one of my favourite pieces of music. His only drawback was that he imbibed not wisely but too well. I have seen him stagger into the orchestra pit, attempt to climb on the podium from the first violin side then stagger over to the 'celli who were sitting the other side, then one of the 'cellists would help him back onto the podium and he would commence. He invariably chose just the right tempo and the dancers loved him for it.

One day just before he died I played for a radio show that he was conducting. He seemed to have D.T's, for he was sweating profusely and his hands were shaking; what a terrible pity.

The ballet being over and as the rehearsals for *Albert* and *Lucretia* were now to be re-located to Glyndebourne, I took my lovesick self thither, after bidding a fond adieu to "D".

The English Opera Group was a small company, everyone being very friendly towards each other. The orchestra consisted of Jack Kessler, a prominent violinist, first violin; Hans Geiger second violin; Bernard Davis, viola; George Roth, 'cello; myself on bass; John Francis, flute and bass flute; Joy Boughton, oboe and cor anglais; Stephen Waters, clarinet and bass clarinet; Eddie Wilson, bassoon; Jim Burdett, horn; Enid Simon, harp and Bert Wilson, Eddie's brother, on percussion, which consisted of practically every percussion instrument used in the modern orchestra including timpani.

The singers were Nancy Evans, soprano, who sang the role of 'Nancy'in *Albert Herring* and alternated with Kathleen Ferrier in the role of 'Lucretia' in the *Rape of Lucretia*; Peter Pears, tenor, as 'Albert' in *Albert Herring*, and the male Chorus in *Lucretia*; Jennifer Vyvyan, soprano; William Parsons, bass; Norman Lumsden, bass baritone; and Joan Cross, soprano, as 'Lady Billows' in *Albert Herring*.

I could remember Joan Cross from my childhood days when I was taken to Sadlers Wells Opera where at that time she was the Prima Donna. She and her partner, Lawrance Collingwood, the conductor seemed to be inseparable. He conducted at Sadlers Wells, spoke fluent Russian and, when I knew him in the Philharmonia, held an executive job with E.M.I. the recording company; for some reason unknown to me the Philharmonia members nicknamed him "Dry rot".

Nancy Evans was previously married to Walter Legge, and had a daughter by him. We were later joined by Ottakar Kraus, baritone, (or "Otto" as we called him) and Ben Britten often used to rib Otto about the villainous parts he sang, especially the part of Baron Scarpia in Puccini's opera, *Tosca*. Richard Lewis, tenor, joined us later and we became very friendly.

Benjamin Britten was a fine conductor and a very good pianist. In my opinion, if he had not been so successful as a composer he might have enjoyed a great career as a pianist or conductor. The only thing holding him back as a pianist was that he would not practice the piano enough, and when we gave chamber concerts together, which was often, he would come unprepared for the rehearsal. However, by the time the concert arrived his playing was truly brilliant.

His conducting was very precise with a clear beat that conveyed everything he wanted to achieve with the music. He also had a good ear and this, coupled with a quick brain and also a quick wit, meant that he could tell in an instant where any problem lay, whether it was in intonation or rhythm. Nobody else could get as good a performance from his operas as he could himself. One might say that it was only natural that he should - but all composers are not necessarily good conductors, I have noticed.

Albert Herring was a very difficult opera to stage mainly because of Britten's demands on singers and musicians alike both technically and rhythmically. There were some almost impossible passages that he wrote for the bass which I admit I encouraged, for if he heard anyone practicing their instrument or going beyond their supposed limit in the voice one would probably encounter it in one of his scores later. His string writing was only just playable, but was always technically correct, for he was a good viola player and knew the limits of string players' capabilities.

During the period when we were rehearsing *Albert Herring* and *Lucretia* we were also rehearsing *Orfeo* with Fritz Stiedry conducting and Kathleen Ferrier singing the part of Orfeo. Stiedry, an Austrian, came with a great reputation. He had a law degree and then after studying music became Kapellmeister of many of the chief opera houses in Europe and directed orchestras and operas in Russia too, but although his performances were sound and solid he never seemed to have the necessary spark that makes for a brilliant performance. He was very pleasant to work with and very knowledgeable and I learned much from him, because as a conductor he was technically perfect. At that time, 1947, he was sixty-four.

Stiedry was a very interesting man to talk to and I chatted with him sometimes during the coffee breaks. He seemed intrigued with the writing of the bass part of *Albert Herring* and remarked that one had to have a fine, sonorous instrument to play it. Fortunately I did possess a good instrument, but I noticed that when it was performed at La Scala, Milan, they used two basses and I often wondered how that came off, as the part is really a solo part, much of it played ad libitum, freely.

Orfeo was a success, and I thought Kathleen Ferrier was delightful in the part. Kathleen was a lovely lady with no "side" even though she had become famous. She had a smile for everybody and was a real Lancashire Lass. She had worked for the Post Office Telephones before taking up a professional singing career. She was keen on tennis and often used to play on the tennis courts at Glyndebourne. Although I was asked to play, I had to refuse because of my inability to play tennis, so I missed out. Bruno Walter championed her and he really made her career but unfortunately she was to die of cancer not long after I met her.

The cast of *Orfeo* was made up of international celebrities and I think this encouraged John Christie, Glyndebourne's owner, to suggest that Rudolf Bing and Audrey Mildmay, Christie's wife, should launch the first Edinburgh International Festival in 1947, using many famous artists.

Ottakar Kraus was good in the part of Tarquinius, the villain in *The Rape of Lucretia*. I can see him now, bouncing around the stage, boasting to all and sundry of what was to be Lucretia's fate; worse than death.

As all the Roman generals are discussing Lucretia around the campfire in the marshes there is the sound of bullfrogs scored for the bass. It was made by plucking and sliding up the string, and in order to better replicate the sound of the frogs and after much discussion with Britten, I made a wooden cover for my finger which gave him the sound he wanted.

The noted ornithologist Ludwig Koch used to broadcast for the BBC, giving lectures on the sounds of the bird life that abounds around Glyndebourne. He is famous for his saying, "Now, if ve listen carefully ve can hear ze zound of ze villow varbler." His son, second bassoon in the LPO anglicized his name to Val Kennedy but his nickname of the"Villow Varbler" stuck to him.

The countryside around Glyndebourne is truly beautiful and I decided to take my bicycle down there to explore all the lovely lanes. I was riding my bike merrily along a lane, the birds were chirping, cows mooing and horses neighing, it was a gorgeous day and it felt almost like Heaven when I espied a very lovely damsel in distress standing by her bicycle trying to fix the chain that had come off its sprocket. Being a Sir Galahad and anxious to help a lady, as well as being full of testosterone at that young age, I dismounted from my iron steed and asked if I could help. As the problem was obvious I took out a spanner and screwdriver from the little tool case behind my saddle and soon had the recalcitrant chain back on the sprocket.

It felt really like Heaven when I took a closer look at the damsel, who I repeat was very pretty. She blushed a thank-you and I plucked up the courage to ask if she would care to ride with me to the nearest pub where I could wash my hands and afterwards we could both have a drink. She agreed hesitantly, having no doubt been warned by her mother about talking to strange men. We both seemed to take to each other instantly and I'm afraid to say it but all thoughts of "D" were forgotten, cad that I am.

We talked about ourselves. Her name was Betty Lusted and she had been raised very demurely, having attended a School for Young Ladies in the neighbouring town, Lewes. Apparently she had been taught how to address the servants (which in those days because of the economy were non-existent) and to entertain in the correct manner but very little else, according to her. I wasn't quite so sure about the latter as she seemed to be au fait on many things. She had been conscripted into the Womens' Auxiliary Air Force during the war and was attached to a radar station spotting enemy aircraft. She told me her hut had been bombed twice and that she had narrowly escaped a bomb which hit a cinema in Dover where she was located. Much later I learned that she had earned more medals than I, but she was very reticent about it.

After the War she volunteered to help returning ex-prisoners of the Japanese, some of whom were blinded or maimed or afflicted by some of the horrible diseases that were rife in the Japanese Prisoner of War camps. She told me that it was quite common for wives to walk away from their husbands because they could not cope with the trauma.

Betty also told me much of Glyndebourne's history. In the 1930's she, her mother and grandmother would often be invited to soirées at Glyndebourne House to organ recitals, or perhaps Mrs. Christie (Audrey Mildmay) would sing.

John Christie was a very rich man. One condition attached to his inheritance was that he take a useful job until he became a certain age, so he taught at the famous Eton College. Later on Christie decided to build a small, intimate opera house for his wife. Betty remembered seeing Fritz Busch the conductor wearing a scarlet lined cloak and also George Bernard Shaw arriving in a red Rolls Royce when the now famous Glyndebourne Opera opened in 1934. I heard of Audrey Mildmay later on for she had gone to Vancouver, Canada in WW2 to stay with the Buckerfields, who were the in-laws of Victor White, the manager of the Vancouver Symphony.

Apparently everyone liked the first manager, a Mr. Nightingale, but Nightingale was dropped in favour of Rudolf Bing, *a singer manqué.*[25]

Betty and I arranged to meet again, but our meetings were infrequent because I was so busy playing the bass.

The premiere of *Albert Herring* was on the 20th June 1947. It was a packed house and was received very well. After the show all the cast and orchestra got together for a kind of *mea culpa* but despite our self-criticism I felt it went very well indeed.

Next day we were rehearsing Lucretia, and in the coffee break I happened to be sitting beside Ben Britten, reading the newspaper critique. Ben asked, "Well Robert, what do the papers say about Herring?" There was an article by Hans Keller, the noted musicologist and scholar wherein he wrote about the Freudian side of the opera - how Britten had used

Albert as a means of conveying the inner meaning of something arcane, and how there was a lot more to it than appeared on the surface. At this, Ben laughed out loud and said, "I only wanted to amuse people."

I should mention that the libretto was taken by Eric Crozier from a short story by Guy de Maupassant called *The King of the May*. The plot is simple; there being no virgin available in the village to be crowned Queen of the May, they decide to crown a King of the May (Albert) with disastrous results.

At the beginning of the season Britten asked me if I would be the Group's librarian, and I agreed. It was a lot of work but I'm glad I did it because I got to meet Ben and so many other people behind the scenes. There was John Piper, the artist, who designed the scenery and Tyrone Guthrie who directed, Ronald Duncan who wrote the libretto to *Lucretia*, E.M. Forster, Imogen Holst and Eric Crozier who wrote the libretto to *Herring* and many more.

Just as Glyndebourne was drawing to a close Britten and I were talking. He confided in me that it was unlikely that any more of his operas would be aired at Glyndebourne in the future as John Christie was keener on the older, more established operas such as those by Donizetti, Rossini and Mozart etc. Ben seemed rather dejected, for he was a very sensitive man, but he was correct, the EOG were not engaged again at least in my time in England, neither was the Southern Philharmonic; the London Philharmonic was engaged in their stead.

Ben went on to tell me that he was thinking of creating a festival in Aldeburgh, where he lived, but there were not many venues except for the Moot Hall, a kind of ancient village hall that was very small, and the Parish Church which was also too small, but he thought it might be possible to inaugurate a festival. Later on the orchestra and cast were sounded out and we unanimously agreed to play for little or no fee, and the next year, 1948, the Aldeburgh Festival was born.

My son and I were over in England some years ago and we made friends with one of the firemen who offered to show us around Glyndebourne for old times' sake. I didn't like the new and improved version, all the old intimacy had gone, added to which Glyndebourne, judging by the price of its tickets had become élitist. True, in the old days it was the fashion to appear in evening dress and have a picnic on the lovely lawns during the long intervals, but even so, many ordinary people seemed to be able to afford it then, but not now.

Glyndebourne ended and we were off to play at the Holland Festival, so I loaded my bike up along with the scenery, said goodbye to Betty, and I was off to Holland.

The Holland Festival went well; we were received warmly and were also invited to play a chamber music concert on Hilversum Radio, then we had two weeks off before making for Lucerne, Switzerland, where we were to play at the Festival, so I decided to make a tour of Holland by bicycle. I looked around Amsterdam then headed north for Friesland passing through some quaint villages and towns where some of the women were still wearing their national dress as a matter of pride. I noticed the food which was much more plentiful than in England although the Dutch still had rationing and currency control as we did in England.

Talking of currency control, I was introduced to Peter Diamand, who, I was told, was a musical entrepeneur and came from Holland. He was later to be connected with the Edinburgh Festival. He sent a telegram to the EOG, who were appearing at Aldeburgh, and we all had a good laugh because the telegram had been mis-spelt; the word "penniless" translated as follows: "Arriving Saturday penisless".

I made many friends on the Holland trip and I was sorry to leave but duty called, I had to be in Lucerne, Switzerland, for the Festival. I sold my bike in Amsterdam and caught the train to Lucerne. Immediately upon arrival I went to the theatre to check on my bass that had travelled in a soft cover; it was undamaged. I claimed my hotel room, had a good night's sleep and was ready for the rehearsal the next day.

The operas went well, also the chamber concerts. There was some time off during the days so I enjoyed myself swimming in Lake Lucerne and taking a trip on the paddle steamer, the "Wilhelm Tell", captained by a bearded blond giant of a man. The steamer also called in at Triebschen where Richard Wagner had lived, and his son, Siegfried, was born to Cosima. It was there that Wagner wrote the famous *Siegfried Idyll* to serenade Cosima outside her bedroom, and it was interesting to see the original scores and other memorabilia.

The shops in Lucerne were full of "goodies" that were unobtainable in the U.K. The women in England were short of stockings and painted their legs instead of wearing stockings so I stocked up on a few pairs of nylons to give to some of my female acquaintances. I was absolutely sure they would be welcomed, which they were!

Lennox Berkeley, the composer, was at Lucerne. His wife had a new baby, and on the boat train from Lucerne to Boulogne I shared the same compartment with them. I don't know what his connection was with

Britten, I never asked him, but a lady of my acquaintance who studied with him gave me some interesting anecdotes. One was that Mrs. Berkeley seemed to be rather jealous of him being alone with his female students. She would interrupt the lesson on some trivial pretext presumably to see whether there were any "goings on".

I was able to get very well acquainted with Berkeley on the long journey. I never liked his music in those days thinking of it as being too milky and watery, but now, after the passage of time I have begun to like it. An interesting advertisement in a magazine recently displayed Lennox and his son, who must now be in his fifties, and is also a musician, featured on a CD of their music.

Back in London there was a long list of engagements waiting for me; some recordings of *Orfeo* and *Albert Herring* plus some radio broadcasts and also concerts with the Southern Philharmonic Orchestra. The most interesting engagement was a season of ballet at Covent Garden with Colonel de Basil's Ballet Russe de Monte Carlo.

Colonel de Basil had connections with Diaghilev's Ballet Russe de Monte Carlo and tried to carry on with much of the Diaghilev tradition. It was by far the most spectacular and colourful ballet company I have ever worked with. Among the many ballets they performed, the *Firebird* and *Coq d'Or* were particularly notable. The Ballet used some of the original scenery by the great artists Diaghilev had commissioned, as well as the glittering costume designs. Unfortunately the audiences were small and the company was disbanded the following year.

One man in the company I wish I had spoken with more than I did was Serge Grigoriev, the régisseur-général;[26] that conversation would have been priceless to recount. I often used to see him at the stage door, a small, thin, aristocratic looking man, well-groomed, and impeccably dressed. He had been a ballet dancer and had helped to arrange Diaghilev's first season in Paris. He was Diaghilev's régisseur for twenty years and had the unenviable job of sacking Nijinsky, presumably because Nijinsky had abandoned Diaghilev for a woman and married her.

I saw Nijinsky, a small, bald little man in his fifties, sitting in a box at a concert in the late 1940's at the Royal Albert Hall. The older members of the orchestra who had seen Nijinsky dance years before told me that his final leap through the window in the ballet *Spectre de la Rose* was truly remarkable - he seemed to levitate.

It was my birthday at the end of August and I was pleased to receive a card from Betty. I 'phoned her and we arranged to meet. I caught the train to Glynde and then began a whirlwind romance. The nylon stockings might have helped too, but it was a genuine case of a love between us that lasted for fifty years and two hundred days.

Not long after, we became engaged and arranged the wedding for December 6th. 1947. An uncle by marriage who worked at Cartier's, the well-known jewellers, was a diamond setter. I suppose he must have been good because he was given the job of cleaning the Crown Jewels, and he made the ring according to Betty's wishes.

It was late November when I received a call from John Francis, who asked me to play in a chamber concert on the BBC Third Programme on, of all days, December the 6th, which was supposed to have been our wedding day. The BBC Third Programme was an intellectual programme devoted to the arts and culture and for this particular concert our names would be printed in the "Radio Times" which would give me great cachet, so I accepted immediately; I had no other choice.

The biggest hurdle I had to cross was to tell Betty. She told me the church had been booked, the invitations printed, the cake ordered, etc. etc. but after a while she agreed to postpone the wedding until December 13th on condition I didn't let her down and leave her waiting at the altar. As it happened I did get another date on the 13th but I turned it down because had I accepted I could never have shown my face to her again!

Then we went house hunting and eventually found one in Mill Hill, a suburb about ten miles from the centre of London, at the cost of £2,500, an exorbitant amount in those days, because housing was scarce due to the heavy bombing London had suffered along with many other cities all over the country.

Then there was the telephone that was to be my lifeline. The telephone people told me that my only chance of obtaining a 'phone was to persuade someone to share a line with me, so I went all the way down the street, everyone refused until I came to the last house; I was in luck.

A big thing in a bass player's life is lugging the instrument around. We were about a mile from the underground station and I needed transport, so I bought a new Reliant three-wheeler van that cost £120. The Reliant was classified as a trade vehicle which meant that one could get an almost unlimited supply of gasoline, which was strictly rationed for private vehicles.

Ben Britten looked down his nose when he saw it because he owned an old Rolls Royce, but the trouble with his Rolls was that it kept breaking down whilst the Reliant just kept going. It was my turn to smirk one day near Aldeburgh when I saw him and his Rolls being towed and

I sailed by, giving him a broad smile and a wave. He looked somewhat discomfited.

The wedding went smoothly; everybody wished us well and we went on a short honeymoon of only three days because I had to get back to London to work. I had promised Betty that we would have a real honeymoon in Holland the next year as we were going on a tour of Holland with the English Opera Group. If she didn't realize it then she was soon to find out what life was like, married to a musician.

For example, a year or two later, when we had two kids, we had arranged to go on a picnic to Marlow-on-Thames where we used to hire a boat. Betty had prepared some delicious food as only she knew how, and we were just leaving the front door when the phone rang; it was the BBC. Someone was sick and could I come immediately and play without a rehearsal for they were sure I already knew the programme. Of course I said I would and was expecting her to be annoyed but she just said, "Well, I suppose that's your life, you have to do it," so I went to the BBC and Betty took the kids to a local park.

Chapter 5 Notes
25. Over the hill
26. General manager

CHAPTER 6

Beginning to make a freelance connection. Some conductors.
The London scene.

In December 1947 we were installed in our new house, fixing it up and buying furniture; I had one or two offers of Messiahs from Doris Greenish but not much else.

My diary was empty except for the Aldeburgh Festival which began in May, and also other engagements with the English Opera Group, but one day in early January I received a call from Morris Smith, "Would I go to play *The Mikado* at Norwich for a week, with Dr. Staitham, the organist at Norwich Cathedral conducting." The money was good so I gladly said, "Yes."

It meant leaving my bride of a month, but she took it very well. I admired her allegiance and I never ever forgot that week. When I arrived back home I found Betty in a state of hysterics for she had not left the house all week and had stayed by the telephone waiting for a call that never came. There were no answering machines, cell phones, fax or email in those days and we were lucky even to have a telephone.

A day or two after my return I received a call from the fixer for the London Symphony Orchestra, who gave me a long list of dates that I accepted. They were not very well paid but at least they helped pay for food and the mortgage.

One of the engagements was to be a recording session at the Kingsway Hall. I asked what was on the programme and he said, "Oh, only a singer and a few arias." I arrived at the Kingsway Hall and was astonished to find that the singer was none other than Beniamino Gigli, the legendary tenor who at that time must have been in his 60's. He very wisely sang Italian love songs, avoiding the difficult opera arias. Far from being over the hill he still possessed an extraordinary voice. He brought his valet with him, a veritable "Figaro"; for in between takes he would spray Gigli's throat with some concoction and then dab his face with eau de cologne, causing much amusement among the orchestra.

The London Philharmonic also gave me a long list of dates and I accepted them all because of the outstanding conductors they were bringing in. There was Bruno Walter, a quiet, avuncular man of rather heavy build, slightly stooped, short, with thinning grey hair. He was very courteous and respectful to the orchestra who in turn gave him of their very best, not because he demanded it but because he earned it.

He had a wry sense of humour. Once he asked the orchestra what time it was and somebody said one o'clock (rehearsals were usually from 10.00 a.m. until 1.00 p.m.). He said, "I'm sure it is not one o'clock alread," and bent over to look at the concertmaster's watch. It was ten minutes before one o'clock and Walter wagged his finger reprovingly, smiled and said, "Musicians' watches, always fast."

We played Mozart with him and it was wonderful. There were no superfluous gestures; nothing exciting or frenetic about him but the end result was stunning - the music just poured out. In one rather sad movement of Mahler's Fourth Symphony, he explained to us that it was Mahler's expression of pain on seeing railcars full of cattle being taken to the slaughter, and my mind went back to my father's respect for the doomed animals. His visit was a great success and we played to packed houses.

Others that came were Paul Paray, who gave a good performance of Berlioz's *Symphonie Fantastique* and Charles Munch who conducted some French music. Both were received very well.

Another conductor was Nikolai Malko. I asked Victor Watson what he thought of Malko and he said, "Yes and no," which just about summed him up. He was tolerably good with some ballet music and the Russian repertoire but never seemed to enthuse the orchestra. At one rehearsal he exclaimed to the principal cellist, "Why you no look at me?" The angry answer was, "I am looking at you" The argument went on and on until Malko shouted, "Everyvere I go, Paris, New York, Amsterdam, uzzer conductors say to me London Philharmonic, "R" no good". Malko wrote a book on conducting, as did Hans Swarowsky, who was a great teacher, having taught Claudio Abbado amongst others, but neither of them, I think, had that sparkle that makes for a great conductor although of course they were more than adequate in everything they did.

Sergey Koussevitsky was a fine conductor and musician besides being a virtuoso bass player. The orchestra agreed amongst themselves that his tempi were just right. All the upper strings roared with laughter when he mentioned that he had been a bass soloist, as the very idea of a bass solo to them was like listening to a cow in labour. Victor Watson knew him well, having played the Bottesini *Double Bass Duets* with him, and had great admiration both for Koussevitsky's bass playing as well as his conducting. I learned much about the Bottesini Duets from Victor.

When I tried to obtain some ideas from Koussevitsky on bass playing all he would tell me was, "You must grip ze bass hard, it is left hand zat makes tone." I always remembered that piece of advice and it served me well although at the time I regarded it as being trivial. He was on a farewell tour and at the concert he gave us all a red carnation to wear in his remembrance.

He must have been in his late seventies but he still had much energy and gave a wonderful concert. In the opening of the last movement of Beethoven's First Symphony there is a slow beginning leading to an allegro, which unfortunately Koussevitsky botched. Some of the violins came in early, some late, but he had the presence of mind to stop and begin the allegro again. Musicians are fond of saying that conductors' batons make no sound, but there are occasions when a clear beat must be given and this was one of them. Despite this little error, Koussevitsky, in my opinion well deserves to be ranked among the greats.

It is an odd coincidence that Sir Adrian Boult was conducting the same piece at the same venue, the Royal Albert Hall, soon afterwards, and he made exactly the same error.

Not long afterwards Georg Solti made an appearance. He had boundless energy and was puffing and snorting on the platform, but the general effect did not back up all these misdirected efforts. One could not say his performances were refined or intellectual but he made a name for himself and was knighted Sir George Solti. Some years later when I was on a tour with the LSO and Solti was conducting, one member of the orchestra referred to him as,"Just a Hungarian peasant" which seemed to sum him up exactly.

Another visiting conductor was George Szell from the Cleveland Orchestra who had a reputation for being a martinet. Musicians around the world have a habit of talking with each other, so anything that might have happened in Cleveland was soon heard of in London.

There is one story that illustrates Szell's character very well: A woman violinist, "A", a fine player who had been playing in New York, went to Cleveland for an audition before Szell. After she had played, and very well too, she thought, Szell patted her on the shoulder and said patronizingly, "Go home and have babies my dear." I shudder to think what the reaction would have been by today's woman. I met "A" later on in Vancouver, British Columbia and she assured me the story was true. Apart from his personality Szell was a great conductor, having that electrifying presence and a very clear beat making him one of the world's finest.

A little later on Erich Kleiber came to conduct a series of concerts with us. I remember his version of Beethoven's Eroica symphony well and he gave some great performances of it. The musicians among my readers will remember the slow movement, *Marche Funèbre*, where the triplet grace notes in the 'celli and basses are usually played before the beat. Kleiber insisted they be on the beat. I am now an aficionado of this rendering but it is rarely played like that, which is a pity I think, because it seems to enhance the dramatic effect. Both orchestra and audiences alike received Kleiber's performances very well. Everybody thought that here was a great conductor.

We used to play these programmes on tour and were so satiated with the constant repetition of the pieces that we sometimes closed the book and played from memory just for the fun of it. Kleiber once glanced at me, saying, "Don't play from memory, (which I suppose is clearly a conductor's prerogative) play from the music."

Looking back, the years 1945 until 1965 must have been the Halcyon years for classical music in London. Apart from the five major symphony orchestras, I played with many others including the London Mozart Players conducted by Harry Blech; the Haydn Orchestra conducted by my friend Harry Newstone. A small orchestra was formed and conducted by Foster Clark who was a member of the family that owned Foster Clark's Custard Company, so he quickly got the nickname of the "Custard King". He wasn't a great conductor, adequate I should say, but he provided a fair amount of work for musicians and must be praised for that.

Then there was the Riddick Orchestra conducted by Kathleen Riddick. She was easily the best of the women conductors for whom I have played, with perhaps the exception of Nadia Boulanger. In those unenlightened days, probably on account of her sex, Kathleen was not given much work, so she formed her own orchestra. An apt pupil of Bruno Walter, she had adopted many of his mannerims. She was cool, calm and collected, nothing ever fazed her, even the most difficult programmes, and she always did her best to reproduce the composer's intentions. Difficult pieces such as Bartok's *Music for Strings, Percussion and Celesta*, his *Divertimento for Strings* and Sir Arthur Bliss's *Music for Strings* she did wonderfully well. She was tallish and stout, her face was always very red and I sensed that she was not in the best of health, but she never spared herself.

The Boyd Neel Orchestra was another small orchestra, formed by Boyd Neel, a medical doctor who had given up medicine to conduct. He later moved to Toronto, and I was to meet him again when he conducted the CBC Chamber Orchestra in Vancouver, British Columbia, Canada. Trevor Harvey conducted The Little Orchestra; the Goldsborough Orchestra was formed and conducted by Arnold Goldsborough and was later to become the English Chamber Orchestra; the Academy of St. Martin in the Fields; the Philomusica Orchestra, the mainstay of which was the harpsichordist and conductor George Malcolm. Then there was the Jacques Orchestra conducted by the genial Dr. "Jumbo" Jacques who used to give the *St. Matthew Passion* twice a year, amongst other things. The Steinitz Orchestra conducted by Dr. Paul Steinitz, who used to perform the St. Matthew Passion every Easter in German at one of the City churches. I was often asked to play principal or sub-principal bass with these and derived much pleasure from doing so. Many of these orchestras were given a start by the BBC Third Programme.

Richard Tauber, the Austrian born tenor who was well known for singing operetta, was also a conductor. "You are my heart's delight" was his signature tune. He concentrated mainly on the German and Austrian classics of which he gave excellent interpretations and had a fine stick technique, maybe a little too sweeping, I thought, but very clear nevertheless. He conducted the London Philharmonic Orchestra and other orchestras and was received very well by the audience and the orchestras. At the end of every concert there were constant calls for him to sing, but he never did.

Vic Oliver, an Austrian born comedian/entertainer/violinist who had married and later divorced one of Sir Winston Churchill's daughters, formed a symphony orchestra that he conducted exclusively himself. He was a moderately good conductor without much fire or panache but he managed to obtain some good results. He always arrived at the concert hall in a chauffeur-driven car accompanied by a youngish woman whom he called his "ward".

I once played a matinée at Birmingham for him; a circus was playing that night. Behind stage there was a performing seal in a tank full of water and just as the clarinet was playing his cadenza in Rimsky-Korsakov's *Capriccio Espagnole* there came an awful snorting from the seal. Somebody found its keeper and we heard no more from the seal who had no doubt been sufficiently bribed by a few herring.

The Southern Philharmonic Orchestra was conducted by Herbert Menges a.k.a "Blank Manges" and gave a concert in the "Dome" Brighton,

Sussex every Sunday afternoon in the winter season. Herbert was a scion of the well-known Menges musical family and although he was not a brilliant conductor he performed everything well and thoroughly. I played principal or sub-principal bass.

Menges conducted the lion's share of the Southern Philharmonic concerts, but two notable conductors came; one was George Szell the other Dohnanyi, who conducted his *Variations on a Nursery Theme*, and also a choral work.

There was also a lot of stage band work at Covent Garden that Morris Smith fixed, and which worked out very nicely for me. The stage band in an opera such as *Der Rosenkavalier* only plays for a short time but is paid a full fee, which was far better than sitting in the orchestra playing the whole opera.

Apart from all this was the BBC who often phoned me to play with the BBC Symphony Orchestra; the BBC Theatre Orchestra, later the BBC Concert Orchestra, whose conductors were Walter Goehr and Vilem Tausky; the BBC Northern Orchestra, conductor George Hurst, now the BBC Philharmonic; the BBC Midland Light Orchestra, conductor Gilbert Vinter; and the BBC Scottish Orchestra, conductor Ian Whyte.

It was always fun visiting the BBC regional orchestras. I went with the BBC Northern Orchestra on a memorable tour of the English Lake District. It is not generally realized that the food in the North of England differs very much from the South, as does their accent. On the way back to Manchester the whole orchestra descended on a famous delicatessen shop where they had ordered in advance all those items of food that make the North famous. They purchased huge orders of chitlings (pigs entrails cooked and spiced), tripe, and blood puddings. I never bought any but the rest of the orchestra were in their seventh heaven. Another thing I noticed was the huge quantity of beer they consumed after each concert (especially the bass players), plus faggots and peas. Faggots are a type of sausage and the peas were called "mushy peas", which were overcooked spiced peas. In Lancashire they also seem to consume enormous quantities of scowse, a kind of stew usually made with the neck end of lamb. I cannot say I liked all these different foods but the BBC Northern Orchestra certainly did.

One day the BBC phoned to ask me if I would fly over to Dublin to play principal bass with the Irish Radio Orchestra. It appeared that the principal bass, a German, had gone over to Germany to try to bring back his fiancée from behind the Berlin Wall. He crossed the border in his car and then he strapped the girl underneath the car and safely made his exit across the Berlin Wall with her. He arrived back in Dublin on time so

I never got to go there. Due to all the media publicity the East German Authorities searched underneath every vehicle ever afterwards.

There were also the amateur societies that often needed a professional bassist. Doris Greenish always contracted these, albeit at minimum rate of pay. One such date which sticks out in my memory was when Doris asked me to play for an amateur society in Surrey that was putting on Handel's *Messiah* conducted by Leslie Woodgate, the BBC Chorus director. I was to be the only bassist. At the rehearsal, which was three hours long, we went right through the whole of it and then after a short break had to play the performance. The *Messiah* is a back breaker for the bass and I was absolutely exhausted at the end of the performance. To add insult to injury, I was paid the bare minimum fee, and ever since, I have taken an extreme aversion to playing it, especially when there is only one bass.

The orchestral players neither liked the conducting nor the manners on or off the podium of Walter Goehr. He had an acolyte training under him who used to look after his every need. He was on medication; one pill to pep him up when he was conducting, another to slow him down when he was not. The legend goes that one day his assistant gave him the wrong pill, which slowed him down with disastrous effect. I was asked to play at a recording of Monteverdi's *Orfeo* for the BBC Third programme and Goehr conducted a good performance. The lutenist, Diana Poulton, a no -nonsense schoolmistress type dressed in tweeds, took part, and the type of lute she was playing was so large and unusual that we nicknamed it the "dinghy". In all the arty-crafty programmes that were put on by the BBC Third Programme, Diana Poulton was always the lutenist whenever one was required. At one programme with the English Chamber Orchestra an unknown guitarist was invited to play; he told me his name was Julian Bream. I often saw him at broadcasts and was to meet him later when he played with the Vancouver Symphony in Canada.

Other musicians who put in regular appearances on the BBC Third programme were Thurston (Bob) Dart on harpsichord and his friend Desmond Dupré on viola da gamba. Dupré wrote some weighty tomes on music, but his musical knowledge, though, exceeded his technical ability.

Mention must be made too of Alfred Deller, the countertenor, whom I often encountered when playing with small groups. In those days counter-tenors were somewhat of a rarity, and I can remember Doris Greenish hinting darkly that there was something 'not quite right' with them. I don't think that was the case with Alfred Deller for he was married with kids. His sound was something like a falsetto, almost a yodel, but he was instrumental in popularizing the countertenor, and nowadays interest in them has grown tremendously. Although maybe there were and are countertenors with a better sound than Alfred Deller I have yet to hear of one that can better him for his exquisite musicianship, artistry and grace.

To say I was busy would be putting it mildly, yet I never considered the money first; that was secondary to the music. I very often played a symphony concert at minimum rates if there was an important conductor or soloist playing. Yes, if I had gone in for it I could have been a "session boy", i.e. one who plays at all the film and commercial recordings and made a lot more money, but looking back, I am pleased I did what I did, otherwise I would not have been able to recount so many stories in this book.

The light music side of the musical business was very tightly controlled. There were such worthies as Charlie Katz, Sidney Sax and Lionel Monte, violinists, who ran most of the work. Personally I found it very boring. True, the money was good but I could never have made a career out of playing "jingles" or film work, it tried my patience, but on the other hand they were very well paid and I liked the money. The players mainly consisted of "fixers", who engaged their fellow fixers for every engagement, the idea being "You scratch my back, I'll scratch yours." A drawback to this was that if ever a "fixer" lost his "fixing" job none of the other "fixers" would engage him.

I should mention that as an orchestral player it seemed as though one had to be impervious to the music, which is probably why so many of the musicians appeared to be so blasé, but most musicians are concerned with the technicalities of trying to make as flawless a performance as possible with no "dominos" or false entries. Of course, they play their best or almost their best at the concert, or "take" in the case of a recording, but it seemed as if one always had to hold something in reserve, only pulling it out on very special occasions, otherwise burn-out occurred.

After I gave an audition before the London Symphony Orchestra at which the Chairman of the Board of Directors, Gordon Walker the flutist, was present, he often 'phoned me for film sessions, but as I had already committed myself weeks in advance for other things (I had to play it safe with a wife, two kids and a mortgage) he gave up 'phoning me.

The conductor who got the lion's share of the film work was Muir Mathieson who is credited with inventing a device that synchronized the music with the action in the film. Apart from that, he was rarely asked to conduct any serious concerts. He had one virtue that he spoke his mind, and one vice, that nothing came out of it.

Another film conductor was Louis Levy, a true Cockney, who used to have a radio programme entitled *Louis Levy and his Symphony*. He made many *faux pas* in pronouncing musical terms. Once he said to all and sundry, "Wot yer got wrote down there boys?" The answer was "morendo", that in Italian, means dying away, upon which he said, "There you are, there ain't enough endo, there should be more endo!" Another word he was fond of was cantabile[27], (pronounced can-tar-bil-ay), however, he would call out, "Nice and cantabyle, boys."

Georges Auric was a pleasure to meet in the film world. He was a member of *Les Six* the famous group of French composers, and he wrote and conducted some delightful film music.

Another light music job that sometimes came my way was the Palm Court Orchestra led by Tom Jenkins, the violinist. Tom was not only a fine violinist but was generally credited amongst the profession as having the largest penis in the business. At every mention of his name the subject was raised. I remember my father listening avidly to the Palm Court Orchestra on the radio when, in my young days it was led by Albert Sandler and in my wildest dreams I never thought that I would get to play with them.

Jenkins was married to the soprano Dorothy Bond, a pretty blonde girl with a "china doll" type of beauty. She was very good in Debussy. I played when she sang the solo part in Debussy's *La Demoiselle Élue*[28] with the BBC Symphony Orchestra and she made an entrancing sound. I thought at the time that she would have made a good Mélisande in Debussy's opera, *Pélleas et Mélisande*. She had been previously married to Michael Dobson who was first oboe in the LPO.

Dobson had a rather haughty manner and earned himself the sobriquet of "Little Lord Fauntleroy". He was short, weedy looking with a pale face and a rather bulging forehead. Although he was a fine player technically, his tone, like himself was thin. Mind you, in pieces like Rossini's La Scala di Seta overture which is a real test piece for the oboe, he could play flawlessly without the "squirts" that sometimes even the finest oboists make, but in a big oboe solo as, for example, in the Tchaikowsky symphonies, or the Brahms' *Variations on a Theme of Haydn* which really need a robust tone, he could never deliver. Friend Brooks who was a director at the time hinted darkly that his puny appearance was all due to masturbation, and when an oboe solo came up in rehearsal that needed to be played strongly, which Dobson never did, the"Barmpot" would nudge Victor Watson, and with a large, sweeping motion of his bow would declare for all and sundry to hear, "There you are Vic, he's been at it again."

Eventually Dobson left the orchestra and was succeeded by Sidney "Jock" Sutcliffe, a very fine player who was also an excellent 'cellist and had given a 'cello recital at the Wigmore Hall. Walter Legge soon snapped him up for the Philharmonia and he can be heard in most of the recordings of their great days.

Acker Bilk, the clarinettist whose one claim to fame was the piece *Stranger on the Shore*, asked me to do a series of concerts with him. They were crowd pleasers and played to full houses, and, of course there were always loud cries of 'Encore' after which he would come out and perform *Stranger on the Shore* and the audience went away happy. Acker Bilk never managed to find another hit to match it so after a while he dropped into oblivion.

A very talented pianist, Arthur Sandford, was very busy in the light music world. He was famous for having written the music for ITMA, a wartime comedy show featuring Tommy Handley the comedian. Unfortunately Arthur was caught having sex with a sailor in a public washroom. It made the front page of the *London Evening News* and he absented himself by going to Australia for a while. When he came back he often played keyboard for the BBC Symphony, but Malcom Sargent treated him with abhorrence. Once when I was deputizing at a show at the Savoy Theatre, Arthur was playing. After the show he asked me to have a drink with him and I accepted. My wife was concerned when I phoned home to tell her I would be late because I was having a drink with Arthur Sandford. Nowadays nothing would be inferred, but that was fifty years ago.

Mantovani conducted his own orchestra, which I sometimes played with, and his records, now on CD are still sold to this day. His music was characterized by the "suspension" i.e. one note held over until it was resolved in harmony, and it became very boring when repeated *ad nauseam*. His trademark, Charmaine, was one of the pieces he flogged to death; however, his large following of devoted fans lapped it up and at a concert would applaud until he finally played it.

If it were a television show he would say after the rehearsal, "Come back a half an hour before the show, boys, and don't forget, black trowsis." Some of the musicians would wear a tuxedo, bow, and white shirt, but were sometimes too lazy to change their trousers because, they thought, nobody would notice them behind the solid music desks. If they hadn't changed pants sometimes a devilish cameraman would deliberately take a sly shot of them.

I played many weekly T.V. shows that Eric Robinson conducted. We were booked "from 9 a.m. till unconscious" which often meant until 11 p.m. and by that time the orchestra <u>was</u> practically unconscious. The very hot lights in those days had a most enervating effect but a little later there was a German invention of water cooled lights, which much improved playing conditions.

Eric's brother, Stanford Robinson, had aspirations to become the conductor of the BBC Symphony Orchestra, although he only just managed to get through the programmes by sheer luck and bluster. Mercifully, the Orchestra themselves intervened and he didn't get the job.

One of the jobs I was offered by Morris Smith was the Old Vic Company's seasons at the New Theatre, London. The beauty of it was that one could send a deputy if anything better came in, which it often did. Herbert Menges was the musical director, and he composed some delightful incidental music to the plays.

Those seasons, 1948 onwards at the New Theatre were wonderful, and are still talked of today. Some of the actors included Alec Guinness, George Relph, Harry Andrews, Laurence Olivier, Peter Copley, Bernard Miles and Mark Dignam. The plays included George Bernard Shaw's *Saint Joan*, Shakespeare's *Coriolanus*, *The Taming of the Shrew*, *Richard the Second* and *Richard the Third*. There was not much music to play in the pit, only the occasional "flourish" when, say, the King appeared and the kettledrums and trumpets played, or perhaps a little tune from the strings, so most of the orchestra would visit the local pub and arrive back in time to play the next entry. I, however, was fascinated by it all, for to have the opportunity to see and hear all those famous actors on the stage was such a great experience that I sat in the pit for the entire performance entranced, and at the end of a play's run I could repeat most of it from memory.

Some of the musicians were hard-boiled old pros, and would bring newspapers into the pit to while away the time between the shorter breaks. The rustling of the newspapers prompted Laurence Olivier to send a note to the orchestra to please <u>not</u> rustle newspapers whilst he was making his big opening speech in *King Richard the Third*, "Now is the winter of our discontent.... " Years later I was to meet Olivier when I was recording some music with a small group for him. He had a great "presence", dressed immaculately and was charming to everybody.

Alec Guinness made a fine Richard the Second and brought real pathos to his acting that tugged at everyone's heartstrings.

Arthur Cockerill was instrumental in having me booked as an extra with the BBC Midland Light Orchestra. It was a fairly frequent well-paid gig and it enabled me to call in home at Leamington to see my mother, my father having passed away in 1948. His passing affected me very much for he was only fifty-seven and I wished I had been closer to him when he was alive.

Gilbert Vinter was the conductor of the BBC Midland Light Orchestra. He was well known as a light music conductor and composer and good at what he did, with a clear beat, even if somewhat exaggerated. The orchestra, however, was fed up with him and wanted a change, partly because his repertoire was very limited, and some years later he left. We played *Swan Lake, Coppelia* and Meyerbeer's *The Skaters*, plus Aaron Copland's *Billy the Kid* and Eric Coates' suite *The Three Bears* until we were sick of it. Vinter's programmes were a steady diet of old chestnuts, but, after all it <u>was</u> a light orchestra.

I remember being stopped by a policeman on my way home late at night from Birmingham, driving the "Reliant". He looked at the bass rather suspiciously and asked me what I had been doing. I told him that I had been playing for the BBC and then he said if I were doing that I should be driving a better vehicle. I bit my lip as I was going to tell him it was none of his damned business, but in retrospect I'm glad I didn't.

Dr. Staitham, the organist at Norwich Cathedral often used to engage me for a concert around Christmas time; Bach's *Christmas Oratorio* was a favourite. Norwich is in Norfolk, the centre of the turkey rearing business, and was the target of turkey thieves at that time of year, so I could always count on being stopped and searched at a police check on the lookout for stolen turkeys.

I'm sure the black van looked sinister, even Ben Britten didn't like the colour. I later changed it to grey and believe it or not I was stopped much less often.

I considered it a great honour to play at a concert with the LPO conducted by Ralph Vaughan Williams on his seventy-fifth birthday in 1947, in a programme devoted entirely to his own works. He was wearing a large, very noticeable hearing aid and looked rather frail, but achieved some marvellous results. At rehearsal he was dressed in rather crumpled tweeds and for all the world looked like a farmer. I thought too, that sometimes his music sounded a little rustic, especially his heavy, rum-ti-tum-tum scherzi which reminded me somewhat of peasants doing a clod-hopping, bum-slapping country dance. I am not making these comments in a pejorative sense but these were the feelings his music evoked in me. Personally I like his music, my favourites being the *London Symphony* and the *Fantasia on a Theme of Thomas Tallis* despite Beecham's acidic remarks about it. I used to notice Ursula V.W., his wife, who was his secretary at one time, faithfully watching over him.

A little later I was asked to play principal bass in an orchestra at Cambridge University where they were putting on Vaughan William's opera, *The Pilgrim's Progress* conducted by the composer himself. V.W. made a very good job of it and the audience received it very well. I was surprised at his vim and vigour, considering his age.

There was a bright young spark named Hugh McLean who was working very hard on and off stage to help make the performance a success. He was later to become organist at Christ Church Cathedral in Vancouver, British Columbia and was on the faculty at the University of British Columbia where I also taught.

Hugh and I recorded Hindemith's *Sonata for Double bass and Piano* for the Canadian Broadcasting Corporation in Vancouver, B.C. He later became Dean of Music, Western University at London, Ontario.

Chapter 6 Notes
27.It. Song-like
28.*The Blessed Damozel*, words by Dante Gabriel Rossetti

CHAPTER 7

The big upheaval in the London Symphony Orchestra. Joseph Krips leaves under a cloud. Ernest Fleischman, a good orchestral manager, takes over.

In contrast to the LPO, the LSO seemed to me to be doing more commercial type concerts. They were given all the Royal Choral Society's work, mainly with Malcolm Sargent as conductor. Once a year around Eastertide they put on Handel's *Messiah* replete with all the appendices, horror of horror to the bass players. It was so long and drawn out that the orchestra was paid a double fee.

My first concert with the LSO was not very memorable for me insofar as the principal bass, George Yates who must have been afraid of his job, kept muttering "Uneasy lies the head that wears the crown," and, "All these young chaps, where's their experience?" He never shook hands to welcome me as is usual when a new face appears in an orchestra, in fact he was quite hostile, as were most of the other members of the bass section which contained such worthies as Samuel Sterling, Arthur Griffiths a very fine young bassist who had no pretensions to becoming principal bass owing to his bad health and Bill Bailey, who was the sub-principal bass, not a very good player, but tolerated because he was no threat to George Yates.

Whenever there was a reception after a concert Bill would bring a plastic bag to take home some of the "goodies", and because of his parsimony he was nicknamed "Money bags Bailey" and reputed to have a long stocking.

At this point, having mentioned Bill Bailey's stinginess, I should also mention another character who was even more tight-fisted; David McCallum, who came to fame as being the first concertmaster of the LPO when it was formed in 1932. I knew him well as a free-lance player and he was always in demand. There is one tale concerning Beecham, who asked David for a cigarette. David drew from his pocket a gold cigarette case, inside were many cigarette butts plus some whole cigarettes, and he proffered it to Beecham with the words, "Go on, Sir Thomas, take a whole one!" On another occasion after a concert he was playing at a large country house, a line was formed with the Duchess shaking hands with the players, thanking them each in turn. When David took her Ladyship's hand, a bottle of champagne he had hidden under his tailcoat fell and smashed on the marble floor. Quick as a flash the Duchess beckoned the butler and said imperiously, "James, another bottle of champagne for Mr. McCallum!"

The LSO's popular concerts included some interesting conductors. There was Efrem Kurz, who conducted ballet music well and precisely. He had a very clear beat but his performances were never very inspiring. His pretty, young wife, Elaine Shaffer, was a superb flutist with whom I recorded Mozart flute concerti.

Other conductors I encountered around this era were Carl Schuricht and Antal Dorati. I only played once or twice for Schuricht but I was very impressed with him, as I was with Dorati, for both were excellent, always came well prepared and obtained good results. Perhaps Dorati came across as being more flamboyant than Schuricht, who conducted the music without trying to inflict his own personality on it, not making any extravagant gestures and letting the music flow, but Dorati was different, a tall, well-built man, he brought much vim and vigour to his conducting but with good results despite his flamboyancy.

I played with the LPO at an Eisteddfod in Mountain Ash, Wales, in 1946. Eisteddfods are a big event in Welsh culture and I can remember seeing the procession of the Bards in their robes, one of whom is crowned, making it altogether a significant event that drew many fervent Welsh Nationalists

The LPO were engaged to play the *Messiah*, but there were so many delays, what with the crowning of the Bard and long speeches in Welsh that everything was running late. James Cooper, the concertmaster, told the organizers we couldn't possibly play the whole of the *Messiah* in the remaining time allotted, so cuts would have to be made. He suggested cutting out the *Amen Chorus* as well as *Land of my Fathers* which is the Welsh national hymn, but there was a near riot at this suggestion so we played them both, but as far as I know the LPO were never invited to play at another Eisteddfod.

Speaking of oratorios, my mind goes back to Sargent, I can see him now, (and I know he enjoyed it) leading women divas on stage, holding their hand high. Usually these singers would be clad in a long dress with a train and wearing sparkling earrings plus a headdress or tiara with an ostrich plume and would make their entrée like a ship in full sail, or, as one wag put it, "carrying all before her". They don't dress like that nowadays but there was something about those divas of yore that makes some of the present day soloists look sloppy.

One such singer was the contralto, Constance Shacklock, a fine looking woman who came on stage often at the last night of the Proms to sing *Rule Britannia* asserting vehemently with a confident nod that "Britons never, never, never shall be slaves!" which brought vociferous applause. I only played the last night of the Proms once, and strangely enough, it was that very performance that was issued by the BBC as a CD with one of their Music Magazines years later.

There was a lot of good-natured humour among the fans at the Proms. On the last night they would often try to slow down the tempo by clapping in the traditional *Sailor's Hornpipe* and also tried other such japes, but they were as quiet as mice when all the rest of the programme was played. Unfortunately there are always some rotten apples in a barrel and sometimes the pranksters went too far by lighting fireworks, fighting, and worst of all one gentleman resorted to throwing toilet tissue rolls at the orchestra. No doubt he thought that it was funny, but the orchestra certainly did not especially when a 'cellist's instrument was cracked. Paul Beard, an excellent concertmaster, could soon get the rowdies under control firmly but humorously, and often what could have been an ugly scene was averted with a smile.

Another conductor I must mention is Royalton Kisch who put on pop concerts with the LSO at the Albert Hall and always drew such a full house that the LSO players nicknamed him "Kisch for Cash". Invariably there would be, say, a Rossini overture followed by a piano concerto, often the Grieg or one of the Liszt piano concerti played by Eileen Joyce, an Australian. In the intermission she would change her dress and come back onto the platform to play another concerto. This went down very well with the audience, particularly some of the females, who just came to see what dress she would wear. Kisch would drool over a Tchaikowsky symphony and then came the grand finale, what else but the *1812 overture* with the band of the Coldstream Guards. This supposedly sure fire winner went on and on, but one day Kisch had taken his pitcher to the well once too often, and, to quote Sol Hurok, "The audience stayed away in droves." That was the end of Royalton Kisch and I never saw him again.

Anthony Collins was another visiting conductor with the LSO in 1953. He had been principal viola for years with the London Symphony Orchestra and had emigrated to the United States in 1939 where he conducted at the Hollywood Bowl and other places and also did some occasional film work.

Some biographers have said that he was in the Army in WW1 but the old sweats in the LSO who remembered him swore that he had been in the Submarine Service and used to call out "Up periscope!" when he came onto the platform. Although he was a fine conductor he doesn't seem to have gone down in history as being a very notable one, but some of his performances, especially of Sibelius were wonderful.

Then there was Charles Hambourg, a.k.a. the "Stepney Slasher" on account of his Cockney origins, who one day appeared at rehearsal dressed as a major in Army uniform and told us he was in "Intelligence", which the orchestra greeted with some scepticism. Rough diamond, Cockney or not, Charlie obtained some good performances. On the other hand, Faith, his wife, a violist and a wealthy woman was just as genteel as Charlie was Cockney, she was very well spoken and quite the lady. Charlie's concerts went on and on, just like the ones with Kisch, but he too met his Waterloo the day petrol (gas) rationing ended, when again the audience stayed away in droves, and like Kisch I never heard of Charlie again.

One 'cellist who came to the LSO and left a lasting impression upon me was Pablo Casals, a quiet, unassuming man, he played a Boccherini concerto. He just sat there and the music welled out. There were several other good 'cello soloists appearing in London around that time but it was the general consensus among the musicians that compared with Casals the others couldn't put the rosin on.

Another famous personality I met at that time, 1953, was Wynn Reeves. He was partly retired and getting on in years, but had a big reputation as a great concertmaster and a conductor. One day he asked if I would play at a Messiah he was conducting at St. Paul's Cathedral. I arrived one day in December where we rehearsed in the freezing cold. At the performance we were provided with white surplices to wear which made some of the old, boozy, red-faced musicians look angelic. I couldn't suppress a smile.

Harry Dugard, a 'cellist in the LSO was the treasurer when I first played with them. At rehearsal intermission the orchestra lined up at a little desk he had set up and he paid them in cash. He never had much of a reputation as a 'cellist, indeed, when Basil Cameron was conducting a Prom rehearsal he looked over at Harry's chair which was vacant and said, "Where is Harry Dugard, he needs the rehearsal more than anybody."

The LSO at that time consisted of many older players who had been very good in their day, but the time was becoming ripe to make a change. My wife came to a concert and declared, "What a collection of white haired old men!" When Harry Dugard was elected Chairman of the Board after Gordon Walker had stepped down, he made the most sweeping changes that I have ever seen take place in an orchestra, and it came about in the following manner.

The principals of the LSO made a lot of money on the side by playing for Gordon Walker's film sessions and in one particular week there was a bad clash. The LSO had a prestigious concert booked, but there was also a week of recording at Denham Film Studios. The principals to a man notified the LSO they would not play the concert, doing so would mean they would lose of a great amount of money.

There was much pressure put on them to be loyal to the LSO but they were all adamant, they wouldn't play the concert, believing there was safety in numbers and that their jobs were secure, even though Harry Dugard had warned them that their jobs would be in jeopardy if they didn't play the concert. They were all fired. There was only one who reneged on his decision, and that was George Yates, who was re-instated, but only for a short time, for Harry Dugard had a long and unforgiving memory.

It is ironic that the LSO was formed in 1904 from players in the old Queen's Hall Orchestra because Sir Henry Wood, the founder and conductor of the Promenade Concerts insisted that the players who came to the rehearsals had to play the concert. This was not an unreasonable request, but the old system of sending a deputy to the rehearsal and playing only the concert was well entrenched in those days.

At the concert many new young faces were seen in the principal chairs; it was a success, and received a good Press. Then came a massive upheaval; even some fine young players were let go, the reason given was that their "persona was not suited to the new LSO". This upheaval lasted for months, after which the LSO became definitely a better orchestra, but this was only achieved after a lot of unhappiness that divided it and also led to Dugard becoming very arrogant, referring to it as "my orchestra" which made him many enemies.

I have dwelt on some of the inner strife of the LSO in detail because the same happened with the Philharmonia Orchestra which in turn became the New Philharmonia and then again the Philharmonia Orchestra, and I can foresee, with all the bankruptcies and disbanding of orchestras in Canada and the United States, that a similar situation might well arise there.

There was a search for a resident conductor. They had been having such conductors as Carl Schuricht, Lorin Maazel (who was also a fine violinist), and Josef Krips; Krips was appointed. He was a fat man, with a dewlap that wobbled as he conducted, and he wore a pair of round eyeglasses that gave him a rather owlish look. He was a first class conductor - Richard Strauss, Mozart, Beethoven and Mahler were his forte, but he was neurotic and he had a nervous habit of spearing his left hand with the end of his baton, sometimes drawing blood, but he had a certain panache together with a good baton technique, which he used to obtain some brilliant performances.

The BBC put on a programme to celebrate the LSO's 50th anniversary in 1954, and John Cruft (son of Eugene) who was the general manager at the time was in the BBC studio together with some BBC dignitaries and members of the LSO board. Krips listened with growing anger and consternation. Because the programme was giving a retrospective of the orchestra's history since it was founded, many conductors were mentioned along with landmark concerts, and only in the last five minutes of the broadcast was any mention made of Krips. He became so incensed that he struck John Cruft in the face.

I heard the whole story blow by blow from Eugene who, fiercely tugging his moustache, told me that John had been an Army officer and therefore was a gentleman, and had been taught never to strike back. That was the end of Krips with the LSO.

On the other hand, his brother Henry was a far more placid individual, a good conductor, but not in the same class as Josef. Henry specialized in Viennese popular music, but I never encountered him conducting any of the classics.

Some time later the LSO engaged Ernest Fleischman, a forthright individual and a very fine manager under whose aegis the orchestra prospered. He later joined the Los Angeles Orchestra as manager. On one occasion I was asked to play in Perugia, Italy, where the Italian organizers put on a very good dinner for us. Barry Tuckwell the horn player, who was then chairman of the LSO, was there together with Fleischman, and mentioned timidly to Fleischman that maybe they should ask for the cheque for the orchestra fee, whereupon Fleischman rose immediately from the dinner table and went up to the organizer, demanded the cheque and came back, waving it in his hand.

CHAPTER 8

The first Aldeburgh Festival. Conversations with Britten. The Proms. EOG Scandinavian Tour. "Busman's holiday'"in Scotland.

In May of 1948, it was time for the new Aldeburgh Festival and an opera season with the English Opera Group. I took Betty with me and we both enjoyed it.

Among the patrons were the Earl of Harewood, Imogen Holst and E.M. Forster. H.M. Queen Mary attended some events too. Imogen Holst was a petite, good-looking lady and multi-talented; she was a pianist, writer, teacher and composer, however, her father, the great Gustav Holst, composer of the *Planets suite*, overshadowed her. She was a big influence behind the scenes, I think, because she and Britten were often in deep conversation.

There was a new work on the programme, *St. Nicolas*, a cantata for tenor, choir, string orchestra, piano and percussion. Peter Pears, Britten's lover, was singing the tenor solo, and at the première, which was given in Aldeburgh Parish Church, he came out resplendent in a square cut Victorian morning coat with a lavender coloured waistcoat, a frilly shirt and a lavender foulard. We were all in fits when Jennifer Vyvyan, the soprano, looked round and whispered "Maternity". Decorum having been restored we began. *St. Nicolas* was an instant success, getting some good reviews.

The EOG orchestra was not very pleased when Norman del Mar was brought in to conduct. He was good at works like Mahler's *Song of the Earth* or the *Gurrelieder* but not at all suited to chamber works. His nickname in the musical profession was the "Mass of Life" after Delius' work of the same name, the reason being that he was a big man, heavy set and with a flailing baton. The orchestra complained to Britten, but he was adamant that del Mar should stay. I don't know if any money changed hands because it was rumoured that his father had given Beecham a sum of money to make him an apprentice conductor with the Royal Philharmonic

Orchestra and the more cynical members of the EOG orchestra surmised that this had again been the case with Britten.

Over the next two years we went on to do performances at Cambridge, where Britten's arrangement of the *Beggar's Opera* was premiered in 1948; among other places, we performed at the Cheltenham Festival, Knocke-La Zoute in Belgium, Holland Festival, Denmark, Norway, Covent Garden, Bournemouth and Wolverhampton.

I asked Britten his views on the future of opera in general and the direction in which it was going and he was very definite. He told me he was convinced that chamber operas would be the thing of the future although there were only a few modern ones such as Holst's *Savitri* in the repertoire at that time. He had some innovative ideas; one was that a marquee could be hired such as the huge one used at the Eisteddfods that would enable chamber operas to be taken practically anywhere but although it was a good idea it was never explored further.

One small company I played with which had a modicum of success was Intimate Opera, run by Frederick Woodhouse. The operas usually demanded only two or three singers on stage and a string quintet plus harpsichord in the pit. Woodhouse's daughter, Francesca, played the violin in the group that had played all over the British Isles as well as Spain, Canada and the U.S.A. Intimate Opera's repertoire consisted mainly of eighteenth century operas and many were real gems such as *The Grenadier* and *The Ephesian Matron* by Charles Dibdin, (1745-1814), which were hilarious.

Joan Cross was in charge of an opera school and she asked me to play at one of the operas the school produced, *Robert the Devil* by Meyerbeer. It is a very humorous opera, well worth reviving, and also does not require a huge orchestra and cast of singers.

When the English Opera Group played at Cambridge, E.M. Forster invited us to his rooms for a party in his beautifully appointed apartment. It was a splendid affair with excellent food and wine liberally served. Margaret Ritchie the soprano and Peter Pears entertained us with some hilarious operatic skits. I spoke with Forster, a quiet, gentle sort of man and the impression I had of him was that of a very cultured *bon viveur*.

At our Covent Garden season Ernest Ansermet, the founder and conductor of the Suisse Romande Orchestra based in Geneva, Switzerland, leaned over the pit rail and asked me if I would care to join his orchestra. Naturally I was very flattered and I met him in his hotel, the very exclusive Brown's in London's West End. Britten urged me to take the job, saying I could play with the Swiss Romande Orchestra in its winter season and with the English Opera Group in the summer, but Betty, my wife, would have none of it; she would not go to Geneva so the idea was dropped and nothing more came of it.

That season, 1948, there was love in the air. Stephen Waters the clarinettist had married Catherine Lawson, a singer in the cast, and Nancy Evans, the soprano, was married to Eric Crozier. But the big event that happened was the wedding of the Earl of Harewood to Marion Stein.

I had met Erwin Stein, Marion's father, a very erudite man who had been a pupil of Schoenberg and had conducted for a while before leaving Vienna for London, where he branched out into musicology and later worked in an administrative capacity at Boosey and Hawkes, the music publishers. Ben had asked me if I would call on Mr. Stein at his office in Regent Street to pick up a cheque; even composers have to live! I only spoke to his daughter, Marion, on one occasion because she was on the other side of the stage to me and both sides rarely crossed, but she was a fine pianist and a beautiful, charming girl.

We were giving a concert at King's College, Cambridge, and my wife mentioned to me that every time she had seen Marion and her mother, a very graceful lady, both were attired in new, lovely dresses. Betty sat next to them at the concert and with a woman's intuition she forecast wedding bells. And so it was. Marion Stein and the Earl of Harewood were married.

Of course, the media made much of the wedding, but alas, it wasn't to be a fairy tale marriage, for they were divorced soon afterwards; the Earl then married the sister of Barry Tuckwell the French horn player and Marion married Jeremy Thorpe, Liberal M.P. and one time leader of the Liberal Party.

One day, Ben and I were discussing our most embarrassing moments, he told me his was when H.M. Queen Mary asked him after a performance of *The Rape of Lucretia* why he chose that story for his opera. He answered, "Well, Ma'am, I like that sort of thing," at which Her Majesty frowned and looked down her nose in opprobrium.

He then said to me, "Well, Robert, and what was your most embarrassing moment?" I replied that I couldn't possibly cap his story but it goes like this: The LPO was down at Brighton, a seaside town on the South Coast of England. I usually arrived there early and took a stroll along the promenade to take a sniff of the briny that was also perfumed with the smell of winkles (a small shellfish) and vinegar wafting up from under the Palace Pier. Suitably invigorated I would take lunch and then walk to the Dome where the concerts took place. As a matter of interest, the Dome is connected by many underground tunnels that led to the various houses of "Prinny's,"(the Prince of Wales, later to become King George IV) mistresses.

Who should I espy walking towards me along the promenade but Dennis Wood, who played English horn, with an older lady on his arm? We smiled to each other, and later, and when I arrived at the Dome I said to Dennis quite innocently, "Did you bring your Mum down for a day by the seaside, Dennis?" He scowled at me which I thought was rude but in one of the tabloid newspapers next day was a photograph of the couple on its front-page encaptioned"25 marries 62".

Britten's homosexuality was an open secret. Everybody knew what was going on between Peter and Ben but nobody mentioned it. It was accepted that they were gay, so what! Nowadays the media makes a great brouhaha about some celebrity "coming out" but in those days things were different; although the law frowned upon it most people accepted it. Social mores are very different now than they were over fifty years ago but I never noticed Ben or Peter engaging in any overt sexual conduct. Britten never made any advances towards me although I was in my twenties and had a lot to do with him as librarian, but I did notice a definite cooling off in his attitude towards me when I married, maybe because I sent him a piece of wedding cake!

Some people have remarked that he was a sexual predator and although there were various boys singing with the Group at times, I never ever noticed anything untoward in his conduct towards them. He and Peter were like an old married couple with Britten being the dominant partner. On one occasion they must have had a lover's tiff, for one evening Peter came down to the orchestra's room to change instead of changing in the room he usually shared with Ben.

There was a revue playing in a London West End theatre called *Salad Days*. In it there was a line that went "Bundles for Britain means Piles for Peers", an obvious double-entendre that neither Ben nor Peter appreciated. I should explain that towards the end of WW2 there was an organization in America, called "Bundles for Britain" which arranged for food and clothing parcels to be sent to Britain, which was short of many necessities due to the War.

At Bournemouth there was an ugly incident. Hitherto we had all been very friendly and everyone treated each other as an equal, however, most of the singers were disgruntled with the huge billing Peter Pears was given compared to the the rest of the cast. Richard Lewis, the tenor, was noticeably upset. A meeting was called at Bournemouth's Winter

Gardens, the orchestra was invited and Eric Crozier presided, but we in the orchestra were embarrassed because it did not affect us -we were all down in the programme in the same type font. Eric tried to mollify everyone but he was not successful and there began the first rift in the lute.

I liked Eric Crozier's *bon mot* when he undertook the task of directing the Bournemouth Festival. He had made some suggestions that were not well received by the Bournemouth Town Council who thought they should have complete control over everything, despite the fact that none of them knew the slightest thing about running a festival. One councillor remarked that Eric should "know his place" to which Eric replied, "I do know my place and it isn't Bournemouth."

After the English Opera Group's Aldeburgh Festival success, followed by a tour of Holland I resumed freelancing and kept very busy. 1949 came and Betty was pregnant with our first child who was expected in the middle of the EOG's season.

At the time when her great day was supposed to happen I was booked for a week at Wolverhampton with the English Opera Group and was worried that I would not be with her when the time came. As things turned out I played on Monday, our opening night, but the next day I was free, so after the performance on Monday night I drove back home, a distance of roughly a hundred miles

The next day was beautiful and there was very little traffic at 6.am. so we sped to the hospital in the West End of London where a very prim and proper nurse dressed in a uniform with starched collar and cuffs met us. She said curtly, "Kiss your wife goodbye," and I felt as though, being the author of my wife's misfortunes that I had to be reprimanded for causing all the trouble. Coincidentally, Britten's sister was in charge of the pre-natal department at the hospital.

Some time later I was told, "It's a boy!" and after being allowed a brief visit with mother and child, I went home and slept. The next day I was back at the hospital for a short visit and then had to drive to Wolverhampton to play the opera. *Let's Make an Opera* was being given the following day and did not require a bass, so I again visited the hospital to see Betty and the newborn.

That season I fitted in both the LSO and LPO Proms. What a glutton for punishment I was! A new work was played at every concert. The Proms, a.k.a. Promenade Concerts were founded in 1895 by Sir Henry Wood, who conducted the bulk of the concerts which were held at the Queen's Hall, London, until it was destroyed in an air raid in 1941. After

Sir Henry passed away the Proms were taken over by the BBC. I think credit must be given to William Glock and others for persuading the BBC to pay for more rehearsal time. Their programming and quality of performance greatly improved due to the extra rehearsals, unlike the pre-war Proms that were only allowed one rehearsal per concert. Conductors and orchestra were understandably on edge, and Eugene Cruft once told me that tensions became so high in the old days that at one rehearsal a horn player took off his coat and challenged the conductor to a fight.

The Proms were well paid, because apart from the concert fee there was an extra fee if it was broadcast or televised, and if it were re-broadcast or re-televised then another fee was paid, and, in addition, the extra rehearsals were another "perk".

There was always a new work on the programme. E.J. Moeran, whose music I admire was well represented, as were Lennox Berkeley, Alan Rawsthorne, Vaughan Williams, Bax and John Ireland among others. Moeran was a toper and it was sad to see him after being in his cups, helped onto the platform by Basil Cameron who held him up to enable him to make his bow.

After four weeks of the Proms I had to catch a flight to Copenhagen where the EOG was appearing the following Monday at the Royal Theatre. Our visit lasted a week and it was sponsored by the Danish newspaper, *Aftenposten*. It was a great success, one performance being honoured by the presence of the King of Denmark who was also a conductor and keenly interested in music.

One day I decided to take an early ferry boat to Göteborg, Sweden, and come back in the early afternoon in time for the opera that night. I arrived at Göteborg and had a good look round, made a few purchases and then went through customs in order to board the boat back to Copenhagen. The Swedish Customs officer was indescribably rude to everybody, especially me when he saw my British passport. He insulted me and sneered at the souvenirs I had bought and I thought I would never catch the boat and be in time for the opera. Although I felt mad I kept my mouth shut, and eventually when he had run out of steam he let me go and I dashed up the gangway. I would be playing the opera in Copenhagen that night after all!

The week following we opened in Oslo, Norway, where we also had a success and I stayed with Sten Sorensen, the owner of a soap factory. Upon leaving he gave me a huge box of baby soap that was difficult to obtain in England in those days. Sten and his friend Lori Ruud came to visit us in London later that year.

We later went to Bergen and visited Hardangerfjord where we were entertained right royally in a rustic setting and were served reindeer steaks. My impression of them was that they tasted somewhat like a coarse beef, but they were delicious and came with an exquisite sauce that tasted of cranberries, or maybe they could have been lingonberries. Whilst we were eating, a musician came along to entertain us by playing the Hardanger fiddle. This instrument is something like a violin but is equipped with a second set of sympathetic strings that vibrate with the notes that are played on the primary set of strings. Its sound was very sonorous and unusual and I thought there was a good case to be made for employing it in our modern orchestras.

We said our goodbyes and caught the boat for our return to England and there were many handshakes and embraces with our newfound friends. Ben Britten was presented with a laurel wreath and we all held a solemn ceremony casting the wreath into the North Sea.

Back in London there were some broadcasts with the London Harpsichord Ensemble, which turned out to be the end of my association with John Francis who ran the Ensemble. Francis, (who drove a Rolls Royce), was in the habit of sawing off part of the fee for "expenses". For instance, if the fee was fifteen guineas, (fifteen pounds fifteen shillings), he would dock the fifteen shillings which he cited as the cost of borrowing the music, and pay the player just £15.00, but I well knew that the BBC supplied the music from their library at no extra cost to him, so I told him I didn't think this was fair.

That was the end of the London Harpsichord Ensemble for me. However, there was much happening in the music scene at that time, and, as Britten was getting fewer and fewer engagements for the Group, I still had a wife, a son and a mortgage so I had to look for fresh fields to conquer. I soon became very busy with other things, indeed so much so, that I desperately needed a holiday.

Holidays for freelance musicians were certainly not considered to be the norm, but I had good connections with all the BBC orchestras and was usually able to arrange a "holiday" with the BBC by playing in one of their regional orchestras and I would take the wife and kids with me. For instance, I would arrange to be asked to play for two weeks with the BBC Scottish Orchestra and would borrow a bass in Glasgow, the BBC's Scottish headquarters, when I arrived. The family would catch a Clyde steamboat to Largs, where we stayed at a B&B, and I would commute by car. The Clyde steamers were magnificently equipped, and the delicious meals were served on silver.

In those days the job was not very onerous and there was a lot of free time. J. Mouland Begbie was the concertmaster and Ian Whyte the excellent conductor. Their repertoire included some Scottish works; Hamish Mc Cunn's overture *Land of the Mountain and of the Flood* always received an airing for political correctness but most of the Scottish pieces played were modern and often first performances. Whyte was a musical legend in Scotland with a catholic repertoire and obtained some excellent readings of the works he conducted.

Alexander Gibson, conductor of the Scottish National Orchestra, was given the nickname "Flash Haggis" by the players. He came down to London occasionally but I didn't think he was in the same class as Ian Whyte. I know comparisons are invidious, but as both came from Scotland there was always the tendency to compare the two of them.

I didn't see Ben Britten for many years after my fallout with John Francis, but one day I was asked by the LSO to play Britten's *War Requiem* in the ruins of Coventry Cathedral. Because of my connections with Coventry in my youth I jumped at the chance. However, I was shocked to see the ruins of what was a beautiful cathedral; nothing remained except for a few blocks of Warwickshire red sandstone with grass growing round them. Was this really the place where the 7th Warwicks had laid up their colours on September 3rd 1939?

I remembered Olivier reciting Shakespeare's opening speech in *King Richard the Third* as he trod the boards on the New Theatre stage: "Now are our brows bound with glorious wreaths, our bruisèd arms hung up for monuments." Unfortunately, our brows were never bound with glorious wreaths and our bruisèd arms were left behind in France although the memory still lingers on in my mind.

Later on I was asked to record Britten's *War Requiem* with Britten himself conducting the LSO. He looked much older, and sick, too, I thought. We shook hands and chatted for a while and that was the last I saw of him. I wrote him in late 1976 from Vancouver, British Columbia, Canada, to remind him of a promise he had made to write me a piece for the bass, but I received a letter from someone telling me that Ben was too ill to write. He died a week later.

CHAPTER 9

The Coronation.

Some time in April 1953 I received a letter bearing the Royal Coat of Arms. It contained a command from Her Majesty Queen Elizabeth the Second for me to play in the Orchestra at her Coronation in June 1953; I was to attend all of the rehearsals, failure to do so would result in my dismissal from the Orchestra. I was to play my five-stringed bass. The dress was to be tails. White gloves, medals and decorations would be worn. I was elated, because it meant that I was now recognized as being a player of standing in the profession.

Everyone in the orchestra had to be or have been a principal of an orchestra. The majority of the violinists were concertmasters drawn from every orchestra in the British Isles; some were leaders of famous string quartets. It was the same thing with the winds; Dennis Brain was first horn, the third horn was principal horn in the Hallé Orchestra and the other horns were principals also. Harold Jackson, principal trumpet of the Philharmonia was playing principal and all the other trumpets were also orchestra principals. This applied to every section of the Orchestra. Paul Beard, concertmaster of the BBC Symphony Orchestra was the concertmaster. All the chorus members were renowned soloists or professors at the Universities.

Sir Adrian Boult was selected as conductor, although I understand that Sir Malcolm Sargent was also in the running and very anxious that he be given the prestigious job. Knowing Sir Adrian, I'm sure <u>he</u> never solicited the conductorship. Eugene Cruft, in co-operation with the organist and music director of Westminster Abbey compiled the list of orchestra personnel.

There was a list of the pieces to be played, many of which were the jingoistic old faithfuls that were dusted off and considered necessary on such occasions. There were two old gentlemen, Doctors of Music and organists at great cathedrals, seated at each side of the orchestra. Each of them had a pack of printed numbers, one of which they were to hold up in view of the orchestra after being given the requisite number from Sir

Adrian Boult, this way the orchestra could find the numbered piece of music which was to be played.

Rehearsals began with the orchestra seated in a gallery called the rood loft, and it commanded the best view of the house, so we were able to look down on the Queen, the throne and all of the surrounding dignitaries. Unfortunately the gallery was not quite big enough to hold us all comfortably and Harold Jackson complained there was not enough room for him to play, at which Boult said acidly, "Neither is there room for anyone else." I'm sure we could have have given a better performance had we arranged ourselves differently.

Another problem that concerned the orchestra was that we would have to be in our seats from six a.m. until about four p.m., and as there was no toilet in the gallery we all wondered what do if we had to answer the call of nature. This concern was mentioned to no less a person than the Earl Marshal, the premier Earl, in charge of the whole ceremony. After much deliberation, and no doubt considering the birds and the bees and the peculiarities of the anatomy of the sexes, the Earl Marshal came to the solemn conclusion that the gentlemen should bring hot water bottles and the ladies should bring sponges and a decree was issued to this effect. Vive la différence!

I spoke laughingly to Marie Wilson, a real old trooper in the profession who had often led the BBC Symphony and asked her if she was going to bring her sponge, she retorted that she was not, because she was not going to drink anything beforehand and also that she would be sure to pee before taking her seat in the gallery. This seemed to be the general consensus of opinion amongst the orchestra.

Boris Ord, organist of King's College, Cambridge, and director of King's College Chapel Choir, failed to appear at one of the many rehearsals, and when he arrived at the Abbey the next day was barred from entry and refused permission to take part in the Coronation ceremony. Perhaps this was done *pour encourager les autres*, as after that there were no more absentees.

There was a final dress rehearsal the day before the event for which lots were drawn for a few tickets that the orchestra was to receive for their relatives. I was unsuccessful but when the rehearsal commenced I looked round and noticed that there was hardly anybody in the Abbey, so they could have given each of us a complimentary ticket - such are the ways of bureaucrats. Some of us took exception to this because we were all performing gratis and we could easily have been granted this small concession as a mark of appreciation.

On top of that, there was a reception held afterwards to which we were all invited, but we all had to pay for admission. This having been said, it was by far the best paying engagement I had ever taken part in by reason of the fact that there were so many reproduction fees paid for by all the media and radio and T.V. stations throughout the world.

Afterwards all the orchestra members were awarded the Coronation Medal, Eugene Cruft was awarded membership of the Royal Victorian Order, fourth class, and the Abbey organist was knighted.

The Great Day arrived and I was up at 4.30 a.m. My dear wife had pressed my shirt which was whiter than white. I pinned on my medals after donning my tail suit and white gloves. My wife gave my suit a final brushing down so that there were no specks of dust to sully my impeccable appearance, and off I drove in the misty, drizzling rain to pick up Gene and Mrs. Cruft. Gene had managed to wangle a ticket for his wife, and had also arranged for me to be given a special pass for my car. He asked me to be particularly careful about the cleanliness of the seats, as Mrs Cruft would be wearing a white gown, which she had purchased especially for the occasion.

I arrived at the Cruft residence and there was Mrs. Cruft in all her finery. She wore a long silk-like dress plus a tiara of sorts in which there was an ostrich feather. I installed her in the back seat of the car upon which I had been careful to put sheets, and Eugene, looking very smart in his tail suit plus his many medals, joined me in the front. We sailed through every street with great ease, being saluted very deferentially by the police after they noticed the official pass on our car.

Nothing had been spared to make the interior of the Abbey look spic and span. For instance when we arrived on the day, Jim Merrett, one of the bassists who sat on a rather worn stool found that it had been re-upholstered overnight in royal blue velvet so as to harmonize with the surroundings.

The Orchestra men looked like penguins with their black tail suits, the ladies were all in white, wearing headscarves, but looking down at the congregation there was a sea of colour. There were the dukes, earls and viscounts etc. wearing their coronets and ermine plus colourful robes, accompanied by their ladies, also beautifully dressed, some wearing blue sashes. There were the heralds wearing their tabards embroidered with coats of arms, the judiciary wearing red robes and full bottomed wigs, many of the congregation wearing full ceremonial dress, generals in scarlet, admirals in blue wearing gold braid and the members of the Diplomatic Corps in court dress. The Asian and African ladies and gentlemen stole

The Bottom Line

the show, attired in their colourful robes. One lady who was conspicuous in her dress and bearing was the Queen of Tonga. Above all, though, was H. M. Queen Elizabeth, who looked beautiful, radiant and confident.

We removed our white gloves and as the dignitaries arrived we played a different tune for each one of them. I forget now whether it was for the Shah of Persia, the Oni of Ife or the Queen of Tonga's entrance but one piece commenced with a tremendous pizzicato forte from the basses. Eugene was in his element and with a magnificent sweep of his hand (known in the trade as feeding the pigeons) he drew his arm in the air with such a flourish that one of his many medals got caught in his strings. He extracted the medal quickly and went on playing as if nothing had happened. I smiled to myself and thought what a great "character" he was.

The service went on and after we had played the anthems etc., we came to the core of the whole affair-the crowning.

There was a boy's choir singing "Vivat! Vivat!" and just at the very moment the crown was being placed upon the Queen's head, a shaft of glorious golden light shone through one of the stained glass windows. The weathermen had been pressed into service and had consulted their oracles to predict the most fortuitous day, weather-wise, for the occasion, but they had failed miserably. It was a dreadful day, save for this one shaft of light, which I and many others looked upon as an augury of future happiness to grace her reign. I prayed then that this would come to be, and although she must have had many sorrows during her reign, she appears to have survived it all remarkably well.

At the end of the service the congregation was filing out and apparently Boult had decided to play one of Elgar's *Pomp and Circumstance* marches a.k.a. *Land of Hope and Glory*. There appeared to be some confusion among the pair of elderly numerologists as they each held up a different number. Boult hissed the name of the tune to no avail, but it was Paul Beard who saved the day by playing the tune fortississimo[29], the orchestra immediately caught on and the error was hardly noticed, which signalled to us all Paul's invaluable experience.

Afterwards, we repaired to the reception. I was sandwiched between Paul Beard and Joe Shadwick, concertmaster of Covent Garden, resplendent in all his medals. We analyzed the day over a few drinks plus some very good "nibbles", and we were greeted with some condescending nods by noble lords and a few gallant knights who were two a penny that day. Never before or since was I in the presence of such a distinguished assembly.

It came time to leave when Eugene and Mrs. Cruft espied me. I took them home and was invited in to tea, but guess what! Being an unpardonable sinner of a freelance musician I had taken on another job playing for Eric Robinson at the BBC Lime Grove television studios. Robinson had agreed for me to arrive late, so I repaired to the studio, played until "unconscious", about 11 p.m. and so home to bed. Looking back I should have gone home immediately after the Coronation, taken my wife out for dinner with champagne and made a memorable occasion of it for us both - but I still had bills to pay.

Chapter 9 Notes
29. Fortississimo, Italian - very, very loud

CHAPTER 10

I am invited to join the Philharmonia Orchestra. Touring experiences. Walter Legge, von Karajan and the big row onstage in Baltimore.

My freelancing connection was flourishing, due in a large extent to my dear wife who ran the business side of it very well. She knew anybody and everybody in the London classical music scene and had an instinctive flair for knowing, when the telephone rang, which dates to accept or refuse. Without boasting I can say that on some days I had as many as five offers of work. It was a very tricky job to juggle with them, but she did, patiently and delicately.

One day in 1953 I received a call from Gerald Brooks. He wanted to meet me for a drink to discuss something. In all honesty I cannot say that we were bosom friends, bearing in mind what had happened in the London Philharmonic, but being curious to know what was on his mind I agreed to meet him in a pub near the Festival Hall.

When we eventually got down to business it appeared that he was coming as an unofficial emissary from the Philharmonia Orchestra. Apparently Herbert von Karajan had hinted that he needed another five-stringed bass in the orchestra. At present Brooks was the only five-string bassist and he was very anxious that I join the orchestra and share a stand with him. I said I would think it over and let him know. The real reason he wanted me there, I think, was that it was better to have a devil he knew sitting next to him than one he didn't.

Although I was doing very well freelancing, the offer to join the Philharmonia was tempting; I would be paid extra for the five-stringer because there were sometimes a few solo notes to play on it and in the 1950's there were not many five-string basses around. I would also be in the core orchestra, meaning I would have all the work they offered but they would allow me to do all the important dates I still wanted to keep, but it would mean giving up some of my independence.

On the other hand I had just bought a better house in a nice neighbourhood, Mill Hill, in North London (it came with a bigger mortgage too!), and I was sending my son to a prestigious, expensive school so I decided to throw caution to the winds and join the Legge Philharmonia. *Kunst nach Brot!*[30] To this day the Philharmonia orchestra of that period - the 1950's and 60's - is still known as the "Legge" Philharmonia. The orchestral personnel were drawn from such far away places as Australia, South Africa, Canada, Poland, Portugal, Italy, Germany, Israel as well as the U.K. Walter Legge, the Founder and Artistic Director could only maintain such an orchestra because of the big pay cheques they took home. He also employed the greatest conductors and soloists. Here I must note that the recording fees we received were paid by the session and that there were no royalties paid to the musicians no matter how many records were sold. This applied also to recordings that were later re-mastered from tapes to CD's that are still being sold to this day.

Concerts and tours were paid at the rock bottom Union rates and for this reason some players tried to avoid them. Jane Withers, previously Legge's secretary at E.M.I., now the manager of the Philharmonia would confront these miscreants with her stock phrase, "Have you no loyalty?'"Most of the orchestra found this rather amusing since there was absolutely no loyalty shown by the management to the musicians. There was a humorous appellation given by the players to these people; they were dubbed "recording artists".

I heard that the classical recording department operated at a loss and it was only due to the huge profits EMI made from the Beatles and other pop groups it had on contract that they were able to keep the Philharmonia going.

Walter Legge was a ruthless man, both in his private life and in his dealings with musicians, whether they were conductors, singers, instrumental soloists or orchestral players, he treated them all with seeming contempt with the exception of those few who were in his good books. In appearance he was of middle height, well built, wearing glasses, leonine looking with a mane of greyish black hair brushed back.

He was a fluent German speaker - indeed, he preferred speaking in German, which he did faultlessly, to his own impeccable English. I was greatly surprised when we were in Italy to hear him speaking fluent Italian.

He had a wonderful ear, and could spot in an instant any flaws in a performance. It is said that he had even been persuaded to conduct the orchestra in a concert in the North of England, but perhaps wisely, had decided at the last minute not to do so and to continue with what was perhaps his real forte, that of a recording producer.

He could be absolutely, unforgivably rude. I remember one occasion when the orchestra was accompanying a singer in some arias. The conductor was a young Italian, and very competent but Legge excoriated him in front of his wife.

There was absolutely no guarantee that you would keep your job. Cecil James, the very fine first bassoon, received his pink slip on a Christmas Day. Probably the reason was that Cecil played French bassoon that in those days was being supplanted by the German Heckel.

Max Salpeter, who was concertmaster before Manoug Parikian came, was also fired. We were on a French tour, playing at Strasbourg. There was a Mozart piece in the programme that contained a very difficult violin solo, and as Manoug was away for that night Max had to step in. He played it beautifully but in a different style to Manoug, and afterwards the orchestra wildly applauded, as did the audience, but it made no difference, he had to go. I asked him what he intended to do and he told me that he was going to take a holiday and then freelance, which he did very successfully.

Other firings were Alf Cursue the fourth horn whom even Dennis Brain couldn't save once Legge's mind was made up. The second oboe was fired as well, besides countless string players who were fired more often than Legge changed his shirt.

Jim Bradshaw, the timpanist took a dislike to Big Harry, who played bass drum and cymbals and had apparently given a clash in the wrong place so he too was fired. But Big Harry didn't take it lying down and went into the recording booth to berate Legge who was not used to being spoken to that way. After some altercation Legge cried, "Get out!" and that was the end of Big Harry.

Every one of the violinists had to have been a soloist or top chamber music player. The concertmaster, Manoug Parikian, whom I had met as the concertmaster in Fistoulari's orchestra was an outstanding player, had a very good presence on stage and, importantly, was an excellent liaison between the conductors and the musicians. Playing at the back of the first violins was a very promising soloist, Tessa Robbins who had played a concerto at the Proms, and sitting very near the front of the first violins was Jack Kessler, whom I had worked with in Britten's English Opera Group. I won't enumerate all of the players, but the first horn, Dennis Brain is legendary. The first trombone, Flascinzsky, was brought over from Poland, but... I could go on and on. With such personnel no wonder the orchestra was received so enthusiastically wherever it played.

The first 'cellist was Raymond Clark, a very fine, consistent player, certainly one of the attributes a good orchestra principal must have. On his very first date with the Philharmonia Orchestra, Franz von Suppé's overture, *Poet and Peasant*, was to be recorded. Legge no doubt chose this as a test piece for Raymond, but he played the difficult 'cello solo magnificently and he was "in".

Another 'cellist in the orchestra was Norina Semino, an Italian lady who very kindly helped me with my Italian pronunciation. She was a soloist and a good chamber music player and had been married to Manucci, the 'cello soloist. She once told me that her ambition when she retired was to return to sunny Italy, she only liked the Philharmonia for the money.

Once I had to give an audition to Legge at his house in St. John's Wood. The door opened and a maid said, "Der Herr Kommt."[31] I played the Dragonetti concerto, which musically he did not think much of, but he seemed to be happy with my playing, and was always pleasant to me afterwards. But you never knew; he could be Quixotic at times.

There were two bassists sitting on the last desk, Roy Watson and Cyril McArthur, who both sported beards; Legge once enquired who they were, saying, "We should keep those bass players with the beards, they look good on stage." Although they were good players neither had given an audition, which all goes to show that playing music is partly showbiz.

I arrived for my first recording session at the Kingsway Hall in Kingsway, High Holborn, which was then the chief recording venue of the Philharmonia and other orchestras. I was greeted by many members of the orchestra whom I had met in the big world outside of the Philharmonia.

On the dais was one, Heribert Karijannis, a.k.a. Herbert von Karajan. He was an aristocratic looking man, well deserving of his adopted aristocratic title of "von". Karajan was lean, of average height and in his mid - forties with his jet black hair brushed back *en brosse* in the old German style, very polite to the orchestra, addressing everyone by name and with a clear beat, good stick technique and getting some good performances from the orchestra. With due respect, I must say however, that for me he lacked the scintillation of a de Sabata, a Beecham or a Koussevitsky. Beecham once said of von Karajan that he was a musical Malcolm Sargent.

I had heard that he was an excellent pianist, but I never did hear him play the pianoforte.

Brooks said to me in an aside, "There he is, Legges's pet boy: God!" This was true, Legge thought the world of von Karajan. Having listened to a post war recording of von K. in the late forties he decided to promote him and from then on, with the help of the Philharmonia, he advanced von Karajans' recognition in the musical world. How he paid Legge back I will explain later.

If the rumours I heard were true, (and I have had no desire to research them) that Legge was the son of a London East End Jewish tailor, I cannot for the life of me understand the unholy alliance between him and von Karajan, a rabid Nazi.

When the orchestra began to play I was astounded to hear the shimmering, mellifluous sound of the strings, the exquisite woodwind and the way the brass fitted in, they didn't overplay as in many other orchestras I had heard.

I should mention the timpani and percussion. Jim Bradshaw, the timpanist was a real artist; his only problem was that he wore dentures which clicked as he was silently counting the bars. This caused the recording engineers some problems until they discovered that the strange noise coming over the microphone was Jim's teeth! One young upstart of a conductor wondered aloud whether Jim was doubling on castanets.

There was another man at HMV/EMI, a Mr. Bicknell, Legge's opposite number, who was also directing some recordings. If he could cheesepare on the orchestra he would. For example, except in recording Mozart or Baroque composers, Legge always employed eight and sometimes ten basses. Bicknell was stingy; he rarely engaged more than four basses and made corresponding cuts in the other string sections. I don't want to make the point that any particular recording survived due to the number of double basses in the orchestra but it is interesting to note that many of Legge's recordings survive to this day, but I don't notice many of Bicknell's. Bicknell married a well-known Italian violin soloist named Giaconda da Vito whom I thought was a real virtuoso when I played some concerts with her.

Legge spared nothing so as to ensure his recordings were perfect. For example, we had been recording all the nine symphonies of Beethoven with von Karajan. One day the Philharmonia office phoned me with instructions to be at London Airport the following day to catch a flight to Vienna. Legge had decided there wasn't a choir in London good enough for Beethoven's Ninth, so we were to record it in Vienna with von Karajan and a Viennese choir in the Musikvereinsaal. Those of my readers familiar with the New Year's Day television broadcasts with the Vienna Philharmonic Orchestra will remember the classical interior of the hall with its caryatids and gilt cherubims, but more importantly it was the wonderful acoustics of the hall that thrilled me.

During one of the recording breaks I ventured outside the hall and saw a big parade of Russian troops including a military band. They were all dressed in immaculate uniforms and I learned that this was their farewell parade prior to leaving Vienna. It was interesting to watch the faces of the crowd, most of who seemed to be showing signs of relief that at last they were no longer to be occupied by a foreign power.

Some time later Legge decided to form his own choir, the Philharmonia Choir, a hand picked group, and every week Wilhelm Pitz, the chorus master at Bayreuth, was flown in to London to rehearse and train them. That is why Legge to my mind must have been one of the greatest impresarios of his day or even any era because he had to have the best, no matter the cost.

Elisabeth Schwartzkopf, Legge's second wife, often sang with us, not because she was Legge's wife but because she was a great artist in her own right. Some people did say that Legge, because of his domineering personality had over-influenced Schwartzkopf in her musical presentation. She had a constant problem with clearing her throat at some recordings and concerts, but I remember her *Exultate Jubilate* of Mozart and her Marschallin in Richard Strauss's opera *Der Rosenkavalier*. Exquisite!

Not long after I joined the Philharmonia I had a contretemps with them over fees that started in a serious manner but fortunately ended in a rather humorous way. The Musicians' Union had raised the fees for concerts; it was the first raise in years and long overdue. Legge, who was only paying the present Union minimum took umbrage over this and was heard to declare to von Karajan that he might even form another orchestra in Patagonia free of any Union interference, von Karajan heartily agreed saying, "We should have our own union."

I was given extra pay for the five-stringer, but after receiving the first pay-cheque since the raise I noticed that Brooks and I were not now receiving the extra for the five stringer at the concerts, although we were paid for the recordings. At the rehearsal for the next concert, to which Brooks and I had decided not to bring a five -stringer, Von Karajan wanted to know where the low 'C' was, but Brooks, usually vociferous, kept mute. I spoke up and informed him that I had been paid for the recording sessions but not for the concerts. A deathly silence came over the orchestra.

Legge sprang up from the back of the hall and said imperiously, "Bring your instrument tonight, you will be paid."

I arrived at the Festival Hall with the five-string bass and who should I come across upon entering the elevator to the concert platform but von Karajan who greeted me with a sarcastic smile and said, "Ah! You brought it, did you get your money?" and rubbed his forefinger and thumb together to underline his remark which insensed me (I was rather hot headed in those days). I replied, "Yes, I will be paid but you are not doing too badly are you, and I'm sure you get a good paycheque." He owned a yacht, a plane and a luxurious villa. I too rubbed my thumb and forefinger together whereupon von Karajan burst into hearty laughter, smiled, patted me on the shoulder and said, "See you on the stage."

This incident had a happy ending, for afterwards, whenever we bumped into each other we both made a money sign by rubbing our forefinger and thumb together and smiled. It all goes to show that many classical musicians, although they may look serious on stage have a different personality off stage. My opinion of von Karajan went up after that because he demonstrated that he, too, could take a joke - and why not with the money he was making.

To publicize the recordings and the orchestra, Legge decreed that we would make one German, one Italian and possibly one American tour a year, besides the occasional trips to France and the yearly round trips to festivals such as Lucerne, Aix-en-Provence, Edinburgh and Salzburg.

When we played at the Salzburg Festival I was leaving the Mozarteum, the concert hall, where we had just finished a rehearsal with von Karajan, when I came across Frau von Karajan, a plump lady sporting a green Tyrolean hat decorated with a saucy feather. She was running round exclaiming,"Wo ist mein Mann, Herbert, Herbert!" I could have told her where he was, in the company of a beautiful, willowy blonde model hurriedly leaving by the back exit and furtively looking round in case his wife spotted him. I believe that von K. and the model were married later on for she was often present at all his recordings and concerts and personally, having encountered both women, I cannot blame him for making the change.

There was one problem as far as the orchestra members were concerned; the take-home pay barely covered the tours. A daily allowance for food and shelter was paid, and, if one elected for them to do so, the orchestra management would book a hotel for you, not caring about the cost; it was all the same to them where they booked you. Say, for example you wanted a hotel in Lucerne they would book you in at the Schweizerhof, the most expensive hotel in Lucerne, and bang went your entire fee as well as the per diem allowance.

There was another downside to staying in the big hotels as well. Sometimes the orchestra would arrive late at an hotel with barely enough time to snatch a meal, change, and then go to the concert. Inevitably there was a long wait in the hotel lobby for the room key; I have waited up to an hour on occasion when the hotel had perhaps overbooked. Staying privately would have saved all that hassle, as well as not having to fork out a tip to the seemingly dozens of menials who stood with their hands outstretched, so I decided to save money by booking at B&B's or "fremdenzimmers" as they are called in Germany, and I built up quite a network all over Europe. Many members of the orchestra asked me if I would book them B&B's too.

There were, among others, a Frau Lehrer in Lucerne; a Signora della Rosa in Milan; a small hotel, the "Rote Hahn" in Vienna and a small hotel in the Rue Serpente in Paris. This enabled us to come back with a profit, and, added to this, I made friends with many people that I would not have done otherwise.

In 1965, just before coming to Canada I decided to take my wife and kids to Vienna by car. We drove through France and we visited Râches where I had been stationed with the Army. I enquired about M. and Mme. Descatoire at the local *estaminet*[32], but they were long since deceased. I was told that Sylvie, their granddaughter, who had been thirteen years old when I last saw her in 1940, was married with a family and living in a nearby village. For old times' sake we stayed at the hotel in the Rue Serpente in Paris but it had changed hands. In Vienna, however, I booked us in at the Rote Hahn and was greeted effusively. "Ah, so, Herr Meyer, bitte herein!" In Baden-Baden and Munich I again renewed friendships and my wife and kids were beginning to believe that I had a wonderful time on tour.

At one Lucerne festival we had a week off, with no pay, of course, just the daily living allowance. Cyril MacArthur, a bass player a.k.a. the "Moor of Venice" because of his dark complexion and black beard, suggested to me that we travel in his car over the Gothard Pass to Lugano. He drove racing cars as a hobby using the name Scott MacArthur.

The Moor and I set off, and after some hair-raising moments arrived at the small town of Bellinzona where we spent the night. We resumed our journey the next morning and arrived that evening in Lugano, which was altogether different to Lucerne. The atmosphere in Lucerne was very severe and "Prunklich"[33] as the Germans say. What a contrast Lugano was to Lucerne! Firstly the weather; it was beautiful in Lugano whereas in Lucerne it always seemed to be raining. There was a saying in Lucerne that if Mount Pilatus, the local mountain, had his hat on, i.e. a cloud on top, it would rain. Well, Pilatus always seemed to have his hat on, and trudging round the streets, looking in the shops and consuming seemingly endless cups of coffee after having viewed all the local points of interest soon palled. But Lugano had a happy, sunny, Italian air.

After a very pleasant stay in Lugano, it was time to head back to Lucerne and the Moor drove off, horn blaring all the way. I was praying all the time and averting my eyes to the sheer drop at the side of the mountain road. There was a German car in front, which the Moor swung out to overtake but inevitably a car appeared from the opposite direction round a bend, and in order for us not to go plunging over the edge of a precipice the Moor cut in front of the German car grazing it rather severely, however, luck was with us and nobody was injured. There was an ugly scene when the German driver got out of his car and swore at the Moor. I was asked to translate, but not wishing to be involved said, "No speaka da ling." Eventually, after papers were verified and insurance cover noted we all went on our respective ways. Thankfully, we proceeded at a slower pace and arrived in Lucerne ready to grapple with Beethoven's Ninth symphony conducted by Furtwängler. I recalled the Lugano incident years later when I was sent a cheque for the repeat of a televised version of the Lucerne concert, so our trip to Lugano ended happily after all.

I was often offered a ride by some of the orchestra, who took their cars over the English Channel by ferry and then drove all the way to our destination. Driving was hazardous in France; the mountain passes and the French Routes Nationales were often overcrowded with heavy trucks and after my experience on the Gothard Pass with the Moor, I usually booked a sleeper train from Boulogne and arrived fresh and in time for the concert.

Then there was the usual foul up over berths on the night ferry crossing the English Channel to France. On one occasion Jane Withers, the manager, announced that there were only seventeen berths and, of course, these would be for the women. By and large, most of the women acted professionally and didn't bring the gender business into it, but there were some women who wanted to have their cake and eat it, despite receiving the same fees as the men.

Nowadays, in a more enlightened climate, women (quite rightly), are being accepted as the equals of men in orchestras. There seems to be a better esprit de corps and more decorum. For instance, the ribald jokes and naughty little ditties sung by the men to some of the tunes are no longer acceptable. But in those days, from the forties right through to the

60's the Philharmonia and the BBC Symphony were the only symphony orchestras to employ women. There were women in the small freelance orchestras such as the Riddick Orchestra, which usually consisted entirely of women, and I remember once being the only man playing with them at the Albert Hall for an annual gathering of the Women's Institute. Imagine an audience of several thousand women, an all ladies orchestra and me the only man. Very embarrassing!

Talking of ferries, we played at the San Carlo Opera House in Naples and after the concert boarded the ferry for Palermo, in Sicily. On arrival, we checked into our hotel on the main street and noticed bullet holes in a wall and some blood. Apparently there had been an assassination just prior to our arrival. Next day, Sunday, there was to be an afternoon concert and we were instructed to put our luggage onto the bus beforehand and afterwards to pack our instruments as quickly as possible in order to catch the bus to the return ferry to Naples, but it was not until after we had boarded the ferry that we discovered the reason for the hurry. The ferry captain had agreed to hold the ferry back from its usual sailing time so we could catch it after the concert, but at a price: he wanted to be given the best seat in the house, and, as an encore, we were to play one of his favourite pieces of music; Verdi's overture *La Forza del Destino*.

The Philharmonia did its travelling on the cheap. It was mainly by train in Europe and the U.K. in those days as planes were considered too expensive, and there was very little time for sight-seeing. After a concert we would stroll through the town and have supper, but concerts on the European Continent usually started late, sometimes at 9.00 or 9.30 p.m. in Italy. Often we had to be up at 6.30 a.m. at the very latest the next morning in order to catch a 7.30 a.m. train. We would have just enough time to grab a cup of coffeee at the railway station before boarding the train and then on to the next stand.

I managed to see all the sights around Perugia and Assisi and we were taken on a little tour of Sicily, but it was frustrating not to be able to see more. I remember strolling the Gallerias in Milan and noting the haughty Gendarmerie strutting in their dress uniforms complete with swords and cocked hats. From the train I managed to catch a glimpse of the Leaning Tower of Pisa, but the train only stopped in Florence en route to the next stop, and I was particularly sad that we were so near and yet so far from all the objets d'art that Florence boasts of.

Whenever we performed at La Scala, Milan, it was the custom for everyone to visit the Duomo, Milan's beautiful cathedral. If I remember rightly there was a cocktail bar you could ascend to in the elevator, but down in the crypt there was a coffin made of crystal containing the blackened bones of an ancient pope. When the sacristan had enough people in the "house" and, of course, after a small financial consideration, he would open the crypt for a short while. We were allowed to view the spectacle, and our exclamations of astonishment together with our largesse made him a very happy man.

One of the worries in a musician's life is to ensure arrival in good time for the concert. I have had some narrow scrapes at times but the following was the worst I ever experienced.

Signora della Rosa's apartment was some distance from La Scala. One had to take a tram, and then change to another tram that went direct to La Scala. One night, after eating at a restaurant highly recommended by the Signora, Brooks and I caught the tram to La Scala, but at the exchange stop, the Scala tram was not waiting there as usual. We both looked at our watches and I wondered whether we ought to catch a taxi. After what seemed to be hours, the tram arrived and deposited us at La Scala just as von Karajan was waiting to go on stage and with all the orchestra already seated. We made a humble apology and walked onstage.

Of all the tours I have ever been on, the 1955 tour of the U.S.A. and Canada was by far the most strenuous. It lasted over five weeks and apart from all the hard work, it proved to be a turning point in the history of the Philharmonia. This was due to an incident that happened at a rehearsal, which I shall explain later.

Of course, there were "goings on" on tour, but I was never tempted to stray from the straight and narrow because I had noticed over the years the havoc it wrought on the lives of so many people.

There was also an amusing incident that occurred. It was the era of McCarthyism and we all had to go down to the U.S. Embassy in London and swear on the Bible that we were not communists. When we arrived in the U.S. we had to sit and wait in a large room together until our name was called and then go up to the desk where an official sternly questioned us.

Imagine our surprise - particularly amongst the women who thoroughly enjoyed the incident and gossiped about it ever afterwards - when the official called out loudly "Mr. and Mrs. ...." Nobody knew until then that one of the lady violinists and one of the woodwinds had been having an affair. He had divorced his wife and married the violinist; they were hoping to keep it private but unfortunately McCarthyism wouldn't let them.

The management paid for and arranged the hotels in the U.S.A. and we were given a dining allowance that just about covered our expenses. In some countries we found that the exchange rate went against us, particularly in Switzerland and Germany. France and Italy were about on a monetary par with Great Britain in those days but higher exchange rates made a big difference in our take home pay since allowances were always calculated in British currency.

Travel in the U.S. was entirely by chartered bus. We had a very friendly driver who seemed to know where all the best rest stops were and we ate in the diners that then studded the highways, but sometimes there was barely time to grab a meal or even to use the washroom due to the line-ups.

I remember one particular day, (it was supposed to be a rest day); we were in that bus for twelve hours from 8 a.m. until 8 p.m. Some days on tour there was hardly any time to wash dress and eat before a concert, yet we were still expected to deliver the goods on the concert platform.

Touring conditions have improved to a certain extent nowadays, but touring still is no joke. Orchestra personalities sometimes clash, and many an enemy has been made, sometimes after a trivial incident on tour. There was an ugly scene in Baltimore towards the end of the American tour, partly because everyone was tired and at the end of their tether. There were Jewish groups carrying placards urging the boycott of the concert due to von Karajan's Nazi membership, and the evening concert was not well attended, unlike the rest of the tour where we had played to packed houses.

At the morning seating rehearsal, Peter Gibbs, a violinist who had been a fighter pilot during W.W.2, stood up and complained to von Karajan that his perfunctory conducting of the U.S. and British National Anthems was an insult to both countries and to the orchestra. This took von Karajan aback, and Legge, who was sitting in the hall, stood up and peremptorily told the violinist to sit down, which he did.

Afterwards, Legge went up to his favourite conductor and in order to mollify him, assured him that the violinist wouldn't be allowed to play that night. This seemed to soothe von Karajan, although he retorted that all the orchestra had applauded the violinist.

At the concert, the basses were seated stage-right so I couldn't see what was happening on the other side. Despite having been told by Legge that he was not to play, the violinist arrived at the concert in evening dress plus his violin, ready to play; von Karajan refused to go on unless the violinist was removed, but Dennis Brain the principal horn and Gareth

Morris, the principal flute among others said they would not go on the platform unless the violinist was allowed to play. The bickering went on and on, and fifteen minutes after the advertised start of the concert the audience began to give the slow handclap. Eventually the whole orchestra came onto the platform including the recalcitrant violinist; then von Karajan entered, and the concert began. At the intermission, however, there was more delay; again there was the slow handclap from the audience and eventually the concert continued.

The next day we were to play in Washington D.C. for our last concert of the tour and to depart the following day for London in our two chartered planes after touring the White House. The orchestra embarked but there was no sign of von Karajan. Apparently he was so miffed that he would not travel back with the orchestra, so he, Mattoni his manager and Legge, caught another plane home.

We had a few days off which we sorely needed and I came down with a bad case of the 'flu which I attributed to my body defences being lowered by the strenuous tour.

Some days later there was a recording session at the Kingsway Hall, and the chairman of the orchestra committee informed us after the session that the committee had received a letter in Pidgin English from von Karajan's Viennese lawyer demanding an apology signed by the whole orchestra. After much debate the orchestra voted that they were not prepared to sign a letter of apology, but instead, as it was nearly Christmastide, voted to send von Karajan a card wishing him a happy Christmas.

The outcome of this was damaging to the orchestra. Von Karajan pointed out to EMI/Angel/HMV records that although he had signed a contract with them it did not stipulate the orchestra to be employed, so therefore, in future, he would be using the Berlin Philharmonic for all the recordings he had contracted to do. This meant a real economic loss to the members of the Philharmonia and it was the catalyst, which later on, amongst other things, caused the orchestra's disbandment, but it was resuscitated as the New Philharmonia with Dr. Otto Klemperer at the helm.

Von Karajan's decision to record only with the Berlin Philharmonic showed that he was a very shrewd businessman. He was already conductor of the Berlin Philharmonic, the Vienna Staatsoper and had most of La Scala's conducting work so why would he need the Philharmonia anymore? It is my opinion that he had used Legge, and through him the Philharmonia, to further his career and was now looking for an excuse to break off the relationship. Certainly any loyalty he owed to Legge for having built him up didn't come into it. No, it was a cold business decision and the violinist's outburst had given him the opportunity he so badly needed to drop the Philharmonia.

Chapter 10 Notes
30. Literally, art comes after bread
31. The master is coming
32. Café
33. Pompous

CHAPTER 11

The Philharmonia Orchestra, continued. Conductors and soloists. Dennis Brain. Legge disbands the Philharmonia but it is resuscitated under Dr. Otto Klemperer. I decide to seek fresh fields to conquer.

Apart from von Karajan there were many other conductors and well known soloists who came to us.

One of the most promising was an Italian, Guido Cantelli, in his early thirties and a protégé of Arturo Toscanini. He stood on the podium gracefully and before he started to conduct, he would look down at his feet, then position himself precisely, taking an inordinate amount of time to do so, as I had noticed many other Italian conductors were wont to do. We made some recordings with him including Mendelssohn's *Scottish symphony* that I thought was particularly good. We gave a few concerts with him including the Edinburgh Festival where he gained much kudos.

He was rather amorously inclined. There was a pretty young girl who regularly attended our concerts and she came to Edinburgh to hear us. Brooks used to travel with her on the London Underground sometimes and we gave her the name of "Miss Hounslow West" that being her stop.

She was introduced to Cantelli who took a fancy to her. She was overawed at being dated by a conductor of his standing and went out with him a few times. I don't know whether the relationship was platonic or not and after nearly fifty years it doesn't seem to matter much but it was cut tragically short by Cantelli's death in an air crash.

Around that time, the mid 'fifties, there were many aircraft crashes. The "Viscount", one of the first jets had some troubles. A young French violinist, Ginette Neveu, was also killed in an air crash in 1949. The musicians gave her the pseudonym "The Girl with Balls" because she had such a big, beautiful tone and was a very musical player. Her death was a great loss to the world of music.

Another violinist to be killed in an air crash in 1953 was Jacques Thibaud, the violinist, who played with the LPO in 1945. He was a sensitive player, with a lush, not overly big sound, but he played with a lot of sparkle. He was a small, dapper little man man, dressed impeccably, and all the violinists in the LPO agreed that he had tremendous talent. He gave some wonderful performances of Lalo's *Symphonie Espagnole* and although he was around sixty-five years of age one would never have guessed it because of his youthful approach to music and life in general.

Some musicians refused to fly, one was Yehudi Menuhin, and I understood that he abstained from flying for many years until it became safer.

Another conductor who appeared with the Philharmonia many times was Eugene Ormandy who came across to me as a rather brash, "New York" type of conductor. He was a shortish man, plump, bald and Pickwickian in appearance. I never experienced any thrill from his performances, but they were good insofar as his tempi were rather brisk and the sound he obtained had a certain sparkle to it; this, coupled with a good stick technique enabled the players to never be in doubt as to precisely where to come in. He was at his best in Shostakovitch and Mahler.

Erich Leinsdorf was an excellent conductor. He was shortish, balding and a man of few words. He could obtain some wonderful performances with seemingly no effort; maybe this was due to his exceptional stick technique, but he was always cool, calm and collected. His Wagner and some of the German repertoire was remarkable.

My life as an orchestral musician has been spent mainly on the concert platform, behind the footlights, and I suppose conductors come across differently to the audience who are on the other side. There is a certain personal magnetism, electricity, penumbra, radiation or telepathy, call it what you will, that seems to exude from a really great conductor. There are many fine conductors who set a good tempo, have a good stick technique and can accompany a soloist but who lack this personal magnetism.

Some conductors attempt to fake this magnetism or try to create the atmosphere by dancing around on the podium and indulging in pyrotechnics. This never goes down very well and also defeats its object; self run orchestras never ask them back again.

Amongst others I met who had this personal magnetism were Anthony Eden, Laurence Olivier, Nadia Boulanger, Victor de Sabata, David Bohm and Jiddu Krishnamurti. It is a quality that no person can assume or try to acquire; either they have it or they do not.

David Bohm, the noted theoretical physicist, was my next-door neighbour in London. He was a pupil of Albert Einstein and famous for his discovery of the "Bohm effect" in atomic physics. Dave introduced me a couple of times to Jiddu Krishnamurti, the great Indian guru who was a friend of his and shared some of his philosophy. Both of these men influenced my life in many ways. Dave Bohm recounted to me the entire goings on of the Theosophical Society as told to him by Krishnamurti, and gave me an essay he had written on his philosophy of the nature of the world.

As there was a paucity of up and coming conductors at that time, Legge and a few others mounted a competition for young conductors that in the event proved to be disappointing. At the end of a cadenza in a Beethoven piano concerto, the general approach by these youngsters was to keep their baton in the air and then bring it down with an enormous whack to bring in the orchestra, as though they were swatting a gigantic fly. Of course it didn't work and the chord was ragged. They didn't know that the trick is to gently beat through the piano scale run leading up to the tutti so that the orchestra is prepared and the chord is precise. After the competition Legge was heard to declare that even the winners were only the best of a bad bunch. Zubin Mehta was one of the winners.

It doesn't hurt either for a conductor to give some silent beats "for nothing" on the finger so as to prepare a tempo beforehand. Maybe many think it looks amateurish, but I have known some fine conductors who used it. Another thing that has crept into conducting is to not use a baton. An experienced orchestra can pull a conductor through whilst he is standing on the podium looking up for a message from on high and engaging in all sorts of capers to the wonderment of a sometimes unsophisticated audience, but there is a certain code of signals that an orchestra expects and must be given by a conductor for a clear performance. Lack of a good stick technique, particularly in opera soon finds them out.

I am glad this practice of hands only conducting has now fallen somewhat into disfavour but there are one or two famous conductors who still conduct without a baton. One conductor I know has a hand problem and cannot hold a stick but still conducts very well and provided he has a good orchestra in front of him can obtain a good performance.

Issay Dobrowen was a very fine conductor, performing with us mainly the Russian repertoire. Winter or summer he always seemed to be wearing an Astrakhan hat and a coat with a collar of the same. He specialized in opera and certainly knew what he was doing; when he accompanied a soloist you always knew where you were for he had a clear, precise beat. Unfortunately he died at the early age of sixty-two.

Artur Rodzinsky was an artist who had that mystique that makes for a good conductor and I thought he was particularly good in Richard Strauss's works. Sadly enough, on one occasion he arrived at the EMI Abbey Road studios to conduct us but he looked very ill, his face was a ghastly white, and halfway through the recording session he had to leave and I never saw him again; he must have been in his early 60's at that time.

We made many recordings of singers and also complete operas. The best of the opera conductors I played for apart from de Sabata was undoubtedly Tullio Serafin who conducted the many arias that Maria Callas recorded with us. He was a short, slight man with thin grey hair and he must have been in his late seventies when I first encountered him. At that age he had a wealth of experience behind him and as soon as he lifted his baton it became evident. He seemed to impart to us that he had been there and done that, which of course he had. As an opera conductor should, he had a very concise beat but with no extraneous movements and was clear, calm and collected. Nothing ruffled him, and when I think how he had to work with a temperamental singer such as Maria Callas, that says a great deal. He seemed to put the singers at ease, not by words but with the quiet, businesslike but artistic way he worked.

When I first saw Maria Callas she was very heavily built but she slimmed down later on, so much so that she acquired a very svelte figure. She always reminded me of a highly-strung tigress who wore her heart on her sleeve and became very emotional at the slightest upset. Her husband at that time was an older, aristocratic looking Italian gentleman named Meneghini who was present at all her recordings, he was always impeccably dressed and looked very distinguished.

We recorded Rossini's opera *The Barber of Seville* with Maria Callas as Rosina, Tito Gobbi as Figaro and Alceo Galliera, the conductor, who was also a distinguished organist. When we started to record Rosina's famous aria "Una voce poco fa" Callas seemed to break up. We made several takes and the atmosphere was electric because one could see that she was becoming gradually more disconsolate as the recording proceeded and eventually she broke down and had a weeping fit. We all felt sorry for her and some of us wondered whether the recording would be discontinued, however, Legge put his arm around her and she went with him and Galliera behind the microphones into the control room. When she re-emerged she was much more composed, and after two more takes the aria was "in the can". Recording is a very nervy procedure especially when an artist knows that he or she is putting his/her reputation on the line. No wonder there are sometimes outbursts of temperament.

Years later in Vancouver, Canada, I played when she sang there together with Giuseppe de Stefano on their now famous ill-fated farewell tour. Twenty years had elapsed since I had last heard her sing; both singers were unfortunately past their prime, and the hall was not full.

Callas was never my favourite soprano despite the fact that nowadays she is a cult figure. But I'm sure that onstage say, in Tosca, she must have radiated an intense presence; her voice and passion were well suited to dramatic opera roles. She is reputed to have tried to correct de Sabata during the recording of Tosca, which I find very hard to believe.

The Philharmonia were booked to record Carl Orff's operas *Der Mond* (The Moon) and *Die Kluge* (The Wise Woman), with Wolfgang Sawallisch conducting. Orff was a pleasant little man, and I liked his operas. Unfortunately I am not aware of any recent availability of these opera recordings, and alas they are now removed from the HMV catalogue.

I was friendly with Walter Jellinek, who used to work as an assistant to von Karajan. Walter was a fine musician, and his wife was an accomplished 'cellist. He asked me if I would play for him in some performances of Mozart's opera *Bastien and Bastienne* that he was conducting, and doing it very well too. After the opera recordings had finished, Walter asked me if I would help him and Carl Orff make a recording of some of Orff's method for music education. There were only the three of us in the studio, Orff was beating a triangle, Walter a tambourine, and I had to make one or two bangs on a timpani. It was a real pleasure to work with Orff and I often wonder whether children are listening to that recording to this day.

Wolfgang Sawallisch was a very competent conductor who gave a very clear direction in every piece he tackled. He had a very good singing voice and I suppose that is why he seemed to be more at home conducting vocal music.

Paul Hindemith came to us for a week to record some of his works, including Mathis der Mahler. I forget the others we recorded, but when I mentioned to him his sonata for double bass and piano, he seemed to be disinterested in it. He conducted well, and, being a violinist and a violist, he had a great understanding of the technique of playing stringed instruments.

Aram Khatchachurian came to record for a week, and we recorded amongst other things his *Gayaneh* and *Masquerade* suites. He must have been in his early 'fifties at the time, a rather heavy man with brushed back curly iron-grey hair. He was very sensitive, maybe even a little neurotic and made all the more so by some of the amused smiles coming from the orchestra at what they deemed to be pop music. I have the greatest admiration for him and his works and I thought it unfair for him to be treated by the orchestra in this manner. Just because his pieces have catchy little tunes does not diminish his greatness, and at least one can leave the concert hall humming them, which cannot be said of many modern composers. I am sure his work will live on, maybe longer than the works of some of the so-called aesthetes.

Igor Markevich came to conduct a few pieces, among them Igor Stravinsky's *Rite of Spring*. The last few pages of the score seem to consist of a frenetic dogfight between the timps and the basses. Jim Bradshaw the timpanist came up to me in the intermission afterwards and told me he had complained to Legge about Markevitch saying his beat was no good. "Ah've got him the bluudy sack," he said in his North Country accent; but I don't think Legge agreed with Jim, as the records were issued and it was a best seller that is still being sold now on C.D.

Markevitch was steeped in the ballet tradition, and besides being a first-rate conductor was also a composer. He had been with Sergei Diaghilev's Ballet Russe. Markevitch was a slight man, nervous and taut on the podium. Despite Jim's assertions, I thought his conducting was clear. I played under him later at another recording session with the LSO when he was standing in at the last minute for another conductor, but he had aged and now wore a hearing aid. Some time afterwards when I was in Canada I formed an artist management company and Markevitch was on my list of artists whom I represented. He was living in Switzerland and we corresponded but I never met him personally after that LSO session.

Carlo Maria Giulini frequently conducted the Philharmonia. He was good in works by composers such as Maurice Ravel, Claude Debussy, Manuel de Falla and Igor Stravinsky. He had an intelligent air about him and he left the impression that he could delve down deeply in to the very soul of the music. There were no histrionics and he was always very calm on the podium; any remarks about the music were delivered in measured, cultured terms and he was a great favourite with the orchestra.

Another fairly frequent visitor to the Philharmonia was the Polish born Paul Kletzki, who was an "all rounder". Very good in Mahler, he once made an excellent recording of Mahler's *Song of the Earth* with the Philharmonia; aside from that he was equally at home in opera where he had an adroit hand in conducting recitatives, always helping the singers. He was also excellent in the symphonic repertoire of which he had an astounding knowledge. Legge did not use him for many concerts but mainly for recording, particularly as an accompanist to the many soloists who came. He was full of *bonhomie* and always got on well with the orchestra who in return gave him some wonderful performances. He was of medium height, often wore glasses and had a gravelly voice. I would not class him as one of the "truly greats", but he was certainly very good at whatever he conducted.

Lovro von Matačič, a Yugoslavian conductor in his mid to late 'fifties, joined us on a few occasions. He was tall and well-built. We were told that he had been imprisoned because of his political activities and had been befriended by von Karajan who recommended him to Legge. His musical background was impressive. As a boy he sang with the Wiener Sängerknaben and made his conducting debut in Cologne; after appointments in Ljubliana and Zagreb he became director of the Zagreb Opera.

His performances were notable for his overall view of the works he conducted. He could control all the subtle nuances and climaxes of any work he tackled, was not given to histrionics and brought a certain tranquility to his direction. Yet somehow there seemed to be an air of sadness about him that may have been the the result of his incarceration. At the time he was conducting us he was musical director of the Dresden Opera and later succeeded Solti at Frankfurt.

I can only mention a fraction of the soloists and conductors who came but standing head and shoulders above so many of the other violinists were Jascha Heifetz and David Oistrakh.

Comparisons are invidious but one cannot help noting the difference between the two men. Heifetz on the one hand was thin, aesthetic looking, of average height with brushed back curly grey hair. He rarely smiled and had an air of coldness, almost frigidity in his manner and he seemed to disassociate himself from the conductor and orchestra and keep in his own cocoon. It was not that he didn't co-operate with the conductor and orchestra, but there was always a sense of aloofness. There is only one occasion I can remember when he let his guard down and cracked a joke, saying that up until the age of forty you are trying to get a technique, and after the age of forty you are trying to keep it.

Heifetz has been criticized for a certain coldness in his playing but I never thought it was cold for he had a wonderful sound, a brilliant technique, and, most of all a great insight into the interpretation of the music that he played. He stood, solid as a rock without moving about or swaying, but the music kept flowing out of this remarkable man.

I had a very good rapport with Bertie Lewis, the "fixer" for the London Symphony Orchestra. He always phoned me to play as an extra if a good concert was coming up, and he once asked me to play with the LSO, Sargent conducting with Heifetz playing the Sibelius violin concerto.

In the last movement, second subject there is a syncopated rhythm for the second bass in the divisi bass part. Things were not going well, so Sargent stopped, and of all things asked me to play the part alone, by myself. This caused me some concern. I wondered if he was picking on me, or perhaps wanted to know how I played. Anyway, I played it, Sargent was satisfied and I noticed that Heifetz gave an approving grin. I mention this because it shows that when one is freelancing one cannot afford to make a mistake. If I had botched it, I would most certainly never have been phoned by the LSO again.

I'll give an example. I was playing in a performance of the tone poem *Till Eulenspiegel* by Richard Strauss, with the LSO conducted by Josef Krips. At the end of the piece there is a scream from the E flat clarinet represnting the scream from Till as he is about to be executed. The clarinettist botched it and I never again saw him playing with the LSO.

Recently I was playing with Ron Patterson, a pupil of Heifetz and he discussed Heifetz's teaching classes with me. You were allowed to tune once and once only before you played to him, there was to be no other tuning during the lesson. It could be that Heifetz had had the experience of his violin slipping out of tune at concerts and had learned to compensate for it and wished to instil this into his pupils.

Ron Patterson was concertmaster of the Monte Carlo Orchestra and knew David Wise who has now passed away. David at one time was concertmaster of the LPO and later principal second violin with the Philharmonia. At the end of one LPO Dutch tour, with conductors Sir Adrian Boult and Edouard van Beinum, we were going through customs and I was in front of David Wise and behind him was Sir Adrian Boult. When the Customs Officer asked David to open his violin case for inspection I noticed that it was full of watches he was trying to smuggle in. Sir Adrian was furious. Later on when his first wife passed away, Wise immigrated to Monte Carlo, married the daughter of an hotelier and played with Patterson in the Monte Carlo Orchestra. It's a small world!

On one occasion David Wise stayed to dinner at my house after we had rehearsed the Bottesini *Duo for violin and bass*. He placed his violin in Nicholas, my son's hands, and said, "Now, you can say you held a Strad in your hands." We ran through it later on in a rehearsal lunch break with Raymond Leppard on piano. He declared, "What a strange piece!"

I played with Heifetz many times, and the concerto I thought he played magnificently was the Tchaikowsky. In the last movement, second subject it gave me a thrill to hear him play glissandi on the G string in a very schmaltzy way.

I think he liked Sir Malcolm Sargent to conduct the orchestra, as he had a very clear beat and was a good accompanist.

David Oistrakh was different altogether from Heifetz. He was of medium build, rather paunchy with a slightly protruding lower lip and thinning black hair. He was a warm man, and his playing reflected his personality. He could play all the "fireworks" too but in the slow movements especially he was noted for his smooth, singing tone and was altogether a great man and a fine musician. If I were asked which concerto I most admired him play it would have to be the Brahms, for he really plumbed the depths of the piece with his warm tone and dignified approach. David Wise told me that he often played duets and chamber music with Oistrahk on their days off, and that he had a wonderful, friendly mien.

David Oistrakh's son, Igor, was also a violin soloist. I played with him once, at the Lucerne International Festival, Switzerland. He was very good, but not in the same league as his father.

Having talked of Oistrakh and Heifetz I must mention other violinists. There was Zino Francescatti, a truly great player; Yehudi Menuhin, who was not entirely consistent with his playing, but when he was on form was wonderful. Isaac Stern had a lovely warm sound as well as a good technique but his performances were sometimes inclined to be patchy. The last time I played with Stern was in New York at the United Nations on United Nations Day. He should be especially remembered for the tremendous amount of work he did in saving the Carnegie Hall, which to my mind is one of the best halls I ever played in, having a rich and resonant sound. Henryk Szeryng and Arthur Grumiaux remain indelibly rooted in my memory, for they were both fantastic violinists.

Josef Szigeti I encountered when he was getting on in years; he nevertheless proved himself a formidable violinist, as was Nathan Milstein who was a short, neat little man, always well dressed even for recording sessions, where musicians usually arrive in casual clothes. He played like he looked, neatly (in the old sense of the word) but gave some of the best interpretations I have ever heard.

Tragically there was a boy named Michael Rabin, round about 18 – 20 years old who recorded two Paganini violin concertos with us. His playing was superb and he showed great promise. He was very exuberant, almost childlike in his playful manner, but he was very overweight. His mother was present at all the sessions and kept perhaps an over-watchful eye on him. I heard years later that he had taken his own life; what a loss to music.

Jelly d'Aranyi was another of the old school of the Hungarian "greats". She played the violin with much aplomb, giving some wonderful interpretations. She had a fine technique, and, even in later years an impressive stage presence.

Before leaving my recollections of violinists I should mention Alfredo Campoli whom I knew well. My father always liked his records, and when I was a kid often played them to me. The story has it that Beecham was eating at a restaurant where Campoli was playing, and Campoli, knowing that Beecham was there played the Mendelssohn violin concerto. Beecham sent him a note correcting his tempi.

One day we were to record the ballet, *Swan Lake*, and Legge decided at the last minute he would not use Manoug Parikian the concertmaster to play the violin solos. Instead he phoned Campoli to come along to the studio immediately and play. Apparently Campoli was in his garden enjoying the flowers and said to Legge that he was having a lovely time in his garden, it being a beautiful day and "No", he would not come. We all admired Campoli for that. The last time I saw him was when I was principal bass with the Vancouver Symphony, and he came to play - guess what - the Mendelssohn concerto! We chatted for quite a while about old times and that was the last I ever saw of him. I noticed that he had put on weight, and no wonder, for like Sir Adrian Boult he could gorge two complete meals at one sitting, although Boult's metabolism still kept his trim figure.

There were many world-class 'cellists in those days and at the forefront of these was Mstislav Rostropovitch. I won't compare him with Casals whom I have already mentioned and who was in a class of his own but Rostropovitch was superb in everything he played. He once played the whole of the 'cello concerto repertoire at a marathon series of concerts in which I played with the LSO. In recording he just seemed to go through everything like a breeze. For example, he was recording Tchaikowsky's Rococco Variations with the Philharmonia wherein is a very difficult section that has some tough double-stopping, i.e. playing on two strings at the same time. Rostropovitch just sailed through the passage and we recorded it in one take. Apart from his technical ability he had a fine tone and played with sensitive musicianship. He was always a favourite with the orchestra.

Gregor Piatigorsky was a giant of a man as well as a giant of the 'cello and I enjoyed his playing and his personality. He brought out a huge tone from his instrument and in order to emphasize a particular note would stamp with his foot as well as put great pressure on the bow.

Paul Tortellier was what I call a "clean" player; every note was neatly there. He made us laugh with his eccentric dancing during breaks in the "takes" of recording sessions at which his young wife was always present. He owned a marvellous instrument that had a fine sound.

Pierre Fournier played the 'cello in a refined, intellectual and musical way. I remember some excellent performances, particularly of the Dvorak 'cello concerto.

Andre Navarra was a swarthy man, blue from the razor, who looked as if he could have been a blacksmith. He played just as he looked, with great passion. He too gave great performances of the Dvorak concerto.

Janos Starker was a frequent visitor and excelled particularly in Bach.

To round off the list with some lady 'cellists last but by no means least, Mme. Guilhermina Suggia, Zara Nelsova and Jacqueline Du Pré were all exceptional players.

When I was with the Vancouver Symphony, Jacqueline du Pré played with us. I have never ever seen or heard any soloist put so much into their playing. She played the Elgar concerto with such gusto that she had the audience leaping to their feet, and I noticed when she took her bows, her back being towards me, she was absolutely soaked with perspiration. She passed away some time later of multiple sclerosis.

Claudio Arrau was indeed one of the finest pianists of my day and Vladimir Horowitz also came into that category, although they each had different personalities and a different approach to the music they played.

Arturo Michelangeli played with us at concerts and recordings and he was well known for his eccentricities. At Abbey Road studios he took great pains to adjust the piano bench, sat down, and then began to play but shortly afterwards he stopped abruptly and there was a pause for about ten minutes, after which he decided to play again. We made a take and then he had another rest. I could see Legge biting his nails, because to record with a big symphony orchestra and a soloist plus all the engineers and back-up men is an expensive proposition. We made another start and recorded a little, and then the session was called off. I don't know whether he was ill or what, but next day we repeated the same procedure eventually finishing the work the day after that.

Walter Gieseking was a superb pianist, especially, I thought, in Beethoven and Mozart. To quote a time worn simile his runs were like a string of pearls. He was a well-built man with thin, greyish hair, and would have been in his late fifties when he performed with the Philharmonia, but was tragically killed in a bus crash in 1956.

Solomon, (Solomon Cutner), one of the finest pianists of his day had his highly successful career cut short in his prime, probably in his mid-fifties. He was a likeable man of medium build, bald except for just a fringe of hair, and clean-shaven.

He was recording all the five Beethoven pianoforte concerti with the Philharmonia and with Herbert Menges conducting, at the Abbey Road studios. The recording sessions went very well until we came to the *Emperor*; concerto number five, when Solomon's playing became very erratic after the first movement. Legge came out of the control room and had words with Menges. The session ended and Herbert asked me if I would give him a lift in my car to St. John's Wood underground station. On the way he confided in me that he was sure Legge would blame him for the disastrous way the recording was going. I felt very sympathetic with Menges because the *Emperor* is a difficult concerto for a conductor to accompany and despite Menges best efforts to keep things together, Solomon seemed to be all over the place. We bade each other goodnight and hoped the next day would be better.

After a seemingly endless number of takes we got it in the can and Solomon, Menges and, most importantly, Legge were satisfied. To celebrate the event Solomon invited all the orchestra for a drink at a nearby pub where his wife joined us - a charming lady who accompanied him everywhere - and we all drank to each other's health. Unhappily we learned the reason why he had been having such difficulties, next day he suffered a severe stroke and could never play again.

Cyril Smith was a wonderful pianist when in his prime. He played the Brahms and Rachmaninoff concerti very well, and produced a huge tone without a thump. Like Solomon he suffered a stroke, and was reduced to playing pieces for three hands with his wife, Phyllis Sellick.

Clara Haskill played with us on many occasions. She was a slight, delicate, frail looking woman, but the music that she made was wonderful, particularly her Mozart.

Victoria de los Angeles was a remarkable singer with a lovely stage presence. Her voice, too, was truly lovely, but not only that, it was the way she delivered the most gorgeous sounds in a commanding manner that made her one of my favourites. I have run out of superlatives for de los Angeles.

I shall now go back to the workings of the Philharmonia and a conductor who had a great influence upon its future: Dr. Otto Klemperer.

Klemperer was a legendary figure when he came to the Philharmonia in the 'fifties. He was steeped in the German/Austrian tradition, having conducted many of their great orchestras and also in their opera houses. After emigrating to the U.S.A he conducted the Philadelphia, New York and Los Angeles Orchestras. He gave the first German performances of Janacek's opera *Katya Kabanova*, Zemlinski's, *Der Zwerg*, Schreker's *Irrelohe* and Stravinsky's *Oedipus Rex* as well as the first performance of Schoenberg's arrangement of Brahms' *G minor Pianoforte Quartet*.

Forgive me as a mere dwarf for criticizing such a giant as Klemperer. If my analysis of him at times appears to be too harsh, it must be borne in mind that these are my memoirs and I have to write down truthfully my recollections. I am sure that in his younger days he must have been a formidable conductor, one of the truly "greats", but when I played for him, Klemperer was in his late seventies and well past his prime.

A good-looking man, tall, with black hair brushed back and streaked with grey, he wore horn-rimmed glasses and had a very noticeable stoop. He had had a stroke which distorted his mouth and therefore his speech was somewhat slurred. At times he used a cane to walk and sometimes had to sit when conducting.

When he laughed, which he did on occasion, it sounded almost maniacal. Apparently in his earlier days he suffered from fits of blind rage; he was indeed a manic-depressive and his doctors chose to resort to heroic measures. For Klemperer it was to be a lobotomy, which is a grisly procedure with a scalpel being gouged around a certain part of the brain after a hole was cut in the head. For him to have been able to conduct with all those impediments was truly remarkable, even more so, to obtain the sweeping monumental performances that he did was little short of a miracle.

His daughter, Lotte, accompanied him everywhere and ministered to all his needs, and she saved his life on one occasion when they were staying in a hotel. In the middle of the night she woke up with a premonition that her father was in trouble. She put on her dressing gown and walked down the corridor to his room where she noticed smoke billowing under the door. She called the management, who called the fire brigade. The fire was put out and Klemperer was rescued, and although he was badly burned he recovered quickly. He had been smoking in bed and had dozed off while his cigarette was still burning. The members of the Philharmonia Orchestra sent him a get well card that he appreciated very much.

He once said to us that in a slow 2/4 beat the audience could listen to it as a quick divided 4/4. The logic of this escapes me, perhaps I heard it wrong, but this did not prevent me in my humble way thinking that often his tempi were far too slow, for example the slow movement of Beethoven's Pastoral Symphony seemed to go on forever; it didn't seem to be like a babbling brook but a turgid slough of stagnant water, moreover he insisted on making all the repeats which are more often than not left out.

If one compares his tempi with Toscanini's Beethoven however, which are like lightning then they are very pedestrian. But, after a time, listening back to Klemperer, his performances had a certain grandeur that Toscanini never attained. I have only listened to the Toscanini recordings, but I have talked with musicians who had played at Toscanini's concert performances as well as those of Klemperer, and they agreed with my observations.

Beethoven, Brahms, Bruckner and Mahler were his forte and I never understood how he managed to get such precise performances, for he conducted sometimes in those days without a baton and his hands trembled. Although he succeeded in part by having such a good orchestra in front of him, it was his own grand overview of a whole work that made him so exceptional. On the other hand I did not care much for his Haydn or Mozart. There was no sparkle or *joie de vivre* and he came across to me in Mozart as being like a Dutch peasant wearing clogs trampling through a field of tulips.

We recorded the Mozart and Richard Srauss horn concerti with Dennis Brain, Klemperer conducting. After the sessions I noticed Dennis almost in tears because of Klemperer's clumsy accompaniment. These recordings were never issued at the time and we re-recorded them later with Wolfgang Sawallisch and von Karajan conducting.

Klemperer's fondness for the opposite sex was notorious and scandalous in his younger days, so I have read, and it was fully in evidence when he was with us. There was a very beautiful auburn haired 'cellist in the orchestra. All the men remarked from time to time on her stunning beauty and lovely figure which Klemperer had obviously noted, for he came up to her one day and said in his gruff voice, "I will buy you a fur coat if you come to bed with me." Really! Only an old man in his dotage would have said such a thing; I don't know what the lady in question replied, but, of course, it was all round the orchestra within five minutes.

He wouldn't take "No" for an answer. Recently I was chatting on the phone with Lorraine du Val, a brilliant violinist playing in the Philharmonia at that time but who is now retired and living in Canada. She told me about the time in the Kingsway Hall when the girl 'cellist came running breathlessly into the ladies' room looking very flustered. When asked what was the matter she replied that Klemperer was chasing her! He had a contretemps with von Karajan who eventually forbade him to come to his sessions because he used to sit at the back of the hall ogling the 'cellist.

Klemperer well knew the wiles of orchestral musicians. At one rehearsal there was no second bassoon and Klemperer in his mixture of German and English enquired, "Wo ist mein second fagott?" The reply was that the man in question was ill, but Klemperer said, "I don't think he is ill, I think he has another job," and he was right!

He was a resigner. Apparently there was an altercation between Klemperer and John Cruft, who was the manager of the LSO. Klemperer told John Cruft in a huff at the morning rehearsal that he wouldn't conduct the concert that night, but John Cruft called his bluff by saying, "Very well, Dr. Klemperer, I'm sorry you won't be conducting the concert, we'll have to find someone else." However, Klemperer <u>did</u> conduct the concert.

During a rehearsal intermission after we had been rehearsing the slow movement of Beethoven's Ninth Symphony that had dragged on interminably, someone quipped that we should have a Beethoven cycle. Everyone groaned but it must have got back to Legge and, sure enough, a Beethoven cycle was arranged. It was so popular that we played several of them. It was back-breaking work for the basses, for besides being technically difficult, the Beethoven works are also very physically demanding. Included were all of the symphonies, the piano concerti, the violin concerto, sometimes the triple concerto, all the overtures and invariably a soprano sailed onstage to sing the aria *Oh Monstrous Fiend* from his opera *Fidelio*.

A tragedy struck the Philharmonia that was to have repercussions later on. We were playing at the Edinburgh Festival in 1957 and after the last concert on August 31st, a Saturday, I took my bass outside the Usher Hall to put it in its shipping case. Most of us were travelling back to London in an overnight sleeper train but I came across Dennis Brain getting in to his Triumph sports car. I asked him if he was going to drive all the way back that night, about 400 miles, a trip I would not have relished especially after a difficult, tiring concert. Dennis was adamant that he was going to drive so we said 'cheerio' to each other and that was the last I ever saw of him. Apparently he crashed his car not far from the outskirts of London.

On arrival in London I travelled on a Tube train together with his brother, Leonard Brain, who had been playing oboe and English horn at Edinburgh. When I entered my front door the news of Dennis's death was being broadcast.

The following Monday just before we were due to record at the Kingsway Hall, Legge stood before the orchestra in tears and gave a short eulogy for Dennis. Alan Civil was appointed as his replacement but although Alan was a fine player he never seemed to me to reach Dennis's standard, Dennis was exceptional.

Besides being a French horn virtuoso, Dennis was also a gifted organist and played the organ in one recording session I played at. He was not in the least bit haughty or conceited despite his great talent, and was, in fact, a quiet, gentle, modest man. At the recording sessions held in the Kingsway Hall, London, the horns and the basses were seated closely, so I had ample opportunity of chatting with him and discovering his subtle wit.

His father, Aubrey Brain, first horn of the BBC Symphony Orchestra for many years was also a virtuoso player; some said he was even better than Dennis. Aubrey could play chords on the horn; I think he played a note on the instrument and then hummed another note in harmony. During the war, in the blackout which was enforced because of air raids, Aubrey had the misfortune to drive his car over a sea wall on to the beach below. His legs were hurt severely and I don't think he ever did fully recover. I remember on occasion playing with him when he was fourth horn at Sadlers Wells Opera, but even that was too much for him so he eventually retired.

Dennis, when I first knew him played the old narrow bore three valve French model horn, but he later changed to the larger bore German double horn which now seems to be universally popular although I always think the sound of the German instrument to be somewhat coarser than the French.

Dennis was an avid fan of motor racing and on his music stand there was always a copy of "Motor Sport" which he used to read intently, but miraculously he always knew when to come in; he just lifted his horn and played perfectly and in the right place. Von Karajan was never happy about this, and once exclaimed icily, "You must have a very interesting book on your stand, Mr. Brain," at which Dennis just smiled.

Dennis told me this story: He was asked by an amateur music society to play two horn concerti with them. A modest fee was arranged (Dennis never charged exorbitant fees although he could well have done) and he arrived at the concert and played the first concerto. During the intermission the president of the society came up to him and said he was afraid his society was in financial straits and could not afford his fee, handing him a cheque for a lesser amount than had been agreed upon. Dennis said nothing but quietly got into his car and left.

Due to the von Karajan affair and the loss of some of our work to the Berlin Philharmonic, our pay was becoming more meagre and I saw the writing on the wall. Because of this and other things that were happening, I thought it had become time to say goodbye to the Philharmonia and resume my freelancing which I really enjoyed better. This was another occasion when one of my hunches paid off, for not long afterwards Legge announced that he was disbanding the orchestra because there didn't seem to be the calibre of musicians available. Looking back I think it was due to von Karajan's desertion of the ship and also Dennis Brain's demise that triggered his decision but there may have been other factors of which I was not aware.

This is where Klemperer came in. Naturally the orchestra itself was against disbandment and Klemperer, who turned on Legge, thereafter referring to him as 'that man', agreed to pilot them into a new future. To avoid any legal action over the use of the name they re-named it the "New Philharmonia", and formed a committee to run it with Bernard Walton, the principal clarinet, as chairman, and appointed Dr. Otto Klemperer as its conductor-in-chief, later to appoint him Conductor for Life. The New Philharmonia went through a pretty tough time. Remember that there were (and still are) five symphony orchestras in cutthroat competition with each other in London, but they weathered the storm, bringing in other conductors such as Riccardo Muti.

Walter Legge seemed to slip into oblivion, but he did much for the London music scene. History should give him all the credit that he deserves as an impresario who brought in great artists, upgraded the orchestral standards, and promoted the Philharmonia through its world-wide tours and its records, many of which have been re-mastered and are still sold to this day.

Chapter 12

After the Philharmonia, back to freelancing and I later join the BBC Symphony Orchestra. Some conductors, including Stravinsky.

I left the Philharmonia with some qualms, and I soon discovered that the freelance world had changed. There was not so much work about, at least for me, but that was understandable since I had given up some of my connections.

Work gradually began to come in, though. Some not very first rate, for example, going down to all sorts of places for Doris Greenish to play principal for amateur societies. I also had a good connection with the BBC partly due to the fact that I had auditioned for them and had been offered principal bass with the BBC Scottish Orchestra. I got as far as arranging to catch a sleeper train up to Scotland to start playing with them, but at the last moment I got cold feet. I considered the upheaval the move would cause my family when it came to selling the house and moving all the furniture up to Glasgow. Oddly enough, my wife was all for the move, a complete about face for her considering she had opposed my going to Geneva, Switzerland, and Santiago, Chile, to join their respective orchestras.

George Willoughby, the BBC orchestral manager, strangely did not bear me a grudge over the Scottish affair, and I was phoned often to deputize with the BBC Symphony Orchestra and other BBC orchestras.

My friend, Gerald Drucker was principal bass of the BBC Symphony Orchestra at the time and asked me if I would care to join them. Willoughby had said there would be no need for an audition as I had recently given one for Scotland, so I agreed.

I reflected that I had tied myself up with the Philharmonia, was now beginning to get my connections back and wondered if I would be making a big mistake. After all, freelancing was in my blood, and apart from earning more money, it was the thrill of arriving, often at the last moment, and being able to pull off a difficult programme. I was also constantly meeting different people and playing a much greater, varied repertoire. Very often there was no chance to look at the music beforehand. Sometimes if I learned that something particularly difficult was coming up in the near future, I would try to obtain the part by hook or by crook and practice it in between breaks in rehearsals and sessions. There was no time to practice it at home as I was always away from morning 'till night. Failing to play impeccably at the session or concert just meant that you were never asked again; it was as simple as that. Nobody complained to you, you were just left out.

The BBC was not a thrilling job; it was more like the civil service. The players were all competent; having been auditioned thoroughly, but there wasn't that spark, that superb sound that I had heard when I was with the Philharmonia. The atmosphere was different too, it wasn't alive.

True, you knew exactly what your hours would be and when you would take your holidays, so that you could plan ahead. But the holidays did not coincide with school holidays, because of the Proms, so we could not go away on holiday together as a family. During the Proms, my wife used to take the kids down to Brighton to stay with her parents. I used to scramble for the last train to Brighton after the concert on Saturday nights, spend Sunday with the family and catch the first train back to London for a morning rehearsal.

The pay was not good. A year or so before I joined the BBC Symphony Orchestra, there had been a strike because the pay had not gone up sufficiently since before WW2 when the pay was eleven pounds a week, a princely sum in those days, but when I joined them in the late 'fifties the pay was nineteen pounds nineteen shillings a week and it had not kept up with inflation; in addition, the workload had increased sharply. Repeats of radio broadcasts and televised concerts were paid extra, though.

When the BBC Symphony Orchestra was formed in 1930 there was much excitement when Broadcasting House was built in Central London. Over the entrance there was a piece of sculpture by Jacob Epstein. A renowned architect had designed the concert hall but had just measured the distance between two chairs and multiplied it by the number of players in the orchestra, and when it came to the first rehearsal there was no elbow room so the space was used for smaller groups and an alternative venue had to be found; Maida Vale, situated in West London.

Before the war the BBC was nicknamed the "lifeboat" because in 1930 there was a big economic slump and coupled with that, all the cinemas that used to employ musicians had gone over to talkies and consequently many musicians were thrown out of employment.

The only other employment open to musicians before WW2 were casual dates in tea rooms or hotels, summer seasons at holiday resorts, theatre orchestras and a little symphony and opera work. There was an office and snack bar at the Musicians' Union club on Archer Street in the West End of London where all the musicians used to congregate to solicit engagements. Everyone carried a business card as there were not many telephones in those days and communication was either by telegram, letter, or through meeting somebody at the Archer Street Club.

Symphony and Opera then were nothing like as busy as today. As I already mentioned, the BBC Symphony Orchestra was formed in 1930, the London Philharmonic Orchestra (not then a full time orchestra) was formed in 1932 and the London Symphony Orchestra, a freelance group, was founded in 1904. No wonder my father used the appellation "precarious" to describe the musical profession.

There were many things to be said in favour of the BBC; one good thing was that they always booked the BBC Symphony Orchestra into the best hotels when they had out-of-town engagements, and if we had a run-out concert they would pay for us to have lunch or dinner in the best available restaurant.

I struck a deal with George Willoughby that I would be paid at casual rates (I missed out on a pension by doing so) that worked out to be more than the weekly wage; in addition I would be allowed to accept chamber music engagements and other important dates outside the BBC.

The resident conductor at that time was Rudolf Schwarz who had previously conducted the Bournemouth Symphony Orchestra and had held other jobs in Germany. He was Jewish, and was incarcerated in a concentration camp in Germany during WW2 where, it was said, he had been strung up by his arms, which impeded his ability to conduct, and although the orchestra was very understanding of his disability, he was very difficult to follow at times. He was a quiet and gentle man, very courteous, but his music seemed to emerge like his personality; it was all rather uninspired and never coalesced into a brilliant performance. Having said that, however, he was a good musician and had an excellent ear.

Jean Martinon, another contemporary conductor, is reputed to have suffered this treatment when imprisoned by the Nazis.

One of the guest conductors who came to the BBC Symphony Orchestra was Hans Schmidt-Isserstedt, the conductor of the German Nordwest Rundfunk Orchestra stationed in Hamburg. He was very good in the German classics and obtained some fine performances. He had an artificial leg and used to limp to the podium. He was also fond of the ladies and formed a liaison with one of the lady violinists. That sort of thing was deeply frowned upon by the BBC hierarchy and I think it all stemmed from its first director-general, Sir John Reith who was noted for his stern, puritanical attitude. Because of all this the Press often dubbed it "Auntie BBC". When it came to the ears of somebody in authority, the offending violinist was let go. She was told that it was because her playing was not up to standard, but we all knew the real reason. I remember when she played her last concert at Maida Vale one Saturday night she came into the studio absolutely hysterical and distraught; Paul Beard tried to calm her down and she left. After the incident with the violinist I don't think Schmidt-Issersedt was often engaged.

Another such occasion was when one of the brass players became over-friendly with a viola player; he too was fired. Archie Camden, the famous bassoonist, once told me that when he was first bassoon in the BBC Symphony Orchestra in the old days he had gone through a divorce and re-married. He wrote to Mr. Pratt the orchestral manager at that time, telling him of his marital status and received a terse letter, which read, "We are not interested." Pratt by all accounts was a martinet; he kept a dossier on each member of the BBC S.O. They all referred to it as their "crime sheet". Even the slightest infringement of the many rules was noted. One woman told me that as she entered a concert hall for a performance, Pratt noticed a thin piece of white piping on the collar of her dress and said to her sententiously, "No piping, if you please." The men were obliged to wear ties and jackets at rehearsals, and when some of them removed their jackets in very hot weather the BBC provided them with light jackets to wear in case the eyes of any visitor would be offended. How different are the dress codes of today. When the Queen came to visit, the offending signs "Ladies" and "Gentlemen" on the washrooms by the entrance were hidden with flowers.

The woodwinds in pre-war days were legendary, many of them over-conceited and a bane to some visiting conductors. For this reason they were nicknamed the "Royal Family". I never found Archie Camden to be at all like this but the oboist Alec Whittaker certainly was; he did not like taking direction from anybody. A famous tale told by all the old hands relates to an incident when Toscanini was conducting them. The maestro asked for something from the oboes and Alec muttered out loud, "Bloody old organ grinder." Apparently there was no reaction from Toscanini; perhaps he had not understood Alec's remark.

Alec left the BBC and I often saw him around freelancing but there came a time when I did not see or hear of him so I thought he had retired. Years later I was playing in the Shakespeare Memorial Theatre, Stratford-upon-Avon. After the rehearsal I crossed the road to get a pub lunch. Behind the bar was Alec, playing the part of Mine Host. As he was fond of his tipple I ruminated to myself what an apt retirement he had chosen.

Another conductor who came to the the the BBC Symphony was Nino Sanzogno, whom I thought to be absolutely first class. He had conducted at La Scala, Milan, and La Fenice in Venice, and his conducting reminded me very much of de Sabata. He could draw out that fire and élan from an orchestra that only the "greats" can do. Paul Beard remarked to me that Sanzogno was an orchestral player's dream of what a great conductor should be.

I ran across Jascha Horenstein on a few occasions in various London orchestras. He was a very experienced conductor, having commenced his career as conductor of the Düsseldorf Opera and later conducted several orchestras in Europe and the U.S.A. He conducted with sweeping strokes of a very long baton. He was a man of few words, everything he needed to convey to the orchestra was with his hands, and they were easy to follow. I thought he was at his best in Schubert, Mahler and Bruckner of which he gave some wonderful performances. In appearance he was tallish, thin with a skull-like face that seemed to inspire a certain mysteriousness, and he never smiled.

One of the greatest artists I have ever encountered was Segovia the guitarist, who came to the BBC round about 1960. He was already getting on in years, about sixty-six years of age, of middle height with rather flowing greyish hair, heavily built and with an unassuming air. His playing seemed to flow so easily from him; it was nothing short of incredible. There were no histrionics, no mannerisms but the music just welled out.

Igor Stravinsky came to the BBC Symphony Orchestra to conduct some of his works. He conducted well and could convey very clearly exactly what he wanted. Robert Craft prepared the orchestra for him and acted as his general assistant.

When he was living in Switzerland during WWI, some publishers had blatantly used his music without paying him for the copyright. This affected him profoundly, and he became very money-conscious in later life, which was illustrated by an event that took place when he came to the BBC.

Our Saturday night broadcasts were usually over around 9.30 p.m. The orchestra had packed up and were leaving, so Edgar Mayes, the orchestra factotum went up to Stravinsky who was still standing on the podium and asked him if he could get his coat and hat and call a taxi, then asked him if there was anything else he needed. Stravinsky replied, "Yes, vere is ze scheck?" Edgar told him that the cheque would be sent to him by mail, but this did not suit Stravinsky who said, "I have heard all zat before, I vant ze scheck now!" Edgar tried to placate him, but Stravinsky would have none of it, so the only thing to do was to try to obtain the cheque by phoning the chief cashier, who lived in a suburb south of London. He caught a train as soon as possible, collected the cheque from Broadcasting House in Central London, and then brought it over to Maida Vale studios in West London. It was past midnight when he presented it to Stravinsky who just said, "Zank you very much," and departed.

I was asked if I would be interested in playing some chamber concerts which were to be directed by Pablo Casals at the Prades Festival in France, near the Spanish border. The BBC granted my request to go to Prades, but shortly afterwards a certain bass player notified Willoughby that the chamber group was to be augmented for one concert at which Beethoven's First Symphony would be on the programme. I was unaware of this until Willoughby told me that as a symphony was to be performed it could hardly be considered to be totally chamber music, therefore permission was now denied.

It seemed to me that I would not advance very far in the profession if the BBC continued to interpret my contract in such narrow terms. Prades was a very prestigious festival and I did not want a denial should another big opportunity present itself, so, after much deliberation I decided to leave the BBC and free-lance again.

CHAPTER 13

Life after the BBC Symphony Orchestra. I become too big for my boots. I am booked as principal bass for the New Opera Company. The Early Verdi Society and the Handel Opera Society. The Philomusica. More ballets. Principal bass for the San Carlo Opera. Tragedy at Sadlers Wells, I am asked to play the season with them as principal bass.

It was with some trepidation that I entered the big world outside the BBC. But I needn't have worried because firstly, I was offered much of the BBC extra work and secondly, Morris Smith immediately offered me a season as principal bass at Covent Garden with their ballet company.

Things went smoothly and there were several other dates that Morris offered me. However, for one performance I put in a deputy because I was offered a really prestigious engagement that clashed with the ballet. Although the deputy was a leading bass player, I should have asked Morris's permission first. In hindsight it was a bad thing for me to have done, for Morris became extremely annoyed. He let me finish the ballet season and then cancelled all the other engagements he had given me, and never ever offered me another date afterwards.

This became a wake-up call for me. I had become too complacent; work came in so readily that I became big-headed with my own importance. I learned the lesson the hard way, that nobody is indispensable, least of all musicians. I went through a tough time and had to sell my expensive car. But one thing about freelancing is that when one door closes, another one opens.

There were several small ventures taking place in London and soon I was booked as principal bass for a number of companies.

There was the New Opera Company, which gave performances of such operas as *Die Erwartung* by Schoenberg, *Il Prigioniero* by Dallapiccola, *A Tale of Two Cities* and *The Moon and Sixpence* by Arthur Benjamin as well as Menotti's *The Unicorn, the Gorgon and the Manticore* and Stravinsky's *Le Rossignol, (the Nightingale)* and *Oedipus Rex*.

Another company was the Early Verdi Society, which gave performances of *Un Giorno di Regno* and *Ernani*.

There was also the Handel Opera Society, which gave amongst others, performances of *Rinaldo*.

John Cage, the famous American composer came to conduct a week of his ballets at Sadlers Wells in the early fifties and I was booked as principal bass. Merc Cunningham, his lifelong friend and collaborator was there. Of course, there was the usual "prepared piano" which Cage had invented; it was achieved by putting pieces of paper between the strings of the piano. There were fun and games in the pit as we were asked to knock over music stands at random, pluck our strings or bang the bow on the fingerboard of the instrument whenever the mood took us. Even the pit door was opened and banged shut a few times, which caused much mirth. I am not condemning this "music", if it could be called that. Perhaps John Cage was a misdirected genius, although his musical background was significant. He had studied with Schoenberg and Varese amongst others and had had a thorough musical education, so he cannot be dismissed out of hand.

Cage was a softly spoken man, with a broad American twang to his voice. He gave me the impression that he was trying to go beyond the recognized norm of the day; he had experimented with electronic music too.

Very often if a person tries to be *avant-garde* as Cage did, they inevitably come in for a lot of derogatory comment, but without experimentation and trying new things, music will surely die. If one looks at the same old programming of some symphony orchestras and opera companies it is a wonder they attract much of an audience at all.

I was engaged as principal double-bass when Roland Petit came over to London with his own ballet company and amongst other things they were performing his ballet, *Cyrano de Bergerac*. Petit was a rather brusque character. At one rehearsal of his ballet, the conductor, who had been principal timpanist in L'Ochestre Suisse Romande, expostulated that one particular tempo was too quick. "C'est la musique," he said, but Petit shouted angrily, "Merde! C'est mon ballet, la musique n'est rien." ("Shit! it's my ballet, the music is nothing.") Marius Constant who composed the music was present and I often wonder what his reaction was to Petit's description of the music.

I had seen Robert Helpmann in his younger days as a solo dancer, but later on he took on such character parts as Dr. Coppelius from the ballet *Coppelia* and he also choreographed some very successful ballets. I played once in Bliss's ballet, *Miracle in the Gorbals*, that was a great success. He could be very painstaking and demanding of the corps de ballet and I remember in one of his ballets there was a cortège in which four dancers were carrying a supposedly dead man. Something went wrong at the rehearsal and Helpmann ranted at them calling them "bloody this" and "bloody that". Nevertheless, he got what he wanted and the ballet was received with acclaim.

The music director of the Philomusica, a very good chamber orchestra, was George Malcolm, an eminent harpsichordist, and also Director of Music at Westminster Cathedral. The Philomusica often used only one double bass, Francis Baines, who was a "character", slightly eccentric, a good musician and a composer. Besides playing the bass he also played amongst other things the hurdy-gurdy. He lived on a barge on the River Thames near Chelsea. I visited him there once and he asked me if I would like some cheese. I said I would and he proceeded to lower a cage with a pulley from the ceiling and then said, "Mice, ye know."

I first met him in the London Philharmonic. Because he needed more time to compose, he and his partner June Hardy, a violinist, plus a baby they had adopted went to live for a year in a small cottage outside London. When he returned to London to take up playing again I asked him if he had learned anything from his experience. His reply was very profound, and one that I will always remember; he said,"Yes, I did. You don't need as much to live on as you think, or are made to think you do."

He had a very loud voice. Once when the Philomusica were playing at Girton College, Cambridge, which in those days was a college exclusively for women, we had to get dressed for the performance behind a curtain; on the other side of it the Mistress of Girton and the Chancellor of the University were seated. We had been invited to dinner before the concert and Francis remarked to me in his loud upper crust voice, "You know, the whole art of attending these functions is to carry on a polite conversation without saying "fuck" once!" I slunk away from behind the curtain, and although I'm sure they must have heard him neither of them raised an eyebrow.

I used to enjoy playing for the Philomusica, sometimes as the only bass when Francis was away. It was a joy to listen to George Malcolm on harpsichord and to glean from him some interesting approaches to the music. He was a shy and retiring man, not saying a lot at rehearsals but what he did say was intelligent and insightful. Most of the music the Philomusica played was from the Baroque period, sometimes earlier. Very often, the music had been edited by self-appointed "experts", resulting in confusion over the rendition of ornaments, i.e. trills, appoggiaturas and other embellishments. His expertise imparted a distinct style to the orchestra and contributed much to its success.

On one occasion the Philomusica played in Italy. There was a randy viola player who decided to visit a bordello. When it came time to pay the Madame (or Signora, I suppose, being Italy) the violist found he did not have enough lire with him. The Signora promptly confiscated his trousers so he couldn't get away. He was allowed to make a telephone call to the manager of the Philomusica, a rather prissy lady who surely looked down upon that type of conduct. However, she took a trip in a taxi to the brothel, embarrassingly paid the Signora and, accompanied by the errant violist, who by that time had put on his trousers, journeyed back to the hotel in time for him to change into concert attire and then play the concert.

Francis Baines' brother, Anthony, was another "character"who played third bassoon and contra bassoon in the LPO when I was there. He had a reputation as a practical joker. Eugene Cruft once told me that before WW2, for a jape, Tony and a group of friends dressed themselves as street repairmen. They put up a sign blocking Oxford Street in London's West End, causing considerable hold ups before the police discovered the practical joke.

Anthony Baines wrote a scholarly book entitled *Musical Instruments through the Ages* published by Pelican Books. He later taught at Stowe School, which gave him more time to pursue his scholarly interests.

I was asked to play principal bass for an opera season in the "Little Italy" quarter of London's Soho district. When I arrived at the theatre for rehearsal I discovered I was to be the only bass. The operas were *La Bohème* by Puccini and *L'Elisir d'Amore*, by Donizetti.

Jack Hylton, the impresario whom I mentioned earlier, had an Italian girl friend, Rosalina Neri. For her birthday present he had engaged the entire cast of the famous San Carlo Opera Company to come over from Naples, Italy, so that she could sing the leading soprano roles.

Even Rosalina's best friends could not call her a singer of operatic calibre. She often appeared on RIA, the Italian television network, singing or rather crooning sentimental love songs, which she did very well. She was pretty and very handsomely endowed. A cast member told me in one of the rehearsal intermissions, "She pusha da boobs almost througha da televisione: Il Papa, he not like, maybe…" and then he gave a sign and wagged his finger as though having committed a mortal sin by baring too much, she might be in trouble with the Pontiff. I never did find out whether the Holy Father had ever watched her performances on television, of course, just to assure himself as to whether or not they were fit for his flock to view.

The first night opened with *La Bohème*, Napoleone Annovazzi was conducting. He was an excellent opera conductor, very precise with his beat, following singers closely and aiding them if they ever strayed from the score.

The cast all had magnificent voices except for poor Rosalina who was to sing Mimi. She must have had stage fright because at the beginning of her aria she let out a strangled croak which got a little better as time went on, but as I had noticed at the rehearsals she was hopelessly drowned by all the other singers.

The audience became restless as only an Italian audience can, and there were boos and catcalls, such as "Neri, cattiva, ma Annovazzi buono!" ("Neri bad, but Annovazzi good "). At length they rang down the curtain and it was announced that Signorina Neri being ill, an understudy would take her place. The understudy had a wonderful voice and when the final curtain came down there was tremendous applause.

The week proceeded and poor Rosalina never ventured on stage again. Whatever happened to her or indeed Jack Hylton I never found out. To quote Felix Apprahamian, "They are probably all dead by now."

Percy Showan, the orchestral manager of the Sadlers Wells Opera Company phoned me one Sunday in the early 60's to inform me that there had been an accident; the brakes had failed on a train carrying all the members of the cast and orchestra, and it had run into the Bradford station buffers at speed. The only casualty was the principal bass and Percy wanted to know whether I would be willing to travel up to Bradford in time for the performance next day to play principal bass with them. I demurred at first but monetarily my trip was to be made worthwhile. I hadn't much in my diary that was really important and, as Percy re-iterated, they <u>were</u> in a bind, so I accepted, farming out the engagements I already had booked in my diary.

I suppose I should have enquired more before I accepted because Percy had only mentioned to me Verdi's *La Traviata* that I knew well. However, when I arrived in Bradford I was informed that Archie, the principal bass was in a far worse state than was originally thought and would be away for some time. I then enquired what the full repertoire consisted of and I was given a list of no less than seventeen operas which I would be expected to play as principal, on sight, many without rehearsal. This was a formidable task, because I already knew from experience that as a principal if you don't come in at the correct entry, nobody else in the section will.

Although I had done most of the "pot boilers" and many modern operas before, there were quite a few which I had never played, including Janacek's *Cunning Little Vixen* and *Katya Kabanova* as well as Richard Strauss's *Ariadne auf Naxos*.

The chief conductor was Colin Davis and I felt at home when playing for him as he has a very clear, decisive beat, particularly in the recitatives. In fact, without a conductor of his calibre it is doubtful whether I could have played as well as I did under the circumstances. I had first met him years before when we had both played together for some school concerts, Colin played clarinet.

I next encountered him at a performance at Chelsea Town Hall, London where he was conducting, and afterwards Colin got his big break in the legendary manner, a conductor was taken ill and Walter Legge sent for him to conduct the concert, the rest is history.

Over the years I met him at various venues. I remember vividly one Prom concert at the Albert Hall; he hadn't been long into his conducting career when he led a performance of Stravinsky's *Rite of Spring* conducting a stunning rendering of the piece from memory that both the orchestra as well as the audience wildly applauded.

When the week at Bradford ended I was asked to stay on with the company for the London season. It was extremely hard work, sometimes with a rehearsal in the morning and then the opera at night. Sundays were free, and I always looked forward to spending the day at home. One Sunday I tried to get out of bed, found I couldn't and had a terrible pain in my back. The doctor was called and he diagnosed a kidney stone, so I was taken to hospital. But even on my hospital bed I had to think of a deputy for Monday, the next day. Fortunately it was Offenbach's *Orpheus in the Underworld*; my friend Gerald Drucker happened to be free and, as he had played the piece before, he agreed to deputize for me and I felt a lot easier in my mind.

At length a doctor appeared and only really seemed to be concerned about filling out a form for me to give to my employers. I patiently explained to him that if I didn't work I didn't get paid and that as the pain had now subsided and if they were not about to give me any treatment I would leave. The head nurse was horrified; "Patients were not encouraged to do this, it was against the rules," and "Be it on your own head, etc." I called a taxi anyway, and went home in my pyjamas.

I went in to Sadlers Wells again on the Tuesday to play the opera. Later on that week I went in for a test, but it appeared negative and I was relieved.

The following week I had booked an engagement in Geneva, Switzerland. It was only a one night stand, and on that particular night Sadlers Wells was playing *Orpheus* again so Percy gave me permission to go and Gerald stepped in once more. When I went to catch the return flight to London the next morning, the aircraft could not take off because we were fogged in. I hung around the airport waiting room consuming endless cups of coffee and the occasional beer when lo and behold I went to the washroom and passed the stone, retrieving it and putting it in a match box to show my own physician. The fog showed no sign of lifting so we were put on a train to Lucerne, then flew immediately to London and I played the opera that night.

When I showed the stone to my physician, his reaction was, "You should show it to that bugger at the hospital who told you nothing was there!"

Reginald Goodall conducted the Wagner operas *Die Meistersinger* and *Lohengrin*. Gioacchino Rossini once quipped that Wagner has lovely moments but awful quarters of an hour. Under Goodall, the operas were, in my opinion, very tedious at times. The reason for this lay in his tempi that were far too slow and pedestrian. I have observed that the best opera conductors keep things moving so that the thread is not lost and the interest is kept alive. An extra bassist had to be engaged for the Wagner operas so I suggested to Percy Showan that Cyril MacArthur be asked. One night he arrived for *Die Meistersinger* and was unable to sit on his bass stool. He had been in a car race at Le Mans France, and the rear end of his racing car had caught fire, singeing <u>his</u> rear end. *Die Meistersinger* is a long opera, so he must have felt extremely tired standing all the time, but he whiled away the very long rests by reading "Motor Sport" and when it was time for us to play I had to remind him that we were ready to leave the pit stops.

Charles Mackerras conducted Janacek's *Katya Kabanova* and *The Cunning Little Vixen*. I had met him before on several occasions when I had played in the English Chamber Orchestra. He was very sensitive to the music's requirements and had a clear, decisive beat. Unlike Goodall, he kept things moving and obtained some really good performances.

Mind you, I am not advocating that all operas be performed at a breakneck pace. The tale is often told of Charlie Corri, a conductor at the Old Vic and Sadlers Wells Operas, who used to say to the orchestra near the end of the last act, "Don't worry boys, I'll get it over before closing time." In those days, just before WW2 the pubs closed at 10.30 p.m.

There were two singers at Sadlers Wells whom I admired, Amy Shuard and Peter Glossop, both of them went on to make a big name for themselves. Von Karajan, recognizing Glossop's talent engaged him to sing Iago in Verdi's *Otello*. Shuard sang well in Menotti's *The Consul*.

Around that time I was asked to play for several ballet companies that included Margot Fonteyn and later with Rudolf Nureyev. I performed one or two TV shows with them as well as the theatre performances. They were easily the finest *pas de deux* that I have ever seen. Margot well deserved her title of *prima ballerina assoluta*.

I met her at the stage door occasionally and she always gave me a radiant smile but I knew she was often in pain with her knee which sometimes caused her to miss a performance.

When she teamed up with Nureyev, who was several years her junior it seemed to give her new life. Unfortunately he died later of AIDS.

Margot was married to Roberto Arias, a wealthy Panamanian politician, she was his second wife. Arias was shot by a rival politician and made a paraplegic. After he died Margot was left on her own on their estate and was living in penury. She had a visitor who noticed the condition she was living in and a benefit concert was given for her in London which enabled her to live comfortably for the rest of her days, but she was only seventy when she passed away.

CHAPTER 14

The Moscow Chamber Orchestra and miscellaneous thoughts

The agent for the Moscow Chamber Orchestra got in touch with me in 1962, regarding a tour of England they were making; they needed another bassist of reputation (he said) to play with them. He mentioned that a famous conductor had recommended me to him and of course I was flattered. I accepted with alacrity and arrived in time for a rehearsal that was set to run through some of the extensive repertoire they were going to play.

Remember that this was in the time of the Cold War, and that describes the reception I received from them when I arrived: Cold. All of them affected an air of superiority and I suppose this was to be expected as they were of Russia's best, but one must also note that these were the days of McCarthyism, Gary Powers' U2 overflight and the Cuban missile crisis.

The orchestra members were drawn from the élite of the Soviet Union and were selected for their place in the profession by the marks they received at the Conservatory. For example, to be in the Moscow Chamber Orchestra you had to graduate with the highest marks, and to be in a chamber group or a principal in a symphony orchestra you also had to be in the top echelon. If, however, you graduated lower on the scale you got a job in a music hall, a band or a travelling show. Top soloists were in another category, their progress was noted throughout their Conservatory days and the truly outstanding ones were groomed right from the start.

Rudolf Barshai led the orchestra on viola. He was a prodigious player and also a good leader of the group, able to convey very clearly to the orchestra his conception of any piece they played. My smattering of Russian enabled me to understand much of what they were saying, and the rest was conveyed by gestures that worked very well.

Their style of rehearsal was totally different from that in Britain; it was more of a consultative process, probably having evolved from the years after the Russian Revolution when the Russian orchestras in the name of *égalité* decided they could manage without a conductor. After some years conductors were brought back and are now re-instated to direct all of their orchestras, but the vestiges of the conducterless system still remained when I played with them.

In a way it was good; everyone had his/her say, particularly the first 'cellist, Tanya. Sometimes they had too much of a say, for they would haggle incessantly over arcane points in the music. This appeared to me at first akin to the House of Commons trying to build a battleship, but in the end Barshai was the final arbiter. That being said the results spoke for themselves, there was excellent cohesion not only in the togetherness of an attack on, say, the first forte note of a piece of music, but also in the sensitive way the various sections of the orchestra blended with each other. For instance, the two horns never obtruded over the rest of the orchestra by playing too loud.

Before any concert most players warm up, and this usually consists of playing a scale or two or playing one of their own party pieces. In the musical profession they are called "Band Room soloists".

At the beginning of most concerts in North America there seems to be a pantomime with the concertmaster pointing with his/her bow to the various sections, followed by a cacophony of "A"'s. The Moscow Chamber Orchestra however, tuned up together off stage and after they had entered and sat down on stage a very quiet "A" was sounded and they tuned again very quickly and very quietly. Off stage before the concert each section of the orchestra would be closeted together playing difficult passages from the evening's programme and creating an ensemble; they really <u>listened</u> to each other.

With the strings, bowings of the parts were not written in before the rehearsal as is the case in many orchestras, but they discussed the various ways of bowing a passage, and the best was finally adopted after trial and error. All these painstaking preparations gave the performances an élan that I had rarely encountered during my career; the cohesion, brilliance and balance were absolutely superb.

After a while the players thawed out somewhat towards me and I became friendly with of one of the violists. Contrary to what we had been told, many of them owned their own instruments, and he owned a beautiful "Granchinsky" as he called it; we would call it a Grancino. He told me that because of their status they were each allotted an apartment in Moscow, and were given six weeks holiday once a year at a resort in the Black Sea. Certainly, they all seemed to be very satisfied with their lot.

They were all beautifully dressed and groomed, exuding an air of prosperity. In England we were led to believe by the Press that all Russians were short of clothes and dressed poorly but that was not my take of the situation. How the serfs back home in Russia were doing I never found out, so I can only vouch for the members of the Moscow Chamber Orchestra.

I asked Feodor, the other bassist to dinner at my house. Either he wouldn't or couldn't accept, the latter probably being the case because their movements were very closely followed in case of defection. In addition, it would not have been politically correct to be overly friendly with a "bloated capitalist". This air of suspicion was noticeable from all of the artists who visited us from behind the "Iron Curtain". Travelling there was always a headache because before leaving home you had to fill out a long series of forms which were accompanied by six photographs; however, upon arrival at one's destination one usually found the locals very friendly. Indeed I look back fondly on my visits to Budapest, then controlled by the Soviets, where there was always a bottle of Hungarian "Tokay" wine placed at my bedside.

On another occasion when I was playing in Berlin, I had to catch an overnight train from Berlin to Hamburg. As we had to pass through the Soviet Zone all the carriage blinds were drawn and there were armed guards on the train to ensure no one left or boarded it.

There is a legendary tale, so often repeated until it has become lore among Czech bassists. It goes like this: The Czech Philharmonic Orchestra was playing in what was then called Leningrad, and were staying at a grand hotel opposite the Leningrad Philharmonic Hall. One night some bass players were having a party in an hotel room, but, being very suspicious of electronic eavesdropping they searched the room for "bugs". One inebriated bassist suddenly gave a cry of triumph. Underneath the carpet he discovered a metal plate held in place by a bolt. Somehow or other a wrench was produced and he proceeded to undo the bolt, but as soon as it was removed there was a terrific crash and a "babushka" came running up knocking on the door. Apparently the bolt was holding a chandelier, which had crashed down into the room below!

When I played for a Polish ballet company in London, they were counted when leaving their bus upon arrival at the theatre and after the performance were all counted back on the the bus by an agent, so as to block any defections.

The Moscow Chamber Orchestra tour came to an end, and we all said a very affectionate "goodbye" to each other, the atmosphere having gone from cold to warm. So we went our various ways. I reflected to myself that that was to be the last I would ever see of them, but as it so often happened during my career, Fate thought otherwise.

The next year the Moscow Chamber Orchestra came back to England for another tour. I reckoned they must have been happy with me because they asked me to join them again, only this time I was received in a very friendly manner.

The tour began and our itinerary included the Bath Festival, where the Bath Festival Orchestra, led by Yehudi Menuhin was appearing. Menuhin was a sympathetic musician with a sense of humility towards the players, although he was by no means pusillanimous when it came to enforcing his musical tastes. He had studied Yoga and once gave us a demonstration by standing on his head and performing other contortions with relative ease.

It had been decided maybe for the sake of *Entente Cordiale* and all that, that the Bath Festival Orchestra and the Moscow Chamber Orchestra would combine forces in a performance of Michael Tippett's *Concerto for Double String Orchestra*. I regard it as being one of the most significant string pieces in the repertoire, and it is very difficult to play, but I was very familiar with it, having performed it with the composer himself conducting, as well as with other string orchestras and conductors. I had also played for Tippett on many other occasions when he conducted his oratorio *A Child of Our Time*, and his opera *King Priam*. He was homosexual, and, as is usual with many gay people, had a very sensitive personality. I really enjoyed working with him and I am a devotee of his music.

At all the other performances of Tippett's *Concerto for Double String Orchestra* that I had taken part in, the two orchestras were placed side by side on stage, the first orchestra being on one side, the second orchestra on the other side, similar to the antiphony at St. Mark's, in Venice. Although the Moscow Chamber Orchestra had never played the *Concerto for Double String Orchestra* before (and it was evident!) they insisted (a) that they play first orchestra and (b) that they would be placed in the front of the stage and Menuhin's group would have to be at the back.

Quiet diplomatic discussions took place behind the scenes, but the Russians were adamant; "Nyet" was the answer. Michael Tippett was brought in to try to persuade the Russians that the first orchestra should be placed on the left of stage and the second orchestra placed on the right but even he could not alter things - the answer was still "nyet".

The Russians got their own way and were placed in front of the stage with the English behind them. Maybe it was a matter of their national pride but, in the event, the performance was a fiasco. At the end of it my

Russian colleague Feodor tried to apologize for his performance, saying "I tired" but I am sure that had we adhered to the composer's wishes things would have been far different.

President Kennedy's assassination took place whilst they were in England and my violist friend confided to me, "Of course they'll think it's our entire fault." He was very worried, as were we in the West, that an open conflagration might take place between the United States and Russia. It became obvious to me from what I heard from my friend the violist that ordinary people on both sides of the "Iron Curtain" just wanted to live their lives in peace.

We all said our "goodbyes" and left each other in a very friendly fashion. That was the last I would see of them.

Later on when I was living in Canada, Rudolf Barshai was appointed conductor of the Vancouver Symphony Orchestra and I now regret not having travelled over to Vancouver to see him. I heard from some members of the Vancouver Symphony that he was not very popular with them; perhaps he demanded too much from them or more than they were prepared or able to give, but I still regard him as a wonderful musician, a virtuoso viola player and a good orchestral trainer, and I felt it was their loss that he didn't stay longer.

CHAPTER 15

Alec Sherman and Gina Bachauer. Rozhdestvensky. The Pro Arte Orchestra. Gary Karr, A one night stand in Venice. Sir David Willcox. The LSO World Tour. I play in Budapest and meet the famous bassist, Lajos Montag. I am invited to become principal double bass of the Vancouver Symphony Orchestra.

After the Moscow Chamber Orchestra's tour I became very busy with multifarious offers from many different sources. I still kept my BBC connection though, because it came in very useful, but I also accepted engagements from the London Symphony and some of the small orchestras which abounded in London at that time. One of these was the New London Orchestra whose conductor, Alec Sherman, was a well-known figure on the London musical scene. In his day he had been an accomplished violinist, having been a member of the BBC Symphony Orchestra for some years since its inception in 1930. With that background he turned to conducting and was very good at it. His gestures were minimal, using a short baton and only using his left hand sparingly yet often he obtained really splendid results.

His musical tastes were catholic, including works by Haydn and Mozart to Debussy and Britten. In fact he made a creditable performance of anything he tackled, but I particularly liked his Haydn and Mozart. He was a good friend to music, having initiated concerts at many different venues and he brought these values to his programmes, giving to the public works that they would otherwise not have had the opportunity to hear.

In appearance he was of slight build, wore horn-rimmed glasses and reminds me in retrospect as having looked very much like Alan Greenspan, the economist, who, incidentally, studied clarinet at Juilliard.

His wife, Gina Bachauer, was a really talented pianist. In my opinion she had that lush, romantic style that was at its best in Tchaikowsky and Rachmaninoff, although she often played Chopin. She was a Junoesque woman and came on stage always wearing a *décolleté* dress displaying an inordinate amount of her ample bosom. Some wag dubbed Alec "The Knight on the Bare Mountain", (after Moussorgsky's piece), a rather cruel if not crude sobriquet, but he was ever after known as that in the profession.

Years later Gina Bachauer played with the Vancouver Symphony Orchestra, Alec was with her and we chatted together. I don't think he was very busy at that time, although he well deserved to be, as he was still very alert and his brain very sharp. But that's the musical profession; you can be "in" and then suddenly "out".

Mention should be made of Gennadi Rozhdestvensky, a truly great conductor who well deserves a place in the Pantheon of the great conductors I have worked with. His interpretations were legendary, particularly of some of the Russian composers. He was coming to conduct the L.S.O. and, although my diary was full with more lucrative engagements I decided to book his concerts, and to this day I'm glad I did.

Rozhdestvensky was an unprepossessing looking man, rather portly, red faced, wearing glasses and very easy to work with. He knew exactly what he wanted - and got it, mainly by his attitude of acting as one artist to another when he worked with the orchestra, but also by his superb insight and latent energy. He possessed a dynamism which only came out in frenzy at a climax in a work. In other words he knew how to husband his considerable energy until the salient moment, gaining a stunning effect. Some inferior conductors throw away this opportunity by "shooting their bolt" too soon, and they lose it.

He conducted Shostakovitch and Prokofiev; Dimitri Shostakovitch's *Symphony Number Five* was a revelation. I have played this symphony many times and I must say that I was certain in my mind that Rozhdestvensky's interpretation was the definitive one. The whole work builds up right from the first movement, until the last page of the last movement. Rozhdestvensky graded this tension gradually and by the time the climax arrived the result was truly electrifying.

Another conductor I came across about this time, the early 60's, was Zubin Mehta who struck me as being a rather brash, brilliant but flashy conductor. He had an excellent beat, and could follow any soloist however erratic they might be, however, I never thought he plumbed the real depths of the music; his readings, to me were superficial. Maybe over time his readings have improved tremendously judging by all the prestigious orchestras he has conducted, but I can only speak of the days when I knew him.

Another one of the myriad of small orchestras that sprang up in London in those years was the Pro Arte Orchestra, a small symphony orchestra that was the brainchild of Eugene Cruft and was also fairly successful. It was composed entirely of free-lance players, and its personnel varied from time to time. The object of its founding was to fill a niche that the major symphony orchestras could not. For instance, if an orchestra was suddenly needed at the last moment for, say, a television show, the major orchestras were usually booked up, sometimes years ahead, and could not accept the engagement. This is where the Pro Arte came in, because it could book freelance players to fill the void on the spot. But its very *raison d'être* also became its Achilles Heel, for if things were slack in the freelance world Eugene could engage the finest players, but conversely if things were busy then he had to put up with the Second Eleven and sometimes this became a source of annoyance to the organizations that were paying for the Pro Arte's services.

At one television show I was booked to play with the Pro Arte as sub-principal bass to Eugene Cruft. There was a young man performing with us as a double- bass soloist, his name was Gary Karr. I had heard of Gary before when he had given a recital at the Wigmore Hall with great acclaim. I would have loved to have listened to this recital but unfortunately I was playing at a recording session that night.

A pupil of mine went to the concert, and he came back full of enthusiasm and a collection of superlatives. All the praise that had been bestowed on him was very well deserved, for he was (and is) a fabulous player. The whole orchestra was overcome with admiration, applauding him loudly after the performance. Eugene, too, was enthusiastic in giving him accolades and I began a friendship with Gary then that has lasted until this day.

Later on Gary came to the Vancouver Symphony Orchestra when I was playing with them and I shall never forget the piece, Paganini's *Moses Fantasia*, which he played with so much artistry. Next day he was to appear in Victoria which is about 20 miles by ferry from Vancouver. I arranged to pick him up at his hotel the next morning; he would have breakfast at my house and then I would drive him to the ferry so he could catch it in time for his afternoon concert. After breakfast, Gary, my son Nicholas and I set off for the ferry but when we arrived at the ferry terminal an official would not allow Gary to board because he was carrying a bass. The whole business was ridiculous and I thought the ferry worker was being overly officious particularly as it was a huge vessel with plenty of room on it for a bass.

After an argument during which the official became very belligerent and threatening, I drew Gary aside, as my son had discovered in the meantime that there was a plane leaving shortly for Victoria. I recommended to Gary that we make for Vancouver Airport right away; we drove quickly to the airport and were just in time for the flight.

We both now live near each other in British Columbia and, as close friends, often meet. I heard him play recently and it was no surprise to hear him play as well as ever – maybe even better.

One day in the early Sixties I was asked to play a concert in Venice with a choir and orchestra conducted by David (now Sir David) Willcox. We were to leave London Airport in the morning, rehearse in the afternoon, play the concert in Venice and fly back to London immediately after the concert, arriving in the wee hours.

In those days Willcox was organist and choir director at King's College Cambridge. A fairly tall, good looking, thinnish man, he represents a dying breed, that of a true English gentleman. His enthusiasm seemed to percolate down to the choir and orchestra, who always gave him of their best, and he also had that knack of obtaining a constant good balance and clear enunciation from the choir.

After the rehearsal I looked round St. Mark's and then crossed St. Mark's Square to a café and sipped the obligatory Campari and soda, watching the crowds go by and throwing some tidbits to the pigeons. I reflected upon Dragonetti and Rossini, leisurely touring from city to city in a coach and four, far easier on the constitution than doing a one night stand in Venice and then back to London.

I knew of a little *ristorante* not far away and invited a friend to dine there with me. It was a wonderful meal and we were in fine fettle to play the concert.

After the concert there was the usual scramble to board the bus to take us to the airport, and when I got on the plane I found myself sitting next to Willcox. We demolished the airline rubber chicken and then proceeded to quaff some airline plonk.

Willcox was a good raconteur and the flight passed very quickly as I listened to some of his interesting tales of happenings behind the scenes at King's College and with the Bach choir.

Upon arrival at London Airport there was a long wait for a taxi, and as it was after midnight there was no set fare, so the cabbie could charge you whatever he liked, which, of course diminished one's concert fee, so there was always fierce bargaining.

The Three Choirs Festival deserves a mention. It is an annual event that alternates between Gloucester, Worcester and Hereford and the concerts are given in the respective cathedrals. It is a time-honoured tradition that the LSO are always engaged for the Three Choirs and if I was free I liked to play· because there was always a new work by, say, Vaughan Williams or any other contemporary composer, and of course, Edward Elgar, being a native of Worcester was well represented. The organists and music directors of the cathedrals, usually musical knights, were given the chance to participate, very often by performing such works as Elgar's *Dream of Gerontius*, *The Kingdom* and *Caractacus* or works by Stanford and Parry

As an aside, I cannot understand why Stanford and Parry are always inextricably linked. To me their music is totally different, although they were contemporaries in the Victorian era. With the culinary arts we always associate ham with eggs and fish with chips, and in the written word we bracket Keats with Shelley and in music Mahler with Bruckner, etc. etc. Maybe it is a human trait to always try linking one thing with another although they often are dissimilar.

Having my BBC connection served me well for I very often fitted in some radio broadcasts with the BBC Midland Light Orchestra and then made the trip from Birmingham to the Three Choirs venues, all of which were not far away.

I struck up a conversation at one Three Choirs Festival with a member of the inner sanctum of the LSO who told me that plans were already afoot for a World Tour to celebrate their 60th Anniversary in 1964. He told me that if I felt like going I should let them know as soon as possible because many musicians were anxious to do it, not only because it was going to be a leisurely tour with absolutely first class accommodation, but there would be several "goodies" to go with it.

Sure enough a call came asking me if I would do the tour. The fixer said it was a case of "speak now or forever hold your peace," I replied that I would let him know as soon as possible, at least before the cut-off date which he gave me.

My wife was very loyal and understanding but did not like the idea of me being away for three months. You see, I was constantly away from home; I accepted everything, or mostly everything that came in because there was/is a myth in the profession that if you turn someone down you will never be asked again. That is not entirely true, but it gained credence because it was repeated so often, particularly by the old hands.

I had made several contacts in North America and other places in the world and I urged my wife to be compliant with my making the LSO tour thereby enabling me to follow up on my contacts and to do some prospecting. I remembered Phil Catalinet, the tuba player, being offered a good job in the United States, also other players emigrating elsewhere in the world and having a relatively easy life, so I contacted the LSO and accepted.

Other things were gradually taking place in London; the five symphony orchestras were fighting a bitter struggle between themselves for a portion of an ever-diminishing pie. The BBC and the many small orchestras were flourishing, but meanwhile a mechanical thing had come into the equation, the automobile.

When I first started free-lancing, gasoline was rationed and there were few cars on the road. I could make the journey of ten miles in my little van from Mill Hill, the suburb where I lived, to Central London in roughly half an hour. Those days were now long past and it was becoming very difficult to fit in some engagements. Because of the ever-increasing volume of traffic it was well nigh impossible to get from, say, a morning rehearsal in West London, where the Maida Vale studios were, to an afternoon engagement that might begin at 2.00 p.m. in the City of London. There was no time to get a meal, so I usually packed sandwiches and ate as I drove; in addition, parking had become a nightmare.

Upon arrival at the next engagement though, one had to appear as fresh as paint even if one felt deadbeat. Fortunately I was blessed with an iron constitution that enabled me to pull through.

With the rising volume of traffic, I had to allow at least an hour and a half to get into town from home and even then it was cutting it fine. Nowadays the journey by car into Central London from where I used to live, takes two and a half hours. There are friends of the Philharmonia who, if they are attending the concert will give the musicians a ride so they are fresh to play upon arrival at the hall. Recently a tax was imposed on cars entering the City of London and freelancing has become even less profitable and more unattractive because of the added expenses. Sometimes I would leave my bass overnight and catch the Underground train, but these were not always reliable and I can tell you it was a horrible situation to be stuck in the "tube", which often happened, hoping and praying the train would soon start and that I could get to my engagement on time.

All this took a toll on me, and more importantly, my family. My kids hardly knew they had a father. True, we had a good standard of living but there are other things in life besides money. It was the rule rather than the exception for me to leave home at 8.00 a.m. and not to arrive back home until midnight. But on the plus side I was now steeped in experience and was confident of appearing anywhere at short notice and "cutting the mustard" as the pop musicians call it. ·

Preparations got underway for the tour. We all had to receive a series of inoculations at the London Hospital for Tropical Diseases. Ernest Fleischman the orchestra manager showed his genius for organization. He made a preliminary tour to inspect the hotels and also the facilities at the various concert halls. He even arranged for a clothes washing machine to be carried on the aircraft that was to join us at Tokyo for the remainder of the Tour.

New fibreglass double bass cases were even made especially for the trip. The wisdom of this was demonstrated at the old Hong Kong airport which was like a finger pointing out to sea and also very much exposed to the considerable wind which blew with ferocity across the tarmac. The eight bass cases were lined up standing back to back when one particularly large gust blew and the bass cases all fell over; miraculously, not one instrument was damaged.

After tearful goodbyes, we departed from London Airport in the fall of 1964 to travel to New York. Following that, we also played in one or two small towns in New York State. Other big cities in the East were on our itinerary and on the West Coast we gave concerts in San Diego, Los Angeles, San Francisco and Seattle where I was very impressed with the Pacific Northwest. We then flew on from Seattle to Tokyo, Japan.

I was surprised to see the prosperity in Japan where we were to have two weeks holiday. I couldn't speak a word of Japanese but undaunted, I set off on the train to see the Great Buddha of Kamakura. I stayed in a "Ryokan", that is, a small private type of hotel of the traditional type used by the natives. Ryokans were reasonable in those days (1964), and were spotlessly clean and usually had an "o funo", a type of hot tub for one to luxuriate in. Nowadays everything is so expensive in Japan but in those days the exchange was favourable to the British Pound, dining out was fairly cheap and always adventurous.

The Bullet Train was then and is even now a "must" to travel on. I visited the Great Temple at Nara, the beautiful buildings of Kyoto and I went to the top of Mount Fuji from where I admired the lovely view.

Eventually I arrived in a small village in the interior of Japan that was graced by a beautiful but expensive hotel. I decided to splurge on a few days' stay but had some pangs of guilt when I thought of my wife looking after the kids back home, and wished she was there with me.

Wearing the distinctive kimono of the hotel was obligatory for it also served as a credit reference; you could buy anything in the shops that catered to the visitors, or if you took a taxi it was also accepted. The hotel was equipped with a beautiful black marble hot pool plus a swimming pool and various other amenities, which made me wonder that this was perhaps the way the Roman emperors of old lived.

Talking of luxury, I ordered a meal to be sent up to my room. There were not one but three kimono dressed girls accompanying the food. They catered to my every (culinary) need, one opening a bottle of beer and proffering me a drink whenever she thought I was ready, another feeding me with fish which I did not like and the other giving me some sort of vegetable concoction. The fish donor was quite upset when I did not eat it all. I was horrified to learn later that it was very expensive, but more importantly that I was playing Russian Roulette by eating it, because one out of so many hundred of them could be fatally toxic.

I rounded off my fortnight's holiday by visiting the Bunka Kaikan museum in Tokyo and seeing all the other sights there. A building boom was taking place, and opposite our hotel a large building was being erected. Every morning I was fascinated to see all the workmen gathered in a circle around the boss, bowing deferentially. It crossed my mind that maybe that sort of ritual might be useful in England where recently there had been some violent labour troubles between the unions and the bosses.

It was time to play our first concert in Tokyo and then to play at Osaka. We were received very well and as we were about to depart I learned that there was an opening for a bass teacher. Apart from there not being much time to arrange anything I dismissed it lightly, because I'm sure my wife and kids would not have fitted in Japan.

From Tokyo we flew to Seoul, Korea, which was totally different to the modernity of Tokyo. Riding in the bus from the airport to the city centre I was amazed to see what looked like holes in the ground covered with thatch, which some poor souls called home.

There was a banquet given for us by the ladies' concert committee. They were all in national dress and a delicious chicken dish was served. We played the concert feeling very well fed.

Arriving in Hong Kong next day I felt ill and I surmised that the Korean meal had not agreed with me but I struggled through the concert and was better the next day. I got a glimpse of the service that was offered in Hong Kong; my dress tailcoat needed to be refaced and I also needed two new white cummerbunds. I ordered them through the concert agent in the morning and they were ready in time for the evening concert - that's service!

From Hong Kong there was a lengthy flight to Calcutta. It was dark when we arrived there, and the first thing I noticed after I got off the plane was the heat. This was a November night, but some of the locals were wearing overcoats. Our bus passed the village of Dumdum on the way into the city and I recollected the infamous dumdum bullets that were manufactured in the arsenal there in the days of the British Raj.

Also on the way I was appalled to see numbers of poor sleeping on the streets; I was told a cart came round every day to pick up the dead. I never ever then expected to see so many of the poor and homeless on the streets of the Western World.

Near our hotel was another older hotel where it was said Rudyard Kipling once stayed. I wandered into its beautiful courtyard shaded with trees and sat down on one of the seats that was sheltered by an overhanging tree. One elderly gentleman, obviously a leftover from the Raj, approached me saying, "Wonderful year for tiger, sir." I could hardly believe my ears and it took some self-control not to burst out laughing at this strange statement, which I put down to the sun.

There was so much to see that if I described it at length it would sound like a travelogue, not just a glimpse of an orchestral tour. However, I should mention in passing that I visited the famous Kali Ghat, Nehru and Gandhi's tombs, and I made an entertaining trip to the Rowing Club.

The concert in Calcutta was in an old building where we played before a packed audience. Although I had seen poverty everywhere there was also much wealth. After the concert I was invited to a fabulous home where there was drink in abundance. I was surprised at this because I had thought that most people there were teetotal, but I was told it was easily available albeit at an exorbitant price.

The next stop was New Delhi. I was very impressed with the way the architect, Sir Edwin Lutyens, had planned the city. I am very fond of curry, and although we stayed in the best hotel, I ate there the worst curry I have ever tasted.

Lionel Bentley, who sat next to the concertmaster, had joined the tour like me, as a freelance player. At one time he was a member of the LSO playing in that same position but had left in order to freelance. I just heard as I was writing this book that he had passed away in London at the ripe old age of ninety-three. We formed a friendship, and decided that we would hire a taxi to visit the Taj Mahal, a few miles away. It was a beautiful day, and after sightseeing at the Taj Mahal, which is indeed one of the wonders of the world we visited Fathepur Sikri, a deserted city where the only inhabitants seemed to be packs of fierce, wild dogs. We had to leave quickly because the dogs, having scented the boxes of food that the hotel had packed, pursued us, baring their fangs. Next day was the concert.

The conductors who came on the tour included Sir Malcolm Sargent, Colin Davis, George Solti, and Istvan Kertesz.

Kertesz had an ebullient temperament; his cheerful manner was infectious and he always got a good show. Despite the outward appearance of nonchalance, his readings of the music were very inspired, and he was a great favourite with the audiences. He met with a tragic death, having drowned in the Mediterranean when visiting Israel.

He was fond of the fair sex and had become friendly with one of the stewardesses. One night he was seen entering her room and a practical joker who had noticed this waited for a while, and then phoned the stewardesses' room saying that Lofty, our aircraft pilot, wanted to see her urgently in the hotel lobby to discuss the next day's flight schedule. A rather dishevelled girl made her way to the lobby, but, of course, couldn't find Lofty.

When we were in the air next day both the girl and Kertesz looked discomfited, whether or not it was a case of *coitus interruptus* nobody ever found out.

We played in rather primitive conditions in Bombay, which was our next stop. On a day off we went on a boat trip and visited the Elephant Caves. These are caves containing carvings of elephants, which were badly mutilated by Portuguese soldiers using them for firing practice.

To get to Iran, our next stop, we had to fly over Pakistan where we were forced to make a stop at Karachi. According to Lofty there was no need for us to put down in Karachi for we had plenty of fuel but what they wanted was a hundred pounds sterling as "baksheesh" for the privilege of flying over Pakistan.

We arrived in Tehran, Iran, where we were made very welcome, but there was a lot of political trouble, many strikes were in progress including the taxis. There were armed soldiers and police patrolling the streets and the general atmosphere was not a very happy one. As I have mentioned earlier in the book, armed soldiers searched my bass and me upon entering the concert hall, probably because the Shah and his consort, Fara Dibah, were in the audience.

We were invited to the Gulistan Palace, an imposing building that was covered inside with mirrors and we were also taken to see the Crown Jewels which were kept in a bank strong-room. There were rubies as big as pigeon's eggs on the Peacock Throne, diamonds aplenty and emeralds and gold in amazing quantities. There were dinner services in pure gold; all this was absolutely mind-boggling and made the collection of Crown Jewels kept in the Tower of London look rather insignificant.

When we flew to Istanbul, Lofty invited me into the cockpit and as we landed I was able to get a good glimpse of that city. We were invited to the home of the famous Janissary Band where they performed especially for us, all dressed in their turbaned uniforms. There was a drum major in front twirling an elaborate pole adorned with a crescent. We found the music very interesting as well as all the various manoeuvres the band made, particularly the drummers. There were also the obligatory visits to Topkapi and Haggia Sophia.

In Israel we played in Haifa, Tel Aviv and Jerusalem and in a kibbutz, Ein Gev. We visited Bethlehem, Nazareth and the Dead Sea, where I dipped, lying on my back floating and reading a newspaper. I saw the Pillar of Salt, which Lot's wife was turned into. At the Sea of Galilee there was a gentleman in a white gown sitting in a boat where he plied his trade as a tourist guide. He asked if we wanted to be taken to the place where Christ walked on the water. On being told his fee, we all echoed, "No wonder He walked on the water!"

In the desert our guide pointed out to us an Arab on a camel, preceded by a woman wearing a veil and covered from head to foot, walking in front. According to the guide there were land mines in the area and the woman would have taken the full brunt of any explosion.

The Israel Philharmonic gave us a reception, where I met Tom Martin, the principal bass. He later returned to England and married the daughter of another bass player, Ernest Ineson.

We were now on the last leg of the tour. It had been wonderful, with lots of sightseeing, hospitality and bonhomie, but we were all pleased to be back home in London. I was glad to sit down, put my feet up, and dispense the various gifts I had brought back, and I was looking forward to the Christmas holiday.

After Christmas I resumed freelancing and soon had a full diary.

I enjoyed a trip to Prague and Budapest, playing in Budapest at the Liszt Akadarnie. I felt honoured to be in the same hall where so many famous musicians had appeared. I was also honoured to meet a famous bassist, Professor Lajos Montag who in those days was principal double bass at the Budapest Opera and also Professor of the Double Bass at the Béla Bartók Conservatory. He invited me to his apartment in Budapest to hear him play. After a delicious meal I looked through his many compositions for the double bass. He was of medium height; balding and very energetic. He was famous throughout Eastern Europe as a virtuoso player and insisted on playing all his of his extensive repertoire for me. I was astounded by his tone and technique. Now and then he would spit out the word "kuss" if he missed the occasional harmonic or high note (which we all do occasionally). His recital went on and on, and I had eventually to excuse myself so as to be in time for the concert, but it was very much worthwhile.

Back in London I was working very hard, and it was becoming more and more difficult getting from one date to another.

One day I set off from home to a rehearsal in Central London. It was the Queen's Birthday Parade and there was a big traffic jam. I knew the streets of London like the back of my hand and I tried all the short cuts but to no avail, so I just had to sit and wait. I was carrying the mail, so I turned off the engine and began to read a letter from Meredith Davies, the conductor of the Vancouver Symphony Orchestra in Canada. He enquired whether I would be interested in coming to Canada as principal bass of the orchestra. Given the state of the traffic I immediately began to give the matter serious thought, so I phoned him later and made an appointment to see him. The terms were good; I would be paid a guaranteed salary, travel to Canada for my family and I would be paid for, and there were other perks as well.

Meredith told me that he was interested in building a world-class orchestra, which other well-known musicians would be joining; they included Simon Streatfeild, who was then principal viola of the London Symphony Orchestra, Norman Nelson, a founding member of the Academy of St. Martin in the Fields and Deputy Concertmaster of the BBC Symphony. There were also to be principal wind players from other parts of Canada and the U.S.A. This heightened my enthusiasm.

I wrote to Jack Kessler, who had stayed on after the Philharmonia's 1955 American tour and had settled in Vancouver as concertmaster of the Vancouver Symphony and also concertmaster of the C.B.C. Radio Chamber Orchestra. He sent me an equivocal reply in which he noted that there was some beautiful countryside around Vancouver, and that it was a nice, clean safe city to live in, but he ended his letter by saying that in any case I would not be crossing the Rubicon; if I didn't like it, I could always return home.

My wife was lukewarm about the whole thing. She pointed out that I was doing well, we had a beautiful home, the kids were in good schools and she had many friends and did not relish pulling up all her roots and starting afresh in an unknown country, but we came to an understanding that if she did not like it in Canada then we would return to England and look upon the move as a temporary change of lifestyle.

The decision having been made, I contacted Meredith Davies, accepted his offer and was given plane tickets to Vancouver. We then went to Canada House and obtained our landed immigrant papers, a process that was easy in those days - at least it was for us.

On October 8th 1965 Gerry Drucker drove me plus my bass, to London Airport to catch the plane to Vancouver, British Columbia, Canada.

In those days there was only one plane a week to Vancouver, run by Canadian Pacific Airlines. As my bass was not in a hard case, Lofty, the pilot with whom I had become friendly on the LSO World Tour, advised me to just walk onto the plane and insist that the flight attendant put it in the front area of the cabin. Fortunately the plane was nearly empty so I did not have any difficulty. Looking back, I cannot believe how lucky I was, especially nowadays after 9/11.

Sitting in the plane after we took off from Schipol Airport, Holland, it hit me that this was indeed going to be a great change in my life, but just how much of a change it was to be I was still to find out.

The Bottom Line

Lajos Montag

The author, age 16, 1936

Sergey Koussevitsky

Eugene Cruft

Wilhelm Mohnke,
1940

2nd left: the author, 3rd left: Jean Pougnet, centre with
lifebelt: Richard Temple Savage, front: David John, Crossing the channel in November, 1945

London Philharmonic Orchestra conducted by Sir
Thomas Beecham, Brussels, 1945, author sitting beneath
tuba player.

Albert Coates, 1946

Benjamin Britten, 1947

Betty and the Reliant at Glyndebourne 1948

Victor Watson and Boris Rickelman (principal cellist
London Philharmonic), 1948

Kirsten Flagstad, late
1940s

Edouard van Beinum,
1949

Wilhelm Furtwangler,
late 1940s

Josef Krips, 1950s

Carlo Maria Giulini, 1950s

Chicago, 1954, Far left: Elizabeth Schwartzkop, 3rd from left: Maria Callas, Walter
Legge next to Callas.

Gerald Brooks, Max Salpeter, the author, on a train in Germany, 1954

Tullio Serafin and Maria Callas, 1955

Sir Malcolm Sargent, 1955

Otto Klemperer, 1956

Victor de Sabata, late 1950s

Benjamin Britten conducting a recording of his War Requiem with the LSO, early '60's

Aaron Copland rehearsing the LSO for the world premiere of his Music for a Great City, author 1st on left, 1963.

Sir William Walton, 1964

Sir Arthur Bliss, Master of the Queen's Music, 1964

Bath Festival Orchestra, Yehudi Menuhin, rehearsal

Sir Adrian Boult

Leopold Stokowski, 1960

Igor Stravinsky and Pierre Monteux, 1962

Guido Cantelli   Ernest Ansermet   Colin Davis

Herbert von Karajan

Sir John Barbirolli

Julian Bream   The author, VSO

The author tours BC by plane, 1968

Meredith Davies, VSO

On tour with Betty, Lourdes, 1970

Gary Karr with the author, 2006

Janos Sandor

Victoria de los Angeles

Dr. Gordon Jacob, who composed
A Little Concerto for the double bass,
dedicated to the author.

George Corwin

Janette Chrysler, the author, and Don Chrysler, celebrating finishing the Rossini Duo recording.

Margot Fonteyn and Rudolf Nureyev

THE BOTTOM LINE

PART TWO

Chapter 16

Vancouver, B.C. Canada. I have mixed feelings. Getting acquainted with the Vancouver Symphony Orchestra, I am invited to be principal bass of the CBC Vancouver Chamber Orchestra by its conductor, John Avison.

It was a beautiful sunny day when I arrived in Vancouver on October 8th 1965. Through the plane's window I could discern trees, mountains and sea surrounding the city that was so much smaller than London.

The plane touched down on the tarmac; there were a couple of other planes standing there and nearby was a cluster of huts over which was a large sign showing to all the world that this was VANCOUVER, and that was all, except for a few cars, one or two taxis and a handful of people who made up the only signs of life. I walked with my bass to one of the huts and after passing Customs and Immigration claimed my baggage and was about to call a taxi when a lady, having noticed the bass came up to me and introduced herself as Mary White, the wife of Victor White the orchestral manager.

She drove me to a large house on South West Marine Drive, the ritzy part of Vancouver where she and her husband were living with her parents, the Buckerfields. Mr. Buckerfield had made his fortune as a farm supply merchant and he owned a chain of stores throughout British Columbia and Mrs. Buckerfield was a patron of the Vancouver Symphony Orchestra.

In the evening Victor came home and Mary, Victor and I had dinner. After dinner Victor showed me round the house with a proprietorial air. We sat down together and Victor told me of his spell in the chorus of Sadlers Wells Opera. Later on I heard him sing. He had a good voice and would give very good renderings of songs such as *Macushla*. Towards the end of the evening Meredith Davies arrived and after a chat, took me to my hotel.

After exploring Vancouver the next day or so, I had a deep sense of *déjà vu*. When I was in Seattle I developed an affinity for the Pacific Northwest and I was feeling it again strongly. The setting sun's rays glowing evanescent over the mountains and Howe Sound, the large variety of birds, the tremendous amount of wildlife and the laid back lifestyle all appealed to me.

The Symphony put on a reception for the newcomers to the orchestra. It was a big affair at one of the large hotels with the Board and their friends being in the majority and few musicians present. My British *confrères* had not yet arrived but the American wind contingent had, plus Doc Hamilton who was to be my stand partner. All the new boys and girls chatted with each other, and as we all came from different backgrounds it was interesting for me to see how the other half lived. I remember remarking to an American that Vancouver was so provincial, and he replied that if you pinched the inhabitants, a week later they would say "ouch". Looking back they were the best days, for we never realized at the time that big isn't necessarily better.

The day of the first rehearsal arrived. I got to the hall early and I greeted my section one by one as they came in.

I learned later that the section players did not understand politeness. It seemed they were used to having a "boss man" as a principal, unlike in Europe where each player treated the other as a colleague and a fellow artist. The attitude of the orchestra to the management was not very healthy either; it was a matter of "Us" and "Them".

I learned subsequently that there had been a disastrous strike the year before in order to gain more weeks of employment for the orchestra, but the population of Vancouver at that time did not justify an increase in the number of concerts. An extraordinary meeting of the Union was organized in order to raise the union dues, or "saw off" as it was euphemistically called, from 1% to 2% of the musicians' fees in order to "strengthen the union" which of course it did not. The only things that happened were that a raise was given to the union president and the office staff was increased with no corresponding gains for the musicians.

Due to their abysmal pay many of the rank and file were forced to take jobs outside of music, and knowing that the imports were being well paid further exacerbated the situation. The union was much stronger and in more evidence than in London. There was a union steward, whose job was to report any infractions however minor, to the union, after each rehearsal or concert.

Generally, the attitude of many members of the orchestra toward the imports was unfriendly, although I tried to be as helpful, co-operative and friendly as possible. Some told me they only really needed a bass and the other imports were not necessary. Whether they told me that for my consumption alone I don't know.

Another thing I soon discovered was that there was no mobility between the union "locals". For instance, if one wanted to play an engagement in Calgary one first had to be a member of the Calgary union "local", and there was a mandatory waiting period even after one had joined, before accepting engagements. This fact made me feel that indeed I had burned my boats and was restricted to Vancouver with no chance of making a move in Canada if things went wrong.

The rehearsal began. There were several good players but many "passengers". The wind was patchy with an overly loud brass section, which, to give him his due, Meredith Davies did his best to control.

The general atmosphere differed greatly from the London scene insofar as there was an air of "Let there be no levity". In London there was always some good-humoured banter and the musicians generally played as if they enjoyed it, however, in Vancouver there seemed to be a stern if not sullen look on most faces. Occasionally I would turn round and try to give some help and direction but was met with a vapid stare. One thing I was thankful for, the rehearsals were for 2½ hours instead of the three hours per rehearsal in London.

Before I came to Canada, Meredith Davies had told me that the orchestra was on a par with the Royal Liverpool Orchestra. I had played with the Liverpool Orchestra on one occasion but on hearing the Vancouver Symphony for the first time, I thought that the Liverpool Orchestra was decidedly the better of the two. Isolated from the rest of the world, and never having the chance of hearing another orchestra, the Vancouver Symphony members deluded themselves that they were a good orchestra, indeed, the music critic of the local newspaper told them so and they all believed him.

The day of the first concert of the season arrived. The next day there was a critique in the newspaper with the headline "Orchestra Bass Heavy". Meredith Davies seemed delighted with this comment because he told me he had never heard anything much from the basses before so would I please keep it up. He suggested that the critic's hi-fi was probably without a bass register so he was now hearing parts of the music he had never heard before.

In between rehearsals I visited Jack Kessler, whom I knew very well from my London days. Jack had resigned from the Vancouver Symphony as concertmaster but was still concertmaster of the CBC Radio Chamber Orchestra, and he gave me an insight into the local situation, some of which was rather disturbing.

Meanwhile in my spare time I was looking at houses, intending to buy one ready for my wife and kids to move into as soon as they arrived in Vancouver. Eventually I found one; it was a new house with gleaming new appliances and in a good area, only ten minutes to the city centre and, moreover, it boasted the best school in Vancouver.

Bearing in mind that Meredith Davies had told me he intended to bring the Vancouver Symphony up to World class level, I plunged wholeheartedly into volunteering as chairman of the orchestra committee, chairman of the auditions committee, organizer of all school concerts in Greater Vancouver and, later, with my wife, a member of the fund raising committee. Incidentally, my wife was the only orchestra wife to belong to anything for the welfare of the organization; the other orchestra wives boycotted all such endeavours. I soon found that my volunteering was to be all pain and no gain, and some of the locals who refused to do anything to help in their own situation openly mistook my efforts as creeping round the management.

The CBC's conductor, John Avison, offered me the position of principal bass in its Chamber Orchestra and I accepted. I needn't have done so because my Symphony contract gave me a guaranteed income; anything I earned outside the Vancouver Symphony would be deducted from it but, as I was so fired up with the idea of making something of the orchestra I believed it to be only fair for me to accept the CBC offer as it would relieve the Vancouver Symphony from the onus of having to pay me my full guaranteed salary. However, some of the other imports turned Avison down; perhaps they were not as altruistic as I was.

John Avison had done a lot for the CBC. He formed the CBC Chamber Orchestra of which I was principal bass for seventeen years. The broadcast recording all had to be done in one four hour session. Frankly, I don't know how Avison stood the strain of conducting a contemporary music programme once or twice a week in the limited time allowed him. It was nerve wracking for the orchestra too, for there was hardly any time to make a second attempt to record anything unless it was a really glaring error.

When I first began playing with them, various works were put on to test my mettle including Mozart's aria *Per Questa Bella Mano* for bass voice, double bass obbligato[34] and orchestra, a frightfully difficult piece for the double bass that was recorded in one take. Another piece, which came up with monotonous regularity was Alberto Ginastera's bass solo with harp accompaniment from his *Variaciones Concertantes*. There were many other big solos for the bass that cropped up from time to time and these pieces were interlarded with a hash of little known 18th century symphonies plus some modern Canadian pieces and most of the standard violin and piano concerti. The choice of programmes was constrained by the Mozart sized orchestra. Six first violins, four or five seconds, three violas, three cellos and two basses plus two flutes, two oboes, two clarinets, two bassoons, two trumpets, two horns and percussion.

There was a regular weekly broadcast, plus one or two extra sessions, also an occasional tour. Avison and Dr. Robert Turner, the producer, were the mainspring of the whole affair, and if it were not for their efforts I don't think the orchestra would have survived as long as it has.

When I first met Avison in 1965, I should say he was in his late forties-early fifties. Of middle height, rubicund, with greying hair brushed back.

Pinchas Zukerman came to conduct the CBC Chamber Orchestra and I thought to myself what a fine violist the world had lost when he changed to conducting. Harry Newstone came regularly, as did Mario Bernardi also Victor Feldbrill, Boris Brott the father, Boris Brott the son and a few others, but Avison did the lion's share of the conducting.

Avison passed away at a relatively early age. I did not attend his funeral but one of the girl violinists did; she told me she went only to make sure he was dead! May God rest his soul, for with all his faults he did a great deal for Canadian music and the Vancouver music scene is poorer without him.

It makes me feel so sad that the CBC Chamber Orchestra is the last radio orchestra left in North America, when once upon a time there were so many radio orchestras. Recently I was glad to learn that an increasing number of people are listening to the radio and maybe it will help this orchestra to remain on the air.

Chapter 16 Notes
34. Obbligato, usually a florid instrumental decoration to a vocal solo

CHAPTER 17

Vancouver continued. The Vancouver Symphony Chamber Players' Tour. I have a row with Arthur Fiedler. Sir Arthur Bliss. I am asked to be principal bass of the Vancouver Opera. Richard Bonynge and Joan Sutherland. I am invited to teach the double bass at the University of British Columbia. I put on a Mini-Festival.

The Vancouver Symphony season continued with Meredith Davies doing the lion's share of the conducting. He was a fairly tall man with brushed back black hair, a longish nose, and a face that the music critic described as "craggy". He was a very capable conductor with a wide repertoire and he was clear with his beat, used a long baton and to good effect. He could address an audience well, and I think he liked doing so.

He had held the post of organist and music director at St.Albans' and Hereford Cathedrals, and his background in choral music came to the fore in performances of such works as Berlioz' *L'Enfance du Christ*, Handel's *Messiah* and Mendelssohn's *Elijah* that had been rarely played in Vancouver before. He made the *Messiah* a yearly event as it always played to packed houses and added to the orchestra's coffers,

During the course of my eight years with the Vancouver Symphony he brought in such conductors as Sir Neville Marriner, Otto Werner-Mueller, Arthur Fiedler and Sir Arthur Bliss plus many others.

I had never had a row with a conductor until Arthur Fiedler arrived. He performed the light music pieces he toured around with very well, but he was an egotist and a great showman. He collected firemen's helmets and would wear one at a concert. On the first day of a rehearsal with the VSO a very young girl pianist was playing a piano concerto. She was very nervous at rehearsal but I thought she was doing well. Fiedler, however, started to bully her unnecessarily, which did not put me in a good mood. He then proceeded to give the back desk of my bass section a bad time. When I told him to quit, and that he was rude and arrogant, he shut up and so did I.

Sir Arthur Bliss was a "character". I had played his ballets *Checkmate* and *Miracle in the Gorbals, the Colour Symphony, Music for Strings* and his *Piano Concerto*. He conducted his *Morning Heroes* with the VSO. It is a work often performed around Rembrance Day.

One funny thing occurred at rehearsal. Bliss wanted the timpanist to play louder. After asking three times and not getting the effect he wanted he lost his temper and cried out "Hit the bloody thing!" which achieved the desired effect. That being said, he was a delightful man. I enjoyed chatting with him about the London scene and also the local fishing.

It was decided by some of the new blood that we should form a chamber music group, and it was called the "Vancouver Symphony Chamber Players". For those who were not playing with the CBC Chamber Orchestra and some of the other concerts that I was involved in I suppose it was a good thing. The work with the VSO was light and they had plenty of time on their hands, but for me it became a chore at times on top of all the other work I was asked to do. The repertoire was long and included Mozart's *Eine Kleine Nachtmusik, A Musical Joke* and some of his *Divertimenti*. Then there was Schubert's *Trout Quintet*, his *Octet*, Beethoven's *Septet*, Spohr's *Nonet*, the Prokofieff *Quintet, Till Eulenspiegel Einmals Ander*, a skit on the Richard Strauss tone poem, pieces by Franz Berwald, the Rossini Sonatas with bass, Roussel's *Duo for bass and bassoon* plus many Canadian pieces. Rehearsing all this took a considerable time.

If the imports were not liked before the chamber ensemble was formed, they certainly were not afterwards. Every year since time immemorial the VSO had made a spring tour of the Province, but the spring of 1966 was going to be with the chamber group and not the orchestra. Understandably this created a furore and though we were barely tolerated before, now we were hated like poison.

Spring arrived and the Vancouver Symphony Chamber Players' tour began. I was anxious to visit for the first time places like Kamloops, Penticton, Vernon, Cranbrook and Rocky Mountain House in Alberta. Forty years ago many of the towns were still primitive, but the vastness of the countryside with its huge evergreens and snow capped mountains made me breathless with wonder.

We were playing in the Okanagan Valley where the Calona winery is situated. Mr. Pasquale "Cap" Capozzi, the owner, an Italian gentleman of the old school was a very gracious host. The winery has a wine tasting room in the style of a refectory, so just before the concert we were invited to sample some of the products.

Some of the group took full advantage of a selection of all the delicious wines laid out on a table just waiting to be sampled. There was just time for us to get a meal before the concert started, which was a good thing, as it somewhat lessened the effect of the alcohol, but when we were seated on the platform waiting to begin the Beethoven *Septet* we just couldn't get started. The first violin gave a signal to commence but nobody came in and a couple of the players started to giggle. At the third try we all came in together, and despite the rocky beginning it was one of the best performances of the Beethoven *Septet* I have ever played.

Back in Vancouver, the situation had gone from bad to worse, particularly as the Vancouver Symphony Chamber Players had had a very successful tour and it was hinted that the tour might be repeated which certainly did not go down well with the Vancouver Symphony Orchestra members. I tried to bring an olive branch to resolve matters between the imports and the local musicians but without much success.

Meredith Davies brought in several famous soloists, among them were Yehudi Menuhin; John Ogdon, who played the Busoni piano concerto; Dame Janet Baker, the singer; Alfredo Campoli, violinist; Jacqueline Du Pré, 'cellist; Phillipe Entremont the pianist who I thought was superb; and the Romero family of guitarists, among many others.

There was a local man of tremendous talents, George Zukerman, who besides being a bassoon virtuoso was also an entrepreneur and ran an artists' agency. He contributed much to the musical side of the city, by bringing in the Canadian Ballet Company, the Royal Winnipeg Ballet and the Bolshoi Ballet, musicals, chamber music groups, soloists etc.

The Vancouver Symphony had long cast an envious eye on the Vancouver Opera as well as the CBC orchestra and the ballets etc. that came, and were actively promoting the demise of George and another influential contractor, but they never made much effort to create new work. The CBC under Avison staunchly held out against it. If it had been swallowed up by the Symphony it would certainly have been the end of Avison. The main problem as I mentioned before, was that the population base was not large enough to support the Symphony fully, and it relied on private and corporate donations to survive; there was not enough income from audiences.

The Vancouver Opera Society usually had five operas in its season. I was asked to be principal bass. They had good artists; I can remember Paul Plishka, Sherrill Milnes and Joan Sutherland among the very distinguished lead singers. The repertoire was mainly all the old favourites such as

Cavalleria Rusticana and *Pagliacci, Rigoletto, Carmen, the Flying Dutchman* and *La Bohème*. The orchestra was fairly good, I thought, and was mainly composed of the best people in the CBC and the Symphony plus one or two freelance players. There were several conductors, mostly Canadian, including Mario Bernardi and George Crum. Other conductors engaged included Kresimir Sipusch, Anton Guadagno, Fausto Cleva and Richard Bonynge. The opera director for many years was Irving Guttman, who made a fairly good job of it although his stage direction was perhaps a little too static.

I remember once when Jack Kessler was concertmaster and we were performing Puccini's opera *The Girl of the Golden West* conducted by Fausto Cleva. He was a miserable individual, sometimes rude to the orchestra. Although he conducted opera well, I think he had a chip on his shoulder because he was not recognized as one of the "greats" of opera conductors. He was living and working in San Francisco at the time. At the first interval, Jack, who was rather irascible, came up to me very excitedly and said, "Bob, I don't know whether to have a go at him now or in the next intermission." I did my best to try to dissuade him from having a row, but I believe Jack did tell him in no uncertain terms that his behaviour was unacceptable. Cleva never came to Vancouver again.

The Musicians' Union was very helpful in funding school concerts. There were two other sponsors, the VSO and the City of Vancouver Schools Department. I was put in charge of it all and named it the "Tri-Sponsored Schools Concerts". It took many hours of hard work to organize, and my wife gave me immense help, so it developed into a big enterprise for which all and sundry congratulated me. Unfortunately, a year or two later the City Council withdrew its support citing a money shortage, and that was the end of the children's concerts.

The Musicians' Union had sent me a nice letter of congratulation but you can't fight City Hall. Down the road as a future audience, the kids would have been invaluable in keeping things like the Symphony alive. Any attempt to explain to City Hall that the Arts brought in tremendous benefits and repaid any subsidy many times over in revenue from tourism, fell on deaf ears. Supporting the Symphony was not on their agenda.

Nicholas Goldschmidt had put on the Vancouver International Festival the year before I arrived in Vancouver. There were such conductors as Herbert von Karajan and many famous artists, but they were expensive. One saving grace was that the VSO was employed, and it brought in some well-needed cash to the orchestra players during the blank summer months, but financially it was a flop and ended heavily in debt. Jack

Kessler who was concertmaster of the Vancouver Symphony at that time told me that von Karajan, who was not thrilled at having to conduct the VSO came up to him and said, "How can you stand it!"

I had played for "Nicki" Goldschmidt with the English Chamber Orchestra in London, and recently I read that he had passed away in his mid- nineties. He was a very affable, musical conductor with a clear direction and sense of the music.

During much discussion with my wife I came to the conclusion that it might be a good thing to attempt another festival, but a more modest one using local talent.

The H.R. Macmillan Planetarium, which had opened not long before, seemed to me to be an excellent site. True, its seating capacity was small, but there were extensive grounds around it that could accommodate many festival activities. The Planetarium Committee was all in favour of a festival happening and promised to arrange for loudspeakers to be fitted outside for the expected overflow. The Musicians' Union came up with a grant from the Music Performance Trust Fund, and also the local Arts Council gave a little. Guess who made up the expected deficit. I named it the Vancouver Mini-Festival, admission was to be to free to all.

There followed many weeks of very hard work, feverish at times. At first my wife demurred, but eventually she came on board. I don't know what I would have done without her.
There were chamber concerts, a violin recital, a small orchestra conducted by Meredith Davies, a ballet especially written and the music composed for the occasion. A series of ethnic dance groups performed including First Nations who entered into the spirit of it. There was also a jazz ensemble, in fact, something for everybody

The Mini-Festival was a tremendous success. The newspapers and the radio were very enthusiastic and giving it much publicity. The crowds were so great that I had to bring in the police to control them, especially at the ballet, which was repeated after much acclaim. When the Mini-Festival ended there was a long, flattering article written by Lawrence Cluderay, the music critic of the Vancouver Province, who thought the whole idea of having a scaled down version of the Vancouver International Festival was a good thing. It also brought in some desperately needed employment for some of the musicians, and, most importantly it ended in the black as well as being an artistic success. A donation of a few hundred dollars from my wife and I had helped too, but the whole thing had been achieved on a shoestring budget, which I thought might encourage its support in future years.

The Vancouver Visitors Bureau organized a special luncheon and presented me with a statuette of Captain Vancouver with my name engraved on it. With all that enthusiasm I fully thought I could do bigger and better the next year, but it was not to be.

I wrote to the Vancouver councillor who was in charge of Arts and Entertainment but I never received a reply. The Vancouver Ballet Society asked me to be its president but there were no funds and not likely to be any forthcoming so I politely refused.

This whole thing, combined with all the other abortive efforts I had made to further the cause of the Arts, and music in particular, was the subject of many debates with my wife and myself as to whether it wouldn't be better to return to London to a really professional environment. I actually booked us all on a boat sailing for England, and sent a letter of resignation to Victor White. I received a warm reply asking me to reconsider my decision, but I continued to make plans for our return to London.

At this juncture, the VSO came back with an offer, again asking me to re consider. My wife, then suggested that we ought to have consulted with the children, now sixteen and eighteen respectively. At those ages there would have to be a considerable re-adjustment for them back in England, so surprisingly, she thought we should stay at least for a few more years whilst the kids were making headway at school. This is what we did; I accepted the VSO offer and we stayed.

Not long after the Mini-Festival I was approached by the Music Department of the University of British Columbia to teach the double bass to about a dozen students. There was an air of smugness about the place, I thought. I only went to one faculty meeting, where I overheard one of them saying, "Well boys, we've got a good thing going, let no-one rock the boat." Most of the faculty were competent, some brilliant, but there were many who should not have been teaching at all, they certainly could not have held down a job in the great big musical profession outside the groves of Academe.

All the bass students were making the bass a second study, meaning that they thought the bass was easy, and it would be a breeze to sail through the term not doing any practice but still obtaining straight "A"s. The double bass is far from being an easy instrument, and when it came to making a proper study of it the pupils were all disappointed that they had to practice and treat their studies seriously.

There was one pupil, "Mark" whom I nicknamed the "Artful Dodger". He would come to the lesson totally unprepared and I was annoyed that I was wasting my time with him. My daughter was in the French

Department and came home one day and told me she had been in the library where she had overheard someone ask Mark who was teaching him at his next lesson. Mark's reply was, "Oh, only old Bob Meyer, I can get around him alright." Mark arrived for his lesson, and as usual was totally unprepared. However, I pressed him on and on so much that he went away rather less buoyant than when he came. Eventually Mark graduated and got a job teaching music in a school. A violinist colleague whose son attended Mark's school complained to me that Mark, who had to teach string instruments, was teaching the violin using bass fingering!

Another such pupil was Fred, who was even lazier than Mark. Things got to such a pitch that just before the end of term I gave Fred an ultimatum that if he could not play even a simple Simandl exercise then I would have no option but to fail him. I reasoned that I had a conscience even if he did not - it did not reflect very well on me to give someone a pass if he really deserved to fail.

The end of term came, and Fred marched in pathetically unprepared so I failed him. This caused some consternation amongst some of the faculty, as in those days the whole name of the game was to keep as many students on the books as possible so as to get more money and grants for the Department. My stock with them went down greatly after that.

I was heartened when some time later, I ran into Hugh McLean, a member of the Music Faculty, later to become Dean of Music at the University of Western Ontario, at London; he told me that it was the best thing that had ever happened to Fred, who was working hard at composition and has now become a recognized composer. He also worked so hard on the bass that he was accepted into the Vancouver Symphony.

In the summer of 1972 I got a phone call from George Corwin who was teaching conducting at the University of Victoria on Vancouver Island. George, a very erudite man who possesses a Doctor of Musical Arts degree, was, and is, a fine conductor. That phone call began a friendship that has lasted for over thirty years. Even today I play in some of the various orchestras and groups that he conducts. He wanted me to go over to the University of Victoria and play in a week of concerts for small orchestra. I was surprised at his innovative programmes and the way he produced such fine performances. If he had not buried himself in a university I'm sure he would have made a great name for himself outside Academe. One thing he did do amongst others was to spearhead the building of a concert hall at the University.

That summer I went to England to see Dr. Gordon Jacob about *A Little Concerto* that he had agreed to write for me and I also saw Eugene Cruft and his wife during the course of the trip. My wife and I arrived at their apartment and I was sad to notice how much Mrs. Cruft had deteriorated in health. Gene, however, looked his old spry self, a little older perhaps, but he was still playing, he told me. Mrs. Cruft drew my wife aside and said, 'There they are, look at them, talking about the bloody bass. Let you and I have our own little chat, my dear'. Mrs. Cruft was quite the lady, and I had never heard her utter the word "bloody" before. It was very evident that she had reached the end of her tether, being married to a bassist.

Until I came to Canada I had had very little to do with symphony or opera boards of directors. After my experiences with various musical boards in Canada I was glad I hadn't. Most boards seemed to consist of the local moneybags plus a few ciphers because they thought it was a "good thing to be on the board". It helped them in business. True, there were one or two altruists who worked very hard for the common weal, and invariably a few elderly wealthy ladies who thought being on the board was to have wine and cheese gatherings and afternoon teas.

The VSO ultimately triumphed by taking over the opera orchestra. Unfortunately, some of its members thought playing in the opera orchestra a bit of a joke, and that it was *infra dig* to be playing in it at all. Then Richard Bonynge came along. There was some derision (undeserved) in that they nicknamed him "Mr. Sutherland", for he was married to Joan Sutherland, but he could stand on his own anywhere in the world as an opera conductor. The lack of attention and even common courtesy was the final straw on the camel's back. Richard decided to revert to the old freelance opera orchestra who at least took the job seriously and were glad to have the job.

One of Bonynge's favourite composers was Massenet. He decided to put on Massenet's *Le Roi de Lahore*, a beautiful opera that was well staged with exquisite costumes. Unfortunately the audiences were very thin. The local critic openly accused Bonynge and Sutherland of using Vancouver as a guinea pig before a possible New York première. I don't think this was true. They were also accused of plunging the opera into debt, but I have it on good authority that they were benefactors of the Vancouver Opera; one cannot believe all one reads in the Press. Bonynge told me he felt very depressed at all this. To cheer him up I gave him a copy of a 'cello and bass duet which he had never seen before and he was glad to add it to his extensive library of Massenet's works.

Bonynge and Sutherland put on a dinner for the new freelance orchestra in appreciation of their co-operation and I had the honour of sitting next to Joan Sutherland. I reminded her that I had played at her first

BBC broadcast in London. It was a Mozart programme and the orchestra was the English Chamber Orchestra. She was delighted that I remembered the occasion. Altogether Bonynge and Sutherland were a fine couple who did much for the Vancouver Opera, but it is a pity that more appreciation wasn't shown them for all their efforts.

I should mention another well-meaning entrepreneur, Yondani Butt, who formed the Orchestra Canadiana. It was a small symphony orchestra that he funded almost entirely out of his own pocket. When I left the Vancouver Symphony, Yondani asked me to play principal bass in his orchestra. There were tours and recordings, but it was short-lived. There was tremendous opposition from the Vancouver Symphony. Yondani took his orchestra on tours to the Yukon and Northern British Columbia, and he also put on a subscription series of weekly concerts. These were fairly well attended but after two or three seasons he had to give up, as his family who were sponsoring him withdrew their support. He also made some good recordings at his own expense. I heard later that he had been engaged to conduct the London Philharmonic Orchestra on occasion.

The Bottom Line

THE BOTTOM LINE

PART THREE

CHAPTER 18

Touring the True North, Strong and Freezing. I give up playing the bass forever (or so I thought). Robert Meyer Artists Management Ltd. The Victoria Consevatory of Music. The Richmond Community Music School. President of Richmond, B.C, Arts Council. I am involved in the building of a new theatre and make plans for a new Arts Centre. Chinese brush painting. Family tragedy.

The CBC Chamber Orchestra had to show the flag all over Canada. This meant journeying as far as Tuktoyaktuk, north of the Arctic Circle in what were then the North West Territories; the Yukon; Baffin Island in the northeast;, Vancouver Island in the southwest and New Brunswick on Canada's eastern maritimes. We travelled to countless places in between, including Hudson Bay, Rankin Inlet, Churchill, Coppermine, Prince Albert, Moose Jaw, Regina, Medicine Hat, Winnipeg, Toronto and Ottawa, in Washington State, Idaho and Wyoming, and even as far as Fairbanks Alaska. This brought the CBC Orchestra recognition from the Canada Council, thus ensuring that it would be given funding. I am glad to have done it for it gave me an amazing glimpse of Canada.

Because it had to be done on the cheap, travel was often by bus which was dangerous on some of the icy roads, but sometimes DC 3s', Beaver's or Otter seaplanes were used and the Royal Canadian Air Force helped at times.

Early one May in the Far North we had to cross the frozen Beaufort Sea in a Bombardier passenger vehicle equipped with tracks to surmount the ice and snow. I was terrified that we might all sink through the ice into the water but eventually we crossed without incident and went on to play the concert. What with the cold and the scariness I think all the string players played with an extra vibrato!

Once I stayed with the head of the local Hydro who told me that he was a volunteer with a housing project for the Eskimos, (now called Inuit). A few bungalows were built to the highest standards. Three coats of paint had to be applied inside, many examinations took place to ensure that all were built strictly according to plan and they were eventually handed over to the Inuit in pristine condition. My host told me he went to inspect them two weeks after occupation and he was nauseated by the dreadful stench coming from one house. When he entered he noticed that the walls of the living room were spattered with blood and there on the carpet was a dead seal in the process of being butchered. Obviously they hadn't taken the central heating into account!

Most of the concerts took place in the school auditoria. In one of the schools in Inuvik I had a chat with one of the teachers. She told me that since pop and candy machines were installed in the schools the children's teeth and health had deteriorated. Their general diet had been changed for the worst since "civilization" had overtaken them.

One incongruous thing I noticed was an Inuit man going out to hunt, driving a snowmobile whilst his Husky dog was sitting behind him on the snowmobile deck!

After playing in Lillooet, British Columbia, we were invited to the magnificent home of a man who had owned a uranium mine and had sold it for a considerable profit. His house was perched on a high hill and it could only be entered by means of a funicular railway. Inside the house were magnificent Persian rugs, Buhle ware, the original bed of Ferdinand and Isabella of Spain and many other antiques. He made copies of antique furniture and employed several machinists in a large workshop.

He was self-sufficient, raising his own cattle and chickens, and he also had an artificial lake. Electricity was generated by a stream flowing from the lake, and he thought he would probably be able to survive if his worst fears of a possible nuclear war were realized. A housekeeper was his only companion and he was very lonely. He invited me to visit with my wife, but I had to decline due to pressure of work.

The Bolshoi Ballet, who came to Vancouver for a number of years, was a highly disciplined troupe with some wonderful solo dancers. The corps de ballet danced with an extreme precision that I had rarely seen before. Their ballet mistress was a real old dragon and as soon as they arrived after a long journey, she would immediately put them through their paces before they could eat. Their conductor, Alexandr Kopilov was one of the finest ballet conductors that I have ever met.

Unfortunately, the Bolshoi stopped coming and I was told that to break even they had to perform in a theatre with a minimum of 4,000 seats; our hall held only 2,000. One of the company with whom I chatted blamed it on the excessive cost of hiring stagehands. The local head stage carpenter would always dictate how many stagehands were required for a particular show. His word was law. Whether the large number of stagehands contributed to their subsequent non-appearance I cannot say, I am only repeating what I was told. It was a great pity, but this, too, was happening with all the other visiting shows.

When I first arrived in Vancouver I imagined that things could only get better but they steadily got worse with fewer and fewer travelling shows coming into the city because of financial difficulties.

On the brighter side, a group called "The Friends of Chamber Music" would bring in world-class chamber music groups as well as individual soloists. They have since expanded and are still in existence. Zukerman brought in the Leningrad String Quartet, one of the finest I have ever heard.

The Vancouver Early Music Sociiety has greatly contributed to the musical life of the city. There are also one or two amateur societies who are going strong.

When I first came to Vancouver, the Symphony played at the Queen Elizabeth Theatre, and later on the old Orpheum cinema was converted to a concert hall for them. Years later the new Chan Hall at the University of B.C. was opened.

Towards the end of Meredith Davies' tenure as conductor of the Vancouver Symphony Orchestra, he seemed to be becoming very disillusioned with the orchestra's lack of progress and so was I. In his view the matter seemed to rest with the Board who had conflicting ideas as to how the orchestra should be run. He told me he might do one more year and then quit, which he did.

There was the usual search for a conductor, and eventually Kazuyoshi Akiyama was chosen for the position, mainly at the wind players' insistence. Meredith told me it was because the winds thought that Akiyama would say "yes" to everything. It is odd that when Rudolf Barshai came on the scene as a conductor who could have improved the general overall standard, he was given very short shrift for attempting to put right the more glaring faults.

Akiyama was a very pleasant man, a fine musician and a good conductor with a clear beat. He excelled at such things as the *Great Gate of Kiev* from Moussorgsky's *Pictures at an Exhibition*, Tchaikowsky's symphonies and tone poems, Ravel, Debussy and in fact all the loud and exciting pieces. I enjoyed working with him.

In 1972 it had already crossed my mind that maybe it was time for me to venture into fresh fields. My mind was finally made up for me by an unhappy occurrence. My wife was diagnosed with cancer; fortunately she survived it and was later pronounced cured, but in the meantime I decided the best thing was to leave the Symphony and concentrate on helping her. She needed someone to be with her at all the radiation treatments etc. and, as she had been so good in helping me in my career it was now my turn to be there for her.

A little later George Zukerman brought in the Leningrad Symphony Orchestra and my wife and I were in the audience. As soon as they started to play the anthems we both thought that this indeed was an orchestra. Its sound was on a par with some of the great orchestras I had played with, and brought tears of nostalgia to my eyes. The nostalgia not only brought tears but also strengthened my resolve to go off in a new direction.

Some time later, after my wife had recovered from her bout with cancer, I had more time on my hands. Although I was still playing principal bass with the CBC Chamber Orchestra and the Vancouver Opera, and also teaching at the University of Victoria and playing a few freelance dates, I decided that maybe it was payback time. I had done very well in my career and there were many projects on my mind in which I could be of service to the Arts community.

The thing uppermost in my mind was that many young Canadian artists had to go to New York in those days to find an agent to represent them, as there were few Canadian artists' agencies. I thought it would be a good idea to help them so I formed Robert Meyer Artists Management Ltd. In this, Yehudi Menuhin was a great help with his enthusiasm, advice and contacts. We met in Vancouver and discussed a plan of action. In his letters to me he made many useful suggestions in regard to a good mix of artists in my future portfolio by including a few established people.

Among the conductors were Kresimir Sipusch, Igor Markevitch and Simon Streatfield. The director of the Vancouver Opera, Irving Guttman, also wanted to be represented as did Béla Siki the pianist and Denis Szygmondi the violinist, Luigi Bianchi an Italian violist, and many young Canadian instrumentalists and singers.

Some time earlier, I had written to the Canada Council, but I did not receive a reply. I decided to visit them in person so I travelled to Ottawa. I asked why my letter had not been answered, and was astounded when I was told that the official in question never replied to letters!

I got the same run-around when a big name on the Canada Council came to Vancouver at Government expense, ostensibly to discuss helping young Canadian artists. I left a message at his hotel but he never phoned me back. This led me to the conclusion that I couldn't expect much help from Government quarters. I did have some success but it was very time-consuming and expensive and when it came to the time to pay a fee to me to cover at least my expenses, some of the artists were reluctant to pay anything at all.

I had to have a long, hard look at the whole situation. I would have been happy to have covered only my expenses but maybe I should have been a bit more hard-nosed in my dealings. I had spent a considerable amount of money on the project and could not see myself as being a philanthropist – I couldn't afford to be anyway, so reluctantly, R.M.A.M. Ltd. met its demise. I was disappointed and sad that it had not succeeded but in later years I was happy to know that some successful artists had emerged as well-known soloists as a result of my efforts.

I was invited to be vice principal/business manager for the Victoria Conservatory of Music and it was the most frustrating job I ever undertook. Many factors contributed to the Conservatory's financial woes. One rich lady on the Board of Governors regularly came up with money to bail them out but I could not see that going on forever. There were some people on the board who agreed that something drastic needed to be done but I could not achieve the necessary changes. After all this and other happenings that I shall not bother to mention, I decided that the Victoria Conservatory wasn't for me, so I left after about three months, which to this day I think was a wise move.

After having had my fingers burned with the Victoria Conservatory of Music I was rash enough to accept the position of Head of the Richmond Community Music School, situated in a suburb of Vancouver.

My worst fears were realized. It turned out as I suspected, all pain and no gain, but at least I was able to set up a syllabus in French and English, introduce new subjects and I even found them a home.

At the time I was also President of the Richmond Arts Council, so in that capacity I was able to twist a few arms on the Richmond Council for a place to house the Richmond Community Music School. We were given a building in an old works yard and the conversion of the building was left to me and some volunteers. The politics were even worse than those I had encountered at the Victoria Conservatory, and in addition, there was opposition from some members of the Registered Music Teachers Association. So, having put them on their feet, I bade them all the best of luck, and left, happily.

I had agreed to taking on the job of President of the Richmond Arts Council with mixed emotions but with the stipulation that it would be for only a year. The job was honorary and at that time the Arts Council was in a very critical stage of its history; I thought that maybe I could put them on the right track. There was a new theatre about to be built, the "Gateway Theatre", and it too came under the aegis of the Arts Council. There were twenty-three arts groups connected with it; sculptors, potters, painters, sketchers, dance groups, theatre groups, debaters, Chinese watercolourists, dance classes for children and adults, ballet, stage and a host of the others. Fortunately I had a paid secretary who took a lot of the load off my shoulders

Of course there was the all-important fundraising to do as well as deciding on the theatre's structure. I suggested that due to economy of scale it would cost less to build a larger theatre that could better pay for itself with the larger audience it would hold. However the answer to that was, "Oh well, we'll just have to engage them (the artists) for two nights instead of one." I couldn't believe my ears and I tried to point out that we would have to pay two fees as well as two nights' accommodation, but it was to no avail, they were all unyielding, so being in the minority I had to let it go.

I found many frustrating ideas coming forth from the board, which at that time consisted of many of what I called the "blue rinse brigade", i.e. ladies, middle aged and elderly who were well off, had a lot of time on their hands and seemed to think that being on a board should be a sinecure and that afternoon teas, cocktail parties and the like should be the main order of business. Some of the ideas they put forth were really laughable. Sometimes one of these ladies would stand up and say, "I think we should do ……" and there followed something absolutely impossible to achieve with our budget and the forces we had at hand. I soon developed a strategy for this, and my stock reply was, "Well, madam, I think that is an excellent idea and we should form a sub–committee with you at the helm'."That never failed. Invariably there was the reply, "I'm awfully sorry, I'm on so many other committees and of course, you know, there's my husband to consider." My invariable answer was, "I quite understand, Mrs. X, and reluctantly we'll have to leave the matter, good idea though it was."

On the other side of the coin there were business people who didn't have much time, would come in late to a meeting, and criticize what was being done and then, having said their piece would depart early, but there were one or two old diehards who would volunteer to do much of the legwork. Unfortunately, as is so often the case, so much work was put on their plate that they often became disenchanted, so I tried to spread the load as evenly as possible in order to hold on to the ones who were the real gems.

After countless hours of working on the new theatre, it was ready, and the Richmond Arts Council handed it over to a theatre committee that proceeded to draw up grandiose plans for the opening. After due deliberation the theatre committee decided that no guests would be invited to the opening; everyone would have to pay for a ticket. The only exception would be the Mayor, but even he would have to pay for his wife! Needless to say I did not attend the opening but wished them well.

Another project I initiated was this; the Arts Centre had outgrown its present premises, a single-floored building taking up a lot of land. The public library next door wanted to expand, but there was no land for them to do so. The head librarian and I quietly sat down together and made a deal that if we, the Arts Council, knocked down our old building and rebuilt a new one on three floors, then the library would have room to expand; in addition, the library trust would give us a grant towards a new arts centre that could easily house all of its many groups.

I arranged a potluck supper for it to be discussed. The paid council employee whose job was to look after the Arts didn't like the idea of this new chap coming in and upsetting the applecart when everything was running so smoothly (for him). His wife was saying, "It would never happen, this wasn't the time, the economy didn't warrant it etc. etc." and I was laughed out. Interestingly enough, a few years later, after I had left Richmond, I was gratified to learn that the new arts centre had indeed been built, along with the new library and all was going well.

There were some funny moments too. One Sunday morning there was to be an adjudication for a ballet prize. I arrived to see that all went smoothly but the judge, an ex-professional ballerina, didn't make an appearance so I was asked to be a judge.

Having no formal knowledge of ballet dancing, I could not be classed as a judge, but there was no alternative, the kids were waiting and we had to start. About half a dozen kids went through their paces and the two or three of us on the panel came to the unanimous conclusion that one little girl was undoubtedly the best, followed by numbers two and three.

When the results were announced the mother of one child came up to the table and exclaimed excitedly that nobody had told her there could be a piano accompaniment, her little girl had danced solo and that it was not fair.

I had to make a quick decision. I had noticed that there was a pile of blank certificates on the table just waiting to be inscribed so I had the bright idea of announcing that the panel had had a very difficult time making a decision and we had come to the unanimous conclusion that all the other little girls without certificates would be given "honourable mention" certificates. All the contestants and their mothers greeted this with great joy. They were presented with their scrolls duly inscribed and left clutching them happily.

One good thing that came out of being president of the Richmond Arts Council was that I was introduced to Winifred Wan-Chun Lee, a world famous Chinese watercolourist who had exhibited all over the Orient. Little did I realize that I would be studying off and on with her for over eighteen years and even now still regard myself as an amateur. Winifred later introduced me to Professor Chan to study Chinese calligraphy; he had taught at Hong Kong University. I was fortunate enough to purchase a chop, i.e. a stamp of my name in Chinese, from Professor Chan that he made especially for me for a very reasonable sum. At the time, I did not know that he was a world expert in chop carving. I discovered this much later at a Chinese art exhibition where I hung some of my pictures. Several of the artists came up to me and asked where I had obtained my chop. I told them it was made by Professor Chan and they all exclaimed in awe "Bob, you have a Chan chop!"

My life had been going along steadily; my wife was volunteering with the Steveston Historical Society and I was also volunteering and doing a fair amount of playing, when a bombshell struck. Julia, my daughter, was a practicing Crown Prosecutor with a Masters degree in Law and also an honours French degree and she could plead in both French and English. She had met her future husband at law school and just before their marriage Julia had gone for a pre-nuptial medical examination and her doctor told her she noticed a small lump on the thyroid, but not to worry, thyroid lumps were mostly always benign. When the biopsy results came back she was diagnosed with medullary carcinoma, a deadly, rare cancer of which we learned later that there was no hope of a cure. I wouldn't accept it and searched everywhere for a possible cure but all in vain. She passed away at the age of twenty-nine. There was one bright spot on the horizon; she left behind a little girl, Isabel, aged eighteen months.

There was an opera rehearsal that night as Julia lay dying and she said to me "Bob, don't do the opera." I skipped the rehearsal. Two days later she passed away, and at the performance, Anton Guadagno the conductor came into the pit, put his arm round me and said, "Bob, I'm so sorry for what happened." This gave me enough strength to get through, but, the show must go on.

CHAPTER 19

Starting a new life in Sooke, British Columbia, Canada. I take up the bass again. Nautical frolics. Sooke Concert Society. Sooke Philharmonic Orchestra. The Victoria Symphony. The Greater Victoria Youth Orchestra.

The trauma of Julia's death had a tremendous effect on me. I was so distraught that I gave up playing the double bass for fourteen years. I reasoned that I had played all the solos, been there, done it and now was the time to give it up and go into retirement.

Vancouver had been expanding rapidly; Steveston, where we lived, had at one time been a small fishing village with its own identity, but it was now being swallowed up as a Vancouver suburb.

In 1987, after searching all over British Columbia, my wife and I ended up on Vancouver Island where we came upon a 2½ acre waterfront lot in Sooke, a village of about six thousand people in those days, and about a fifty minute drive from Victoria, the Capital. We decided to build our dream house and I set about designing it myself.

I advertised my basses. There was a Betts, an Old Italian and a solo bass built for me by Ernest Lant, an English maker; as well there were five bows made especially for me by the English bow-maker P.W. Bryant, together with an airfreight case. I received many replies. Bryant had been the first hand at Hill's, the stringed instrument dealer in London, and had opened a shop of his own to make bows just after WW2. Unfortunately he could not obtain Pernambuco wood from Brazil, which is essential for a fine bow, because of currency restrictions. I contacted Sir Thomas Beecham who wrote to the British Board of Trade to enable a shipment of Pernambuco wood to be delivered to Bryant, who was eternally grateful to me afterwards.

A bass player from the USA came to Sooke to view them and after playing on them said he felt like a kid in a candy store. I gave him a deal he couldn't refuse so he bought the lot. As he was leaving he asked me if I wanted to keep perhaps one of them, but I was firm in my resolve and said 'No'. I was looking forward to continuing with my painting with which I had been so active since giving up the bass.

As the basses were going down the driveway in the hired truck, I could hardly believe that I was now bass-less. I remembered a line from George Bernard Shaw's *Saint Joan*. After Joan has been burned at the stake, someone says, "You have heard the last of her," and the reply was, "The last of her? Hm! I wonder!'" Somewhere at the back of my mind was the nagging thought that maybe, just maybe, I might play the bass again, but I'd sold them all hadn't I?

Soon afterwards I was approached to be president of Sooke's Arts Council, which I politely refused, but, however, I did promise to arrange for a barge to be towed to Sooke Harbour, and engaged the Naden Naval Band to play at the opening of the newly dedicated Whiffen Spit Park, now renamed Quimper Park after Manuel Quimper, the Spanish naval captain who had discovered Sooke over 200 years ago.

The barge was safely anchored off-shore and the Band went aboard. After playing one or two numbers it was the politician's turn. The record crowd was told how lucky it was to receive the necessary funding for the park but he forgot to tell us it was really some of our own tax money being returned. Then he went on to make a strong political pitch. After that, we were treated to a long and boring history of the area; a suitable blessing was followed by *O' Canada*. That being done, the Band erupted into the usual navy classics - *A Life on the Ocean Wave, the Sailor's Hornpipe* and *Hearts of Oak* plus *Anchors Aweigh*. Everyone then repaired to the numerous refreshment tents to partake of grilled salmon, hamburgers and fish and chips washed down with copious draughts of beer and wine. This went on until dark when the stars came out and the fireworks began. People were sitting round camp fires, the older ones sleeping it off while the young ones were kissing and canoodling which made one old dear mutter something about Sodom and Gomorrah.

As Betty and I tried to slip quietly away, one of the locals called out to us that we had 'done real good', which meant more to us than anything.

Some time later I was asked to start a concert society in Sooke. I accepted with the proviso that I would only do it for a year and once it was up and running the Arts Council was to take over. There was a considerable amount of work to be done with the usual "helpers" who were on the board in name only but full of unworkable suggestions. In the event it boiled down to my wife and I doing the lion's share of the work involved. We sat at the shopping malls fundraising and trying to sign up memberships of the concert society and managed to sign up 230 or so members, enough to put on a small season but not quite enough to engage the Victoria Symphony Orchestra, for which we would have needed 250. I talked to the manager of the VSO and he agreed to bring the orchestra at a cut rate, hoping that we could sign up more members for the following year..

I approached George Zukerman who was still running Overture Concerts, his booking agency, and decided to follow his pattern of signing members up for the whole series so that we would have the necessary money in hand before the season started, and not be in debt.

There were about half a dozen concerts in all and they varied from classical trios to Ukrainian folk dancers to the VSO. They were held in the gymnasium of the local high school. It had a small stage, and the space was adequate, if somewhat stark.

We had our ups and downs. Some members of the Arts Council complained to me about the fact that the stage drapes at the back were not drawn. I patiently explained that I had being trying hard to have this done but protocol demanded that we go through the School Board, not the janitor.

Another lady complained there were no flowers on stage and it looked awfully unsightly, so I suggested to her that perhaps she could arrange for the flowers. She agreed, but on the night of the concert there were no flowers.

Then there were problems with the janitors, or in politically correct language, custodians. If one wanted the slightest thing done, one had to grovel and say, '"Please sir," and according to their mood at that particular moment they would or would not agree to do it. One gentleman was sweeping the corridor by the hall and had his radio blaring while the concert was on. He shut it off with very bad grace after I asked him to; indeed, he looked very aggrieved as though his rights were being trampled upon.

The season was a great success so I handed it over to the Sooke Arts Council, but unfortunately the concerts only ran for another year. I was asked to fill in the breach again but having had my fill of do-gooding, I declined and determined then and there that I would never again be connected with anything musical, but Fate played a hand again.

One day I espied someone coming down the driveway to my house. Of all people, that someone turned out to be Norman Nelson. After greeting me with "Dr. Livingstone, I presume," Norman told me he had retired from the University of Alberta at Edmonton and was now living in Sooke with his wife, Jenny. It was years since we had seen each other, dating back to our Vancouver Symphony days when he had been concertmaster, so we had much to talk about.

Then the bombshell dropped; he said he was thinking of starting an orchestra that would be called the Sooke Philharmonic. I gasped and wondered out loud where he would get his players. First he said he would like me to be principal bass. I refused out of hand explaining that I hadn't played the bass for over fourteen years and, I added smugly, that anyway I didn't have an instrument, having sold them all.

Norman did not take "no" for an answer, for a week later he phoned to say he had borrowed a bass from Mary Rannie, the principal bass of the Victoria Symphony and would I re-consider? From this I established a wonderful friendship with Mary and was honoured to be present at her wedding reception in Gary Karr's house.

After much urging from my wife and my son who both said it would be "good for me", I relented and agreed to play for Norman.

I took delivery of the bass and I realized then how gracious Mary was to lend me such a fine instrument, so I dug out Simandl's very difficult *Gradus ad Parnassum* from my library and practiced it assiduously for hours on end. I think it went a long way in assuaging the grief I still felt from the loss of my daughter.

When the day of the first rehearsal of the Sooke Philharmonic Orchestra arrived, it felt wonderful to be sitting in an orchestra again. I presented myself, complete with my borrowed bass, and settled down in good time beforehand to observe the players as they arrived. I didn't feel out of place after all those years of not playing the bass. It just felt like "same old, same old".

They were a motley crew drawn from every strata of society. I wondered how on earth Norman had assembled them. Norman's wife, Jenny, had worked in the BBC Symphony's office and has a very good knowledge of concert organization which helped tremendously; nevertheless it must have been an immense task. Among the players were fishermen, home-makers, teachers, scientists, artists, authors, plumbers, carpenters, computer experts, retirees and many other trades and professionals; there was even an astro-physicist among them. Some were fine players, others mediocre and some just downright bloody awful. There were hiccupping horns, screechy strings, bellowing brass and deafening drums.

The rehearsal began. There was utter chaos and cacophony and I wondered how on earth we could possibly give a concert, but by dint of cajoling, threatening, shouting, pleading, begging and joking and after many rehearsals, Norman gradually licked the orchestra into reasonable shape and we were ready (or almost ready) for the concert, which was to be on June 20th. 1998. It was a great success, and the future of the orchestra was at once assured.

I went with Norman to the Provincial Arts Council offices to enquire whether we could obtain a grant for the conversion of an old barn to a concert hall, but there was no money available, so the orchestra continued to play in a school auditorium that was less than satisfactory. Later on different venues were tried out and the orchestra was reduced in size to form a chamber orchestra. Nevertheless, in addition to the Sooke Philharmonc Chamber Players, the Sooke Philharmonic Orchestra still gives a few concerts, and a Sooke Philharmonic Chorus has been formed.

Soon I was being contacted by various musical organizations including the Victoria Symphony Orchestra. I was very surprised at the high standard of the playing in the Victoria Symphony; some of the players could take their place in any orchestra in the world. Of course, they are not all virtuosi, but considering their pay and the relatively short season, it is a good orchestra.

When I arrived at one rehearsal I was taking Mary's bow out of the cover, and horror of horrors, it broke! I was mortified. I didn't know how to tell her that I had broken her bow and took it immediately to Jim Ham, a local luthier whom I was fortunate to find. Gary Karr plays on one of his basses.

Jim told me the bow could not be repaired but he consoled me with the fact that there was a flaw in it, and that it would have been bound to break sooner or later. I offered to buy Mary any bow of her choice but she told me it was already insured. I gave a sigh of relief, but my son was horrified. He said that after all my years in the business I should have known better than not to have the bass and bow insured. I resolved then and there to buy a bow and bass of my own.

This proved to be a difficult task. I telephoned my old friend in England, Gerry Drucker, who had been principal bass with the Philharmonia Orchestra of London. He painted a pretty grim picture. There were not many basses on the market and these were very highly priced. It struck me that I had sold my basses for a mere song. I hunted around but was not successful in finding a suitable instrument.

One day I was visiting Vancouver and my son suggested I try a local music store where they had several basses for sale. I went along, and as I had expected, found nothing suitable. My son then looked up the Yellow Pages and found a stringed instrument store in Vancouver that might have a bass for sale. I patiently explained that I had never bought any of my basses at a store, and that in England good instruments were usually handed down from player to player.

I was dragged kicking and screaming to this store where we were greeted by a surly individual who claimed to have played 'cello in the Calgary Symphony Orchestra. I tried out an instrument, but it was dreadful and very highly priced. Then he said he had another bass downstairs that was not as good, but it might suit me. This bass was equally dreadful, and I was despairing of ever finding anything suitable, but then, just as we were leaving, he called out that he remembered there was yet another instrument in the depths of his basement, although he did not think I would find it to be suitable for what I wanted.

Reluctantly I agreed to try it and as soon as I started to play I was pleasantly surprised; my son, who had often had to endure listening to my practicing, was also enthusiastic. I looked inside at the label; it read "Eberhart Meinel" and it was made in Markneukirchen, Germany. I had often heard my father mention Markneukirchen as it was not too far from where he had lived and I thought what a coincidence this was.

The ribs and back were of maple with a nice flame, and the belly was of close-grained pine. It was very well made and there was a touching little note with it written in German that roughly translated said, "I have made this instrument for you and hope you have many happy hours playing it".

I told the dealer I would buy it and he told me that a cover, bow and resin went with it. I paid him, and just as we were leaving, he called out to me that a tutor also went with it. I politely declined, telling him I thought I could manage without it.

Once outside we struggled to put the bass in the car, a sedan. My son said it would be dangerous to drive that way, as there was no all round vision. This was a problem I had not prepared myself for, but he suggested that what I needed was a station wagon, so we set off immediately to see what was available at the local Ford dealership. We selected a station wagon, traded my old car in, paid for the new one, loaded the bass in, and I set forth with new bass and new car en route for the ferry to Vancouver Island. I was now seriously in business as a bass player.

In the meantime, however, my wife became sick with a brain disease that eventually led to dementia. This meant spending most of my time at home looking after her. Occasionally it was possible to engage a home help for a day or so which gave me much needed respite and on a few occasions I could take time off to play an engagement. Sadly, her condition gradually worsened and eventually she had to be placed in a care facility.

I visited her every day and spent my spare time practicing. Then came the sad news that she was dying, and I was absolutely devastated for we had been married for over fifty years and had had a wonderful relationship.

After the funeral there was time to sit down and think. My thoughts were that maybe Fate had yet again played a significant part in my life by steering me in the direction of the double-bass.

I was alone in the house with the bass plus a dog I had rescued from the SPCA. There was nothing for it, I thought, but to practice and try to bring myself up to my previous standard. I was then seventy-eight years old. Meanwhile I made the re-acquaintance of Gary Karr and we are very good friends.

There were a couple living in Sooke, Don and Janette Chrysler, who came originally from Texas and became very close to me. Janette is a very fine 'cellist who could make her mark anywhere in the musical profession if she so chose. Don, a successful retired businessman, was very supportive of Janette's 'cello playing, so much so that he had built a beautiful concert hall attached to their house seating upwards of 100 people.

I joined them when they were touring California. Through Janette's widespread connections with the chamber music world throughout the American Southwest, we joined forces with a number of groups of string players to perform different works. I lost count of how many performances of Schubert's *Trout Quintet* we played.

Other chamber music tours with various groups were very interesting and I made many friends as a result. The world of music is remarkably close-knit. One is always bumping into old friends or colleagues in unexpected places. I was on a tour of the Gulf Islands of British Columbia with the Victoria Chamber Orchestra under the direction of Yariv Aloni, an excellent violist and conductor from Israel. Accommodation was limited on some of the smaller islands, so at one we were put up at a camping resort. I shared a cabin with Yariv and Peter Smith, a keyboard artist. As we were chatting just before going to sleep,

Peter mentioned that he had played with the BBC Northern Orchestra during the period when he was teaching at Manchester University. I cast my mind back, and then remembered him as a young man playing the harpsichord. He is now retired and living in B.C. and I later pressed him into service to accompany me in my solos, some of which can be heard on my CD, *Discovering the Double Bass*.

I was asked to coach the basses in the Greater Victoria Youth Orchestra whose conductor is János Sándor, a Hungarian. He is known worldwide, having been conductor of the Budapest State Opera and the Györ Philharmonic Orchestra among many others. One day when we were chatting together I was surprised to learn that he had met and played with many of the people I had come across in England, and also some I had encountered in Hungary and elsewhere. It's a small world, music.

The young people in the GVYO give me a sense of humility. There are some excellent players among them but hardly any want to become professional musicians. One thing I do advise my students is to become reasonably proficient, because to play a musical instrument is a great social asset and they could meet many new friends through it, so when their brains become fogged after a day spent in their chosen profession what a wonderful escape music could be.

CHAPTER 20

Closing thoughts.

There is a malaise affecting the musical profession at present with serious unemployment, and even the demise of some orchestras. Various solutions have been suggested; for instance, Benjamin Britten's idea of concentrating on chamber operas and mine of forming chamber orchestras for smaller communities. The orchestras that are doing well are those with adequate endowment funds and that is what all orchestras should aim for.

Scarce as jobs are nowadays in orchestras, there seems to be an over supply of candidates. After reading the hiring advertisements in the Musicians' Association newspaper I am amazed at the degree of competence required and the low salaries offered. Again, I know that nowadays workers in any field are aware that they may have to change their job description several times in a lifetime and this applies to music also.

The standard of playing has improved tremendously since I entered the musical profession. Of course, there were and are and always will be the giants of the profession, musicians whose names become household words, but however talented one is, this is never accomplished without hard work. To become a surgeon, for instance, also requires much study, but I venture to suggest that in order to be successful, a musician probably has to study as long as or longer than a surgeon to achieve competency.

One anachronism that still persists is the overly generous fees paid to some world-jetting conductors and soloists. Although many of these people deserve a good fee, some of the orchestras they conduct or play with live in penury, and grossly overpaying them in relation to the orchestra doesn't seem to me to be conducive to an orchestra's survival. There is a glut of very good young soloists and conductors just waiting for a break, why not give it to them.

A variety of factors have contributed to the lowered attendance at concerts. The rapid development of visual and aural technology has resulted in a boom in home theatre entertainment. Leisure opportunities have become more varied and attractive. Unfortunately this, coupled with the decline in discretionary income and an increase in street crime has translated into smaller audiences and less work for musicians, though there have been some interesting attempts to rectify this.

Some people declare that they are not keen to go to a concert because the soloist never sounds as good as the CD they bought. I know of one violinist who recorded the Beethoven violin concerto and I was told there were seventy, yes, seventy splices in the cadenza alone. This must make an audience more critical, but nothing can beat a live performance. There's the hushed expectation, the chemistry that evolves between soloist, orchestra and audience and a sense of being there which you don't get with a CD. True, it may be a cold, rainy or foggy night, but once inside the auditorium you enter another world.

One of the latest technological advances is the invention of the virtual orchestra, which is being resisted by musicians. Some concert halls will not give it house room and, also, the Musicians' Association is fighting it although some virtual orchestra proponents are accusing them of being Luddites.

Grants to the Arts have been cut in many countries throughout the world and many orchestras are in a deficit situation. Perhaps there is a surfeit of music. In stores, elevators, airports, bus stations etc. one is always greeted by piped music. Then again, every little hamlet in the world has its own music festival or summer music school and schools of music seem to have sprung up like mushrooms.

The Powers that Be rarely seem to realize that the Arts contribute a financial benefit to the community and should be looked at as a money producer and not a liability. While they use orchestras for the opening of gala events and other occasions when pomp and circumstance is required they do not seem to be interested in supporting what could be a cash cow for the community.

The continuing cuts to music in schools give me great concern. The children are our future audiences and if they learn an instrument and listen to an orchestra, their life will be enriched by it. The juvenile delinquency rate is alarming and very costly to deal with, and I am sure school music programmes would actually save money by keeping kids occupied and directing their energies into doing something worthwhile, and they would cost a fraction of what is spent on the delinquency problem.

I have attended symphony performances in many parts of the world and am sometimes disappointed by the way some, not all, symphony orchestras appear on stage. The players slink on randomly, some of the women wear boots, not always black, that give one the impression they are about to scale Mount Everest, their dresses look tatty and their hairdo leaves much to be desired. The same goes for some of the men who wear short socks exposing some bare calf, they wear clumpy, dirty shoes, their evening dress has seen better days and their shirts are crumpled. Mind you I'm only talking about a very few orchestra members, but they need to remember that they are on stage to convey a message to the audience that this is truly a special event put on just for them, one that they can enjoy and that will transport them into another world; the world of classical music.

Recently I went to a performance by the Cirque du Soleil. It was held in a marquee holding 2,558 people. The audience was bowled over by the lavish costumes, scenery, lighting and direction to say nothing of the artistes' extraordinary skills. The capacity audience gave them no less than six recalls. As I left, I pondered upon the present plight of modern day symphony orchestras and wondered that perhaps we are doing something wrong. We seem to lack that phantasmagoria that draws the crowds; but there are exceptions.

I'm not saying that it should all be Cirques du Soleil, fireworks and guns or Roman Carnivals but we need to do some re-thinking in the light of what is happening rapidly around us.

Many attempts have been made in the past to attract an audience. Sir Henry Wood, the founder of the "Proms" was one individual.

Recognizing that some fillip was needed to boost audiences Sir Thomas Beecham was experimenting even in the 1920's with lantern slides being shown during music performances. He mentioned it once to the members of the London Philharmonic and writes about it in his autobiography, *A Mingled Chime*, which also happens to be a good read.

When I was a kid I remember being taken to a vaudeville show. The orchestra played while on-stage there were tableaux of topless women. The Lord Chamberlain, the English censor, decreed that this was permissible provided the women didn't move, so they had to stand like statues. It certainly drew in the crowds. My mother and grandmother were less enthusiastic about it than me. They called the women "Shameless Hussies". I remained wide-eyed at such a spectacle, but they didn't think it was morally good for me to be corrupted by seeing all those bare breasts on stage.

Son et Lumiére was in vogue in Europe in the 1970's. It consisted of lighting up the façades of ancient castles etc. while an orchestra played appropriate music. It quickly dropped out of fashion but you can see that even in those early days, with the examples I have given, innovative attempts were being made to increase audiences.

Another attempt that was made to promote opera seems to have fallen by the wayside. A year or two ago, some impresarios were bringing in grand operas, such as *Aida*, and staging them in big arenas with expensive casts. The cost of the tickets was enormous and unfortunately some of the audience told me they were placed behind pillars and could hardly see the stage. To compensate for this, television screens were used, but many people left disenchanted because they could easily have bought a video of the opera and saved money by staying at home.

Recently the Vancouver Symphony erected giant television screens on stage at their concerts, and attendance went up, and I heard that their success led other orchestras to do the same thing.

In Europe, sometimes orchestras bring on a pair of ballet dancers to perform a *pas de deux*; that too has been received well by audiences.

Last year I played with the Victoria Symphony Orchestra at what was called the "Symphony Splash". The orchestra played on a barge that was fitted with a decorated band shell, had good lighting, and relayed sound in the Victoria Harbour. The men in the orchestra wore white jackets and black trousers, the women wore white tops and black skirts; altogether there was a sense of occasion and it was free to all. There were over 4,000 in the audience including many children

During the deafening applause I mused to myself that maybe, just maybe, some of the crowd would attend the Symphony's regular performances during the season now that they had a taste of what a symphony orchestra sounded like.

Shortly afterwards I was present at a VSO concert when they played Beethoven's Fifth Symphony. Tania Miller, the orchestra's resident conductor led the superb performance and the packed audience gave it a standing ovation. Perhaps the Symphony Splash helped to inspire such a large turn-out.

Next time you hear some beautiful music being performed I hope you will remember my attempt in this book to give you some idea of all the work, hardship, frustration and joy that becoming a professional musician entails. Good listening.

Vancouver, British Columbia, Canada, February, 2008

The Bottom Line

DISCOGRAPHY

Introduction

It would be impossible for me to list all of the recordings I have made in my long career, which must have amounted to thousands, but I have compiled a fairly long list which I think is representative.

I carried a diary, only noting the engagements I was to perform and did not note the music, or the artists and conductors present. On two occasions I worked for over three months without a day off, sometimes playing three sessions a day. My main objective was to keep the diary full of engagements as I had a wife, two kids and a mortgage. *Kunst nach Brot*! You never knew when the engagements would dry up, but, fortunately for me they never did.

Often you were not told what you were going to record; you were expected to know the entire standard repertoire and sometimes there was no chance of obtaining the music beforehand so you had to sight read, and if you didn't "cut the mustard" you were out. Walter Legge, the Founder and Artistic Director of the Philharmonia Orchestra was also in charge of the recordings, and he changed violinists more often than he changed his shirt. We were paid very handsomely but there were no residual or repeat fees. Some of these recordings have been re-mastered but the musicians have received nothing, for as musicians from all over the world were clamouring to get into the Philharmonia Orchestra because of the big take home pay, (they came from the USA, Germany, Italy, Portugal, South Africa, Australia, Poland, Czechoslovakia etc. etc.) the management could easily find a replacement if you did not like the conditions of employment.

I was told by an official of EMI/Angel that it was only possible to afford all of these classical recordings because they had the Beatles on contract which brought them in a huge amount of money.

It was hard work and like treading on eggshells, you had to be on your toes all of the time, also there was the travelling: I had to leave my home in Mill Hill, about ten miles from the centre of London, at 8.30 a.m. and would often not arrive back home until midnight.

Legge made things a lot more difficult for most of the orchestra by booking his sessions from 10 a.m. -1.00 p.m. and 6.p.m.-9 p.m. saying that the orchestra was fresher by having the long gap in between. I, for instance, had to allow six hours a day for travelling and would have much preferred 10-1 and 2-5. so I was not fresher, quite the reverse. I arrived back home past 2 p.m. and after a rest and an early dinner left home about 4.30 p.m. (you dare not be late) for the 6 p.m. session

Half way through the recording sessions or rehearsals there was a statutory Musicians' Union break of 15 minutes. A few of the musicians listened to the "takes" but the majority scrambled out for a coffee, or sometimes a beer in the evening.

When I first started recording it was on the old 78's made of a type of brittle plastic. This was very nerve wracking because they had to be perfect and recorded in one "take" lasting about 13 minutes or so.

Later, vinyls came in at 33 $^1/^3$ RPM and when tape recording was introduced it made things a lot easier, for the tape could be spliced and edited. Sometimes the editing can be overdone. I know of one violinist who made 70 splices in the Beethoven Violin Concerto cadenza alone!

Nowadays with advanced technology a good tonmeister can tweak recordings so as to alter pitch, sound and resonance etc. No wonder people who attend concerts say that it is not as good as the CD.

The 'fifties and '60's were truly the Halcyon days of recording in London. The main reason was that stereo recording had been introduced in the 'fifties causing the entire repertoire to be re-recorded in stereo. Another thing was that the British musicians had a good reputation for sight reading, and recording companies throughout the world saw it as a financial asset – the recordings were completed in much less time.

At the present time, however, I am given to understand that there is very little recording happening in London. Much of the work is being done in the Czech Republic and Bulgaria because their fees are much lower and also their musicians are first- rate. I have a friend who is a composer and he wanted to have one of his works recorded. The fees in Canada were prohibitive; also a royalty fee had to be paid for every performance so he had it recorded in Sofia, Bulgaria, where there was a fine orchestra, choir, conductor and technicians in a beautiful studio. When he asked them if they had a good piano they replied 'Yes, we have three Steinways!

The Kingsway Hall acoustics were very good, it was a central location but sometimes when the red light went it was impossible to make a "take" because of the external noise caused by adjacent building works. I saw Legge occasionally go outside and give a workman a ten shilling note (a lot of money in those days) to bribe him not to use his hammer for the next twenty minutes!

Most of the recordings were made in the Kingsway Hall, London, but sometimes recordings were made in the suburbs and I have noted these venues.

As many of these recordings I have listed are over fifty years old, I can only approximate the recording date and sometimes cannot trace the conductor or soloist.

I have divided the list into Symphonies, Collections of various pieces, Concertos, Opera/Operetta and Vocalists.

Often the records were released much later than the actual recording date, so my given dates have had to be approximate.

Discography

Overtures

Beethoven; *Leonora#1, Leonora #2, Leonora #3, Coriolanus,* Philharmonia, Klemperer, EMI, late '50's

Berlioz; *Overture Roman Carnival,* Philharmonia,von Karajan, Angel, mid '50's
*Overture Roman Carnival,*London Philharmonic, de Sabata, London FFRR, Walthamstow Town Hall, Essex

Brahms; *Academic Festival.* Philharmonia, Klemperer, EMI, 'mid '50's

Mozart; *Six Overtures,* Philharmonia, Klemperer, EMI, mid '50's

Rossini, Giachino; *William Tell, Tancredi, La Cenerentola, La Gazza ladra,*Philharmonia, Carlo Maria Giulini ,EMI, early'50's
L'Italiana in Algeria, Barber of Seville, Signor Bruschino, La Scala di Seta, Philharmonia, Giulini, Seraphim, early '50's

Turner, Robert; *Children's Overture,* CBC Vancouver Chamber Orchestra, Avison, CBC Vancouver Studios, early seventies

Verdi; *La Forza del Destino, La Traviata (Preludes Acts 1& 3),* Philharmonia, Giulini, Seraphim, early '50's
Overtures Nabucco, Aida,Giovanna D'Arco, Philharmonia, Tullio, Serafin, Seraphim, mid '50's

Weber; *Overtures,* Philharmonia, Wolfgang Sawallisch, EMI, mid '50's

Wagner, Richard; *Overtures Rienzi, Der Fliegende Holländer, Der Meistersiger von Nürnberg, Tannhäuser,* Philharmonia, Klemperer, EMI, mid '50's

Symphonies

Bach, C.P.E.; *Symphony #1,*CBC Vancouver Chamber Orchestra, John Avison, Ace of Diamonds, CBC Vancouver Studio, early seventies

Beethoven; *Symphony #3(Eroica)*,London Philharmonic, de Sabata, London FFRR, Walthamstow Town Hall,1946
Symphony #7 in A, Philharmonia, Guido Cantelli, Seraphim, early '50's
Symphony #8 in F, Philharmonia, Klemperer, EMI, late '50's
The nine Symphonies, Philharmonia, von Karajan, EMI, mid '50's
The nine Symphonies, Philharmonia, Klemperer, EMI, late '50's (Ninth symphony recorded at the Musikvereinsaal,Vienna)
Symphony #9, Philharmonia/Furtwängler,(Live TV recording at Kunsthaus, Lucerne, Switzerland) early '50's

Brahms ; *Symphony #2*, Philharmonia, von Karajan, EMI, mid '50's
Symphony #3 in F, Phillharmonia, Erich Leinsdorf, Pickwick,'50's
Symphony #3, Philharmonia,Klemperer, EMI, mid '50's
Symphony #3, Philharmonia, Giulini, Seraphim,late 50's

Bruckner, Anton; *Symphony #7*, Philharmonia, Klemperer,EMI, mid '50's
Symphony #8 in C minor, Philharmonia, Klemperer, EMI, mid '50s

Elgar, Edward; *Symphony #1 in A flat*, Philharmonia, Sir John Barbirolli, Seraphim, '50's

Mahler, Gustav; *Symphony #4 in G*,Philharmonia/Loose, Paul Kletzki,EMI, early 50's

Mendelssohn, Felix; *Symphony 34 (Italian)*, Philharmonia, Cantelli, Seraphim, early '50's

Mozart; *Symphony #10*, CBC Vancouver Chamber Orchestra, Avison, Ace of Diamonds, CBC Vancouver Studios, early '70's
Symphonies#40/41, Philharmonia, Klemperer, EMI, mid '50's

Prokoviev, Sergey; *Classical Symphony*, Philharmonia, Kurtz, early '50's

Schubert, Franz; *Symphony #8 (Unfinished)*, Philharmonia, Cantelli, Seraphim, early '50's
Symphony #9 (Great C major), Philharmonia, Klemperer, EMI, mid '50's

Tchaikovsky; *Symphony #2 (Little Russian)*,Philharmonia, Giulini, EMI, mid '50's
Symphony #4, Philharmonia, Klemperer, EMI, mid '50's
Symphony #6 (Pathétique), Philharmonia, Klemperer, EMI, mid '50's
Symphony #6 (Pathétique), Philharmonia, Giulini, Seraphim, early '50's

Collections, Tone Poems & Miscellany

Bartok, Bela; Concerto for Orchestra, Philharmonia/von Karajan, EMI, mid '50's

Beecham, Sir Thomas; Love in Bath, (a balletic entertainment) , Handel-Beecham, Royal Philharmonic, EMI, late 'forties , Abbey Road

Beethoven; Triple Concerto, Philharmonia/David Oistrakh, Knushevitzky, Oborin/Sargent EMI early '50's

Berlioz, Hector; Selections from "Les Troyens" (Royal Hunt & Storm etc.), "Damnation of Faust", (Ràkòcky March etc.), Philharmonia/Richard Kapp, Vox, early '50's

Bizet, Georges; Suites "Carmen" & "L'Arlésienne", Philharmonia/von Karajan, late '50's

Brahms: Double Concerto, Philharmonia/Christian Ferras violin/Paul Tortelier cello/Paul Kletzki, EMI, early 50's

Brahms; " Variations on a Theme of Haydn" , Philharmonia/Erich Leinsdorf, EMI, Pickwick, early '50's

Britten,Benjamin; Four Interludes from "Peter Grimes", "The Young Person's Guide to the Orchestra", Philharmonia/Giulini, EMI, mid '50's

Britten; "War Requiem",London Symphony Orchestra/Pears, tenor/Britten, Decca, early 60's

Butt, Yondani, conductor; Barber" 2nd Essay", Saint-Saëns "Danse Bachanale"; Sibelius "Lemminkainen's Return", Liszt " Mazeppa" Symphonie Canadiana , Orion 1981, Centennial Hall, N.Vancouver, B.C.

Chabrier, Espana; Chabrier "Joyeuse Marche", Weber arr. Berlioz "Invitation to the Dance", Verdi "Aida' Ballet Music, Waldteufel "Les Patineurs", Weinberger Polka from "Schwanda the Bagpiper" Farandole from "L'Arlésienne", Ponchielli, Dance of the Hours from"La Giaconda", Tchaikovsky Waltz from"Sleeping Beauty", Philharmonia/von Karajan, EMI, mid '50's

Coronation of H.M. Queen Elizabeth II Music, Coronation Orchestra/Sir Adrian Boult, BBC Recording

Copland, Aaron conducts his own works, London Symphony Orchestra, Decca early '60's, Wembley Town Hall

Debussy, Claude; "La Mer", "Three Nocturnes", Philharmonia/Giulini, EMI, mid '50's

Debussy; " La Mer, Nuages & Fête", Prelude "Faune", Philharmonia/Guido Cantelli , Seraphim, early' 50's

Haydn, Joseph; Divertimento Op. 2 #5, Vancouver Symphony Chamber Players, CBC ,Ace of Diamonds, N. Vancouver Centennial Theatre, 1969

von Karajan; Ballet music," Gaité Parisienne", Offenbach (arr. Rosenthal); "William Tell", Rossini; "Faust", Gounod, Philharmonia/von Karajan, EMI, mid '50's

von Karajan; " Stereo Showpieces for Orchestra" Tchaikovsky"1812"; Mussorgsky "Pictures"; Resphigi "Pines of Rome"; Liszt "; Sibelius "Valse Triste"; Philharmonia, mid '50's

Khachaturian, Aram; "Masquerade" & "Gayaneh" suites, Philharmona/ Khachaturian, EMI, mid '50's

Kodály; "Háry János" Suite, Philharmonia/Leinsdorf, Seraphim, early '50's

Last night of the Proms; various pieces, BBC Symphony Orchestra/Malcolm Sargent, BBC, early '60's

Leoncavallo, Ruggiero; Intermezzo from "Pagliacci", Philharmonia/von Karajan, EMI, late 50's

Liszt, Franz; "Les Préludes", Philharmonia/von Karajan , EMI, mid '50's

Mahler, Gustav; "Song of the Earth", Philharmonia/Fischer Dieskau/Dickie/ Paul Kletzki, Seraphim, early '50's

Mendelssohn; Complete incidental music to "A Midsummer Night's Dream, Philharmonia/ Heather Harper/Philharmonia Chorus/Klemperer, EMI, mid '50's

Mozart; Divertmento #7, K.205, Vancouver Symphony Chamber Players , Ace of Diamonds, N.Vancouver Centennial Theatre, 1969

Mussorgsky, Modest; Dance of the Persian Slaves from "Khovanshchina" , Philharmonia/von Karajan, EMI, late '50's

Mussorgsky; "Night on the Bare Mountain",Philharmonia/Giulini, Seraphim, mid '50's

Mussorgsky; "Pictures at an Exhibition", Philharmonia/von Karajan, EMI, mid '50's

Ravel, Maurice; "Rhapsodie Espagnole, "Pavane pour une infante défunte", Philharmonia/Giulini, Seraphim, mid '50's

Prokofiev, Sergey; "Peter & the Wolf"," Classical Symphony", "March from the Love or Three Oranges ", Philharmonia/Kurtz, Seraphim, early '50's

Prokofiev, " Lieutenant Kijé" Suite, Philharmonia/Erich Leinsdorf, Seraphim, mid-'50's

Prokofiev; Excerpts from ballet "Romeo & Juliet", EMI, mid '50's

Rossini; Duo for 'cello & bass, Ian Hampton, 'cello/Robert Meyer d.bass, CBC Festival Vancouver, early seventies

de Sabata, Victor ; Sibelius "En Saga", "Valse Triste", Wagner "Ride of the Valkyries", London, FFRR, Walthamstow Town Hall, 1946

Schmidt, Franz; Intermezzo " Notre Dame", Philharmonia/von Karajan, EMI, late '50's

Smetana; "The Moldau", Sibelius; "Finlandia", etc. Philharmonia/von Karajan, EMI, mid '50's

Strauss, Richard; "Die Frau ohne Schatten" - Suite, "Till Eulenspiegel", "Salome's Dance", EMI, early 50's
"Salome", Philharmonia/Klemperer, EMI, mid '50's

Stravinsky; "Firebird", Ravel; "Mother Goose Suite", Bizet; "Children's Games", Seraphim, mid '50's

Stravinsky; ballet "Petroushka", London Philharmonic/Ernest Ansermet, Decca FFRR, 1946

Stravinsky; "Rite of Spring", Philharmonia/Igor Markevitch, EMI, mid 'fities

Stravinsky; "Septet", Vancouver Symphony Chamber Players, Ace of Diamonds, N. Vancouver Centennial Hall, 1969

Symphony Splash, Variety of small pieces, Victoria Symphony/Peter Mc Coppin, 1999, GSP Records

Stokowski conducts orchestral favourites; London Symphony Orchestra/ Stokowski, Decca, Wembley Town Hall

Tchaikovsky; Suites from the ballets "Sleeping Beauty", "The Nutcracker", Philharmonia/Yehudi Menuhin Violin/ Efrem Kurtz, EMI, Early '50's

Turner, Robert "Nocturne" CBC Vancouver Chamber Orchestra/Avison CBC Vancouver Studio early seventies

Verdi Giuseppe, Overtures Philharmonia/Tullio Seraphin EMI Watford Town Hall

Wagner, Richard; Music from the "Ring", "Tannhäuser', "Parsifal", Philharmonia/Klemperer, EMI, mid '50's

Wagner ; Flagstad, Kirsten Made C.1946., LPO, I cannot remember them being issued, Decca

Vaughan Williams; "Magnificat"," Partita for Double String Orchestra", "An Oxford Eleg", "Five Tudor Portraits","Partita", CBC Festival Orchestra and Chorus/Harry Newstone, CBC, 1971

Vocal

Bach; " Jauchzet Gott in Allen Landen" (Cantata, BWV 51), Scwartzkopf/ Philharmonia/von Karajan, EMI, mid '50's

Callas, Maria; Opera Arias, Philharmonia/Tullio Serafin, EMI, mid '50's, Watford Town Hall

Falla, Manuel de; " El amor brujo" excerpts, Victoria de los Angeles / Philharmonia / Giulini, Seraphim, early '50's

Mozart, Wolfgang Amadeus; Concert aria for bass voice with double bass obbligato "Per Questa Bella Mano", CBC Vancouver Chamber Orchestra / William Reimer, bass / Robert Meyer, D. bass / Avison, CBC recording, late '60's

Mozart; " Exsultate Jubilate", Philharmonia / Schwartzkopf / von Karajan, EMI, mid '50's

Various opera arias, Schwartzkopf / Philharmonia / Galliera, EMI, mid '50's

Opera

Britten, Benjamin; "Albert Herring", English Opera Group Conducted by Britten, British Council, 1948

Janácêk; " Jenůfa", Philharmonia / Vilem Tausky, BBC, late '50's, Camden Theatre

Rossini; " Barber of Seville", Philharmonia Orchestra & Chorus / Callas, Gobbi, Alva / Galliera, EMI

Monteverdi ; "Orfeo", Ad hoc orchestra / Walter Goehr , BBC, '50's

Strauss, Richard; "Der Rosenkavalier", Philharmonia / Schwartzkopf, Ludwig, Stich-Randall, Wächter / von Karajan, Angel, mid '50's

Verdi; "Falstaff", Philharmonia / von Karajan, EMI, 'mid 50's

Operetta

"Die Fledermaus", Johann Strauss, Philharmonia / Schwartzkopf, Gedda, Kunz / von Karajan

"Merry Widow", Franz Lehar, Philharmonia / Schwartzkopf, Kunz, Gedda, Loose / Otto Ackerman, EMI, mid '50's

"Der Zigeuner Baron", Johann Strauss , Philharmonia / Schwartzkopf, Gedda, Kunz, Prey / Ackerman, EMI, Mid '50's

Flute

Mozart; The Two Concertos plus Andante in C Philharmonia / Elaine Shaffer, Flute / Efrem Kurtz, Hampstead Studios, early 50's

Violin

Brahms; Concerto, Philhar.nonia / Nathan Milstein / Anatole Fistoulari, Seraphim, early '50's

Bruch, Max, Concerto in G minor , Milstein/Philharmonia/Barzin, Seraphim, early '50's

Chausson; "Poème", Philharmonia/Milstein/Fistoulari, Seraphim, early '50's

Khachaturian, Aram; Violin Concerto ,Philharmonia/David Oistrakh/ Khachaturian, EMI, late 50's

Mendelssohn; Concerto in E minor, Milstein/Philharmonia/Barzin , Seraphim, early '50's

Paganini, Niccolò; Concerto # 1 in D, Michael Rabin/Philharmonia/Sir Eugene Goossens, Seraphim, early '50's

Saint-Saëns; Concerto , Philharmonia/Milstein/Fistoulari, Seraphim, early '50's

Wieniawski, Henryk; Concerto in D minor, Philharmonia/ Rabin/Sir Eugene Goossens, Seraphim, early '50's

'Cello

Tchaikovsky; "Rococo Variations" Phiharmonia/ Rostopovitch, EMI, mid '50's

I was with the Philharmonia in the '50's and with the BBC Symphony Orchestra in the early '60's and recorded much of the 'cello repertoire with the following: Starker, Fournier, Navarra, Tortelier, Rostopovitch, Nelsova etc. and their recordings are possibly in the archives.

Double Bass

"Discovering the Double bass" (Orchestral tuning) Robert Meyer, Double bass/ Janette Chrysler' cello/Josh Layne harp/ Deborah Rambo piano/ Mary Rannie d. bass/ Peter Smith piano/Christopher Symons Harpsichord/Nancy van Oort bassoon.
Solos including Paganini "Variations on a Theme from Rossini's Moses in Egypt"; "A Little Concerto for Double bass" Second Movement, Gordon Jacob (Robert Meyer, dedicatee); Albert Roussel "Duo for Bassoon & Double bass"; Duet for 2 Double basses, "Polacca"; Aria from "Il Trovatore" Verdi arr. Bottesini; Rossini, Duetto for'cello & bass; plus several orchestral excerpts, 2007

Hindemith, Paul; Sonata for double bass & pianoforte, Robert Meyer, double bass, Hugh McLean pianoforte, CBC Vancouver Studios, late' 60's

Guitar

Segovia; Various solos including a concerto, Maida Vale Studios, 196l, BBC Symphony Orchestra

French Horn

Mozart; The Four horn Concertos, Philharmonia/Dennis Brain/Klemperer, EMI, mid '50's , Hornsey Town Hall. A far as I know these recordings were never issued.

Mozart; The Four Horn Concertos, Philharmonia/Dennis Brain/von Karajan EMI, mid '50's, Hornsey Town Hall

Richard Strauss; 2 Concertos , Philharmonia/Dennis Brain/Wolfgang Sawallisch, EMI, mid'50's, Hornsey Town Hall

Pianoforte

Beethoven; The five pianoforte concerti, Philharmonia/Solomon/ Herbert Menges, Seraphim, Abbey Road, mid '50's

Beethoven; Concerto #5 (Emperor), Philharmonia/WalterGiesekimg/Galliera, Seraphim,early '50's

Brahms, Johannes; Concerto #2 in B Flat, Philharmonia/Claudio Arrau/Giulini, Seraphim, early '50's

Liszt, Franz; Concerto #1 in E flat, Philharmonia/Annie Fischer/Klemperer, Seraphim, early '50's

Michelangeli; Various Concertos, Philharmonia, EMI, Abbey Road, late '50's

Schumann, Robert; Concerto in A minor, op. 54, Philharmonia/Annie Fischer/ Klemperer, Seraphim, early 50's

ILLUSTRATIONS

Photographs in this book have come from the collection of the author and the kind participation of many who are represented here. Gratitude especially goes to to G. Macdominic for his photographs of Stokowski, Barbirolli and Klemperer.

Illustrations in order of appearance:

The author, age 16, Lajos Montag, Koussevitsky, Eugene Cruft, Crossing the Channel in November, 1945, Wilhelm Mohnke, London Philharmonic conducted by Sir Thomas Beecham, Albert Coates, Benjamin Britten, Betty and the Reliant, Victor Watson and Boris Rickelman, Van Bienem, Josef Krips, Carlo Maria Guilini, Kirsten Flagstaff, Edouard van Beinum, Wilhelm Furtwangler, Chicago 1954, Schwartzkopf, Callas and Legge, Gerald Brooks, Max Salpeter, the author, on a train in Germany, 1954, Tullio Serafin and Maria Callas, 1955, Sir Malcolm Sargent, 1955, Otto Klemperer, 1956, Victor de Sabata, Benjamin Britten conducting a recording of his War Requiem, Aaron Copland rehearsing the LSO, Sir William Walton, 1964, Sir Arthur Bliss, Master of the Queen's Music, 1964, Bath Festival Orchestra, Yehudi Menuhin, Sir Adrian Boult, Igor Stravinsky and Pierre Monteux, 1962, Leopold Stokowski, 1960, Guido Cantelli, Ernest Ansermet, Colin Davis, Herbert von Karajan, Sir John Barbirolli, The author, VSO, The author tours BC by plane, 1968, Meredith Davies, VSO, On tour with Betty, Lourdes, 1970, Gary Karr with the author, 2006, Janette Chrysler, the author, and Don Chrysler, Victoria de los Angeles, Dr. Gordon Jacob, George Corwin, Janos Sandor, Margot Fonteyn and Rudolf Nureyev.

The Bottom Line

INDEX

Nelson, Norman 176, 207
Nelsova, Zara 139
Neri, Rosalina 155, 156
Neveu, Ginette, 129
New London Orchestra 165
New Opera Company 152
New Philharmonia 127, 145
New York Philharmonic Orchestra 141
Newnham, Michael 60
Newstone, Harry 86, 184
Nijinsky 80,
Noble, Dennis 29
Nureyev, Rudolf 159

Octobass 26
Ogdon, John 187
Oistrakh, David 135,137
Oistrakh, Igor 137
Old Vic Company 93, 158
Oliver, Vic 87
Olivier, Laurence 93, 109, 130
Orchestra Canadiana 193
Ord, Boris 106
Orff, Carl 130
Ormandy, Eugene 136,

Palm Court Orchestra, 91
Paray, Paul 84
Parikian, Manoug 117, 138
Parsons, William 74
Partös, Ödon 50
Patterson, Ron 136
Pears, Peter 74, 103, 105, 106
Petit, Roland 153
Philadelphia Orchestra 141
Philharmonia Orchestra
36, 37, 48, 53, 63, 64, 66, 67, 74, 92, 100,
110, 115, 116, 118, 119, 124, 127, 128,
129, 130, 133, 134, 140, 141, 142, 143,
145, 146, 208
Phillips, Mr. & Mrs. H.B. 32
Philomusica 87, 152, 154
Piatigorsky, Gregor 139
Piper, John 78
Pittsburg Orchestra 54
Pitz, Wilhelm 120
Plishka, Paul 187
Polish National Radio Orchestra 60
Pougnet, Jean 42
Pouishnoff 34
Poulton, Diana 89
Prades Festival 151

Price, Harold 11, 12, 27
Primrose, William 50
Pro Arte Orchestra 165, 167
Promenade Concerts ("Proms") 52, 53,
57, 98, 100, 102, 106, 107, 147, 157, 214

Queen Elizabeth 2$^{nd.}$ 110
Queen's Hall,(Orchestra) 51, 100, 106
Queen Mary 102, 104

Rabin, Michael 137
Râches 19, 22, 23
Rankl, Karl 51
Rannie, Mary 207, 208
Rawsthorne, Alan 107
Reeves, Wynn 99
Reiner, Fritz 37, 38
Richmond, (British Columbia) Arts
Council 196, 200, 201, 202, 203
Richmond Community Music School
196, 200
Richter, Hans 59
Riddick, Kathleen 86
Riddick Orchestra 86, 124
R.M.A.M. (Robert Meyer Artist
Management Ltd.) 32, 196, 199, 200
Robinson, Eric 60, 93, 114
Robinson, Stanford 93
Rodzinski, Artur 132
Romero 187
Rostropovitch, Mitislav 138
Rothwell, Evelyn 57
Royal Academy of Music 30
Royal Albert Hall 35, 42, 50, 52, 55, 56,
80, 85, 124, 157
Royal Choral Society 54, 96
Royal College of Music 29, 31, 35
Royal Festival Hall 58, 121
Royal Liverpool Orchestra 182
Royal Opera House, Covent Garden
51, 57, 72, 88, 103, 152
Royal Philharmonic Orchestra (RPO)
48, 60, 61, 102
7th Royal Warwickshire Regiment 15,
19, 109
Royal Winnipeg Ballet 187
Rozhdesvensky, Gennady 165
Russell, Thomas 60

Sabata, Victor de 61, 62, 63, 64, 65, 66,
67, 68, 118, 130, 132
Sadlers Wells Theatre and Opera

DISCOVERING THE DOUBLE BASS

To accompany this book, Robert Meyer created a CD which demonstrates the range, capacity of sound, harmonics and other subtleties that can be expressed through the orchestral double bass tuned GDAE. It is rare that an orchestral bass is performed in a solo capacity using orchestral tuning, as for solo playing the bass is usually tuned up a whole tone.

Meyer's masterful performance is imbued with his vast experience playing with the greats of the 20th century. In his chamber operas, Britten often wrote bass lines with Meyer's playing in mind. On this CD, in the Bottesini duet and the Roussel Bassoon duo, Robert Meyer's performance is based on practical advice he received from Koussevitsky himself and Victor Watson. The excerpt from Otello by Verdi is based upon Victor de Sabata's personal comments and suggestions to Robert. Robert Meyer is also grateful for the concerto by Dr. Gordon Jacob composed directly for his expertise.

Each piece features a spoken introduction with historical, humourous and interesting notes on the composer, the times or the piece itself.

CONTENTS

Beethoven Symphony No. 9 recitative
Bottesini, Polacca for two double basses
Bottesini, aria from Il Trovatore
Ginastera, Variaciones Concertantes
Gordon Jacob, A Little Concerto for Double Bass,Second Movement, with piano accompaniment (Robert Meyer, dedicatee))
Mahler, Symphony No. 1
Marais, La Matelotte
Paganini, Moses Fantasia, arr. for double bass and piano accompaniment
Prokofieff, Lieutenant Kijé
Rossini, Duet for 'Cello and Double Bass
Roussel, Duo for Double bass and Bassoon
Saint Saëns, The Elephant
Verdi, Otello and Rigoletto excerpts

To order *Discovering the Double Bass* by Robert Meyer,
go to www.robertmeyerbass.com.

ISBN 141208970-0